# GUIDEBOOKS TO SIN

IS ONE place in the Tenderloin District you can't very well afford to miss. The Countess Piazza has made it a study to try and make everyone joval who visits her house. If you have the "blues", the Countess and her girls can cure them. She has, without doubt, the most handsome and intelligent octoroons in the United States. You should see them; they are all entertainers.

If there is anything new in the singing and dancing line that you would like to see while in Storyville, Piazza's is the place to visit, especially when one is out hopping with friends—the women in particular.

The Countess wishes it to be known that while her mansion is peerless in every respect, she only serves the "amber flued."

"Just ask for Willie Piazza."

PHONE 4832 MAIN.

# GUIDEBOOKS TO SIN

The Blue Books of Storyville, New Orleans

## PAMELA D. ARCENEAUX

with a foreword by Emily Epstein Landau

THE HISTORIC NEW ORLEANS COLLECTION

The Historic New Orleans Collection is a museum, research center, and publisher dedicated to the study and preservation of the history and culture of New Orleans, the lower Mississippi valley, and the Gulf South region. The Collection is operated by the Kemper and Leila Williams Foundation, a Louisiana nonprofit corporation.

© 2017 The Historic New Orleans Collection
533 Royal Street
New Orleans, Louisiana 70130
www.hnoc.org

Editor: Dorothy Ball
Director of publications: Jessica Dorman
Executive director: Priscilla Lawrence
Design: Alison Cody Design

First edition.
All rights reserved.
Printed and bound in Canada by Friesens.

21  20  19  18  17    1  2  3  4  5

ISBN: 978-0-917860-73-7

Library of Congress Cataloging-in-Publication Data

Names: Arceneaux, Pamela D., author. | Landau, Emily Epstein, 1969– | Historic New Orleans Collection.
Title: Guidebooks to sin : the blue books of Storyville, New Orleans / by Pamela D. Arceneaux ; foreword by Emily Epstein Landau.
Description: New Orleans, Louisiana : The Historic New Orleans Collection, [2017] | Includes bibliographical references and index.
Identifiers: LCCN 2016035869 | ISBN 9780917860737 (alk. paper)
Subjects: LCSH: Prostitution—Louisiana—New Orleans. | Storyville (New Orleans, La.)—Guidebooks. | New Orleans (La.)—History—19th century. | New Orleans (La.)—History—20th century. | New Orleans (La.)—Guidebooks.
Classification: LCC HQ146.N6 A73 2017 | DDC 306.7409763/35—dc23 LC record available at https://lccn.loc.gov/2016035869

To those long-ago ladies of Storyville.
They have been very, very good to me.

*Honi soit qui mal y pense.*

# CONTENTS

Preface
9

Acknowledgments
13

Foreword: How to Be Wise
by Emily Epstein Landau
17

Introduction: Storyville and the Blue Books
27

Provenance: The Historic New Orleans
Collection's Storyville Guides
55

## BIBLIOGRAPHY OF PROSTITUTION GUIDES
65

Editions of *Blue Book*
66

Alternative Storyville-Era Guides
106

Fakes and Facsimiles
122

Key to Nos. 1–25
146

Works Consulted
147

Image Credits
150

Index
153

View of Basin Street
ca. 1908

# PREFACE

## *"A word to the wise"*

The author of this Directory and Guide of the Tenderloin District has been before the people on many occasions as to his authority on what is doing in the "Queer Zone"—Tenderloin.

Everyone who knows to-day from yesterday will say that my Blue Bood is the goods right from the spring.

### Why New Orleans Should Have This Directory

First. Because it is the only district of its kind in the States set aside for the fast women by *law*.

Second. Because it puts the stranger on a proper grade or path as to where to go and be secure from hold-ups, brace games and other illegal practices usually worked on the unwise in Red Light Districts.

# PREFACE

"Everything goes here. Fun is the watchword." This language from madam Emma Johnson's 1908 advertisement in *Blue Book* piqued my interest when I first became acquainted with Storyville. One of the few New Orleans–related books I had read prior to my interview for a position as librarian with The Historic New Orleans Collection in August 1981 was *Storyville, New Orleans* by Al Rose, about the city's legally designated red-light district that existed between 1897 and 1917. In it was a chapter describing the publications of Storyville, especially the little directories of female prostitutes and houses of prostitution collectively called blue books. I was fascinated by the lists of names, the advertisements, and the flowery, saucy, but also quaintly coy descriptions of the better brothels and their madams. I discovered that the research library at The Historic New Orleans Collection housed a rather large number of these unusual guides. My interest in them led to writing an article, "Guidebooks to Sin: The Blue Books of Storyville," first published in 1987 in *Louisiana History*, then revised for *The Historic New Orleans Collection Quarterly* in 1995, and subsequently published in 2000 in a scholarly compilation, *Visions and Revisions: Perspectives on Louisiana Society and Culture*. I contributed the entry on blue books that appears in *KnowLA Encyclopedia of Louisiana*, an educational online resource of the Louisiana Endowment for the Humanities, and for several years I have also presented a popular illustrated lecture on the history of prostitution in New Orleans entitled "A Red-Light Look at New Orleans History," which includes material on the blue books.

A previous bibliography of these guides, *The "Blue Book,"* was privately printed in 1936 by rare-book dealer Charles F. Heartman. Years later, The Historic New Orleans Collection acquired Heartman's collection of Storyville guides, in addition to editions not described by either Heartman or Rose. With the publication of this book, I present a fresh look at this group of New Orleans brothel directories, which I have worked with for so many years. Along with a bibliographic description of each of the Storyville-era blue books now housed at the Williams Research Center of The Historic New Orleans Collection, I note errors in Heartman's and Rose's publications that my observations and research have uncovered, and I include a section on fakes and facsimiles in our holdings. This book is also an opportunity to correct errors and misconceptions that I have discovered about Storyville and the blue books since my initial article appeared so long ago.

I am certain that there are more New Orleans prostitution guides beyond those I have examined. No one has yet identified the number of editions produced, nor how many copies of each edition were printed, nor is anyone likely to. While I have tried to make this bibliography

Typography from preface, from No. 4

as complete and accurate as possible, invariably as soon as ink touches paper, heretofore-unknown editions of these guides to Storyville—almost all that's left of that bawdy world—will surface, new information will come to light, and pronouncements once taken as fact will be disproved. I hope I have not strayed too far from the mark. ✖

Doorway of the Star Mansion in 1945

## *ARLINGTON.
### JOSIE ARLINGTON,
225 Basin.

Annie Casey, M. Beach, Helena Clayton, Frankie Sawyer, Eunice Deering, Marie Cole, Marie Barrett, Minnie White, Ollie Nicholls, Freda Dunlap, Madelene Vale, Amber Shepherd, Myrtle Rhea.

## *FISHERS.
### LOTTIE FISHER,
313 Basin.

Etta Ross, Marie Gates, May Howard, Effie Russell, Neda Nelson.

## *THE STUDIO.
### FRANKIE SHERMAN,
331 Basin.

Ruth Atwood, Josephine Howard, Clara Morris.

## *THE CLUB.
### MISS FLO MEEKER,
211 Basin.

Margeret Roux, Cleo Strauss, Bert Palmer, B. Montgomery, Anna Cook, Mattie Fisher, Kate Tremper, Camille Walton, May Spencer, Eunice Deering, Mattie Forster.  Cumberland Phone.

## *McDOWELLS.
### NELLIE McDOWELLS,
221 Basin.

Gloria Ely, Gladys Harris, Mona Desmond, Josie Howard, Kay McDonald.

## *SIMPSONS.
### GRACE SIMPSON,
223 Basin.

Annie Mills, A. Ellis, Dottie Lewis, Marie Best, Beatrice Allen, Reta Bonds, Ivy D. Preston, Jean Lawrance.

# ACKNOWLEDGMENTS

**N**o one toils alone on any venture such as this, and I was fortunate to have assistance, support, encouragement, and technical expertise from many sources. Every piece of information, regardless of how exhaustively or how casually imparted, has helped spur me along the path of discovery, challenging me to question and explore further. Colleagues at The Historic New Orleans Collection, especially Viola Berman, M. L. Eichhorn, Aimee Everrett, Kevin T. Harrell, Tere Kirkland, John H. Lawrence, and Robert Ticknor, were unfailingly helpful, and without my dear friend John T. Magill, I may have thrown in the towel before even getting very far. I also thank The Historic New Orleans Collection's Executive Director Priscilla Lawrence, Williams Research Center Director Alfred E. Lemmon, and Director of Publications Jessica Dorman for their belief that *Guidebooks to Sin* would be a worthy project and for their belief in me. Senior editor Dorothy Ball's thoughtful and intelligent questions, professionalism, and unflagging enthusiasm enabled me to envision aspects of this subject beyond my initial proposal and buoyed my spirits when I felt overwhelmed and discouraged. I cannot praise her highly enough. Designer Alison Cody insightfully captured the sense of fun and whimsy about these little guides that drew me to them initially, and I thank her for this beautiful book you hold in your hands.

Librarians, archivists, and academics at other institutions were immensely helpful and patient in responding to numerous mail, email, and telephone queries on my often-obscure tangents of thought as I tracked down blue book enigmas. I especially thank Sean C. Benjamin and Bruce B. Raeburn, Tulane University; Florence M. Jumonville, University of New Orleans; the late Lester G. Sullivan, Xavier University; Michael Taylor, Louisiana State University; Missy Abbott, Christina Bryant, Yvonne Loiselle, Jenny Rogers, and Irene Wainwright, New Orleans Public Library; Sean Farrell, Library of Hattiesburg, Petal, and Forrest County; Sarah S. Fisher, George Miles, and Timothy Young, Yale University; Barbara Pilvin, Free Library of Philadephia; Peggy Price, Jennifer Brannock, Cindy Lawler, and R. Eric Platt, University of Southern Mississippi; Eliza Robertson, National Humanities Center (North Carolina); and Jeanne Solensky, Winterthur Museum, Garden, and Library.

I am grateful to the many friends, acquaintances, authors, and professionals in the rare-book trade who also shared invaluable insight and information—Sally Asher, John R. Bass, Ralph and Jodi Beatty, Cordelia Frances Biddle, Bailey Bishop (formerly of Goodspeed's Book Shop in Boston), the late Eric J. Brock, Emily Clark, Sacha Borenstein Clay, Bruce Coates, Nancy Sharon Collins, Katy Coyle, John J. Dee III,

*Typography from directory, from No. 2*

Bill Grady (Hughes Books), Claudia Kheel (Neal Auction Company), William Reese and Teri Osborn Kolton (William Reese Company), Emily Epstein Landau, Alecia P. Long, Nancy H. Luedke, Jay Moynahan (Chickadee Publishing), Wayne and Debbie Pitt, the late Gaspar J. "Buddy" Stall, Kirt Stall, Christine Wiltz, Justin D. Winston, and Phil Zuckerman (Applewood Books).

A special thanks goes to Sari Brandin, my husband's cousin and a good friend, whose gracious invitation to spend a relaxing week in December 2012 with her at her Orange Beach, Alabama, condo provided the impetus for me to finish the first draft of *Guidebooks to Sin*.

I can never thank my father, the late W. P. "Dave" Davis, and my mother, Elizabeth Brown Davis, enough for their love, their encouragement, and the educational opportunities they provided, even though they could little imagine that it would lead to this line of study. My sister, Mary E. "Betsy" Davis, has always been and continues to be an inspiration to me.

Most importantly, I commend my husband, Paul L. Arceneaux, whose patience and constructive suggestions throughout the entire writing process contributed so much to the final result. "Dear, I'm finally at a good stopping point!"

Advertisement for Champagne, from No. 4

# FOREWORD
## HOW TO BE WISE
by Emily Epstein Landau

"To know a thing or two, and know it direct, go through this little book and read it carefully." These words come from Storyville's infamous blue books, and one would be wise to follow this advice with regard to the present volume, ably written and composed by Pamela D. Arceneaux: to know a thing or two *about* the blue books, read on!

**Why New Orleans Should Have This Directory**
First. Because it is the only district of its kind in the States set aside for the fast women by *law*.
  Second. Because it puts the stranger on a proper grade or path as to where to go and be secure from hold-ups, brace games and other illegal practices usually worked on the unwise in Red Light Districts.[1]

The blue books were tour guides to Storyville, New Orleans's notorious turn-of-the-century red-light district. They were directories of prostitutes and houses of prostitution, and they provide a rare window onto this infamous demimonde. They also help us situate Storyville within larger cultural contexts, like the development of big business and advertising as part of America's transition into a consumer society during the same time period. And so, the books reveal something about Storyville's place in these broader transformations.

The blue books promised to put the visitor on the right path, to steer him away from cheats and scoundrels, to lead him toward the "cream" of tenderloin society. Typically, the books listed women and their places of work by address and by race. "W" was for white; "C" for colored; and "Oct." for octoroon, meaning one-eighth "black." In some editions, Jewish women were listed too, designated with "J." Stars were awarded for "first class bordellos" or "wine mansions," "B" signaled houses that served beer, and in some editions the number "69" was used to distinguish "French" houses. Other than this oblique reference to oral sex, the books did not include sexual services, prices, or any other such coded details.

Outside of its Storyville context, the term "blue book" often indicates official documents. "Blue book" has also historically referred to the social register, a directory of so-called "blue bloods." The first edition of Storyville's *Blue Book* has the words "Tenderloin 400" on its cover, likely a reference to Ward McAllister's New York social register and the four hundred elite guests who received invitations to Mrs. William Backhouse Astor Jr.'s 1892 gala ball. Another resonance is with the French Hachette guidebooks known as *Guides Bleus*, or "blue guides." These guides did not begin publication until 1918, as Arceneaux points out, but they nevertheless make a useful analogy. Roland Barthes wrote that as tour guides, the *Guides Bleus* are

View of Storyville between 1904 and 1908

extremely selective in their content, revealing "nothing historical," reducing geography to the "picturesque."[2] Similarly, the blue books played up elements of Storyville that the authors most wanted their readers to imagine. They created a fantasy world and invited their readers to enter it.

Like all guidebooks, the blue books taught the reader to perceive the world in a particular way and, in a sense, constructed their own ideal tourist. By highlighting certain features and diminishing or omitting others, guidebooks not only make assumptions about their readers, but also educate them as to what to see and how to see it. Along with Barthes, historians Donna Haraway, Lawrence Levine, David Nasaw, and Robert Rydell, among others, have described museum exhibits and world's fairs as configuring the thinking of tourists in the same way.[3] Clearly, the proposed reader of the blue books was a man, and the blue books represent a particular distillation of the "male gaze," in feminist film theorist Laura Mulvey's powerful formulation. Mulvey argues that in watching movies, the viewer identifies with the male lead and sees the action through his eyes. She argues further that commercial cinema normalizes this "cinematic" gaze as all viewers', male and female. Women in film exist to respond or to appear in fragments—legs, a face, a tone of voice—and not as human beings through whose perceptions the viewer may understand the action.[4] Whether the blue book reader was a john in search of sex or not, the books configured him as a "man-about-town," or, as they put it, a man "out on a lark."

Thus, as Arceneaux reminds us, the blue books do not tell us very much at all about women's lives. They tell a particular kind of story. The books, while presuming to cater to the reader's desire, in fact may have played a role in creating and inflaming that desire. In a sense, the world evoked by the blue books resembles the French fashion magazine *Elle*, which Barthes called "a world without men, but entirely constituted by the gaze of man."[5] The blue books offered an enticement to men to enter the "female world" (gynoecium) they constructed and to possess bodily the women within it. The books themselves never put it that way, of course.

The blue books also configured their readers as white. Bordellos, along with all other sites of commercial amusement, were for whites only; this was the convention in the South at the turn of the century, including in New Orleans. There were no guidebooks to the "Uptown Storyville," sometimes called "Black Storyville," which was created as a concession to a neighborhood already irredeemable in city officials' eyes. Storyville's cribs, the one-room shacks where women worked alone, sometimes in shifts, and where black men could visit prostitutes, are not featured in most of the guides. The women labeled "colored" or "octoroon" in the blue book directories were there for the paid pleasure of white men.

In addition to the directories, blue books contained advertisements for particular bordellos. "Read all the 'Ads,'" the books advise, "as all the best houses are advertised and known as the 'Cream of Society.'" The ads describe the décor, furnishings, entertainment, and jolly ambience of Storyville's best bordellos. According to these tour guides, they were all "absolutely and unquestionably" the most lavish and expensive such houses in the nation and the world. To be sure, "popular convention

Photographs taken of prostitutes upon their arrests in the Storyville era

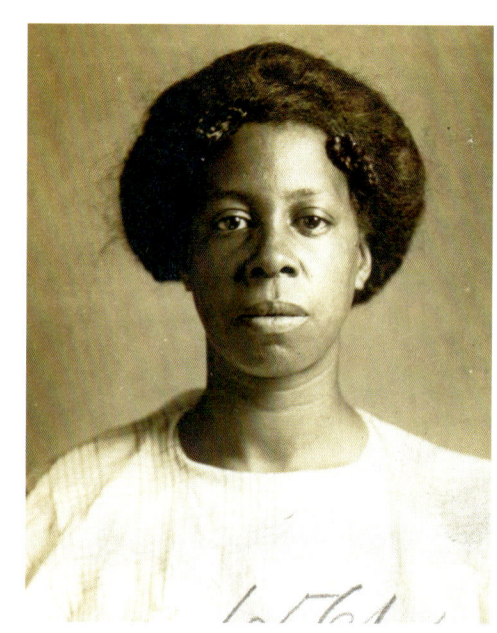
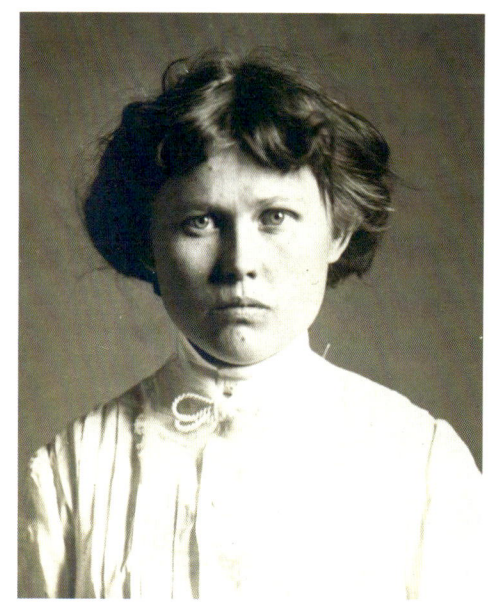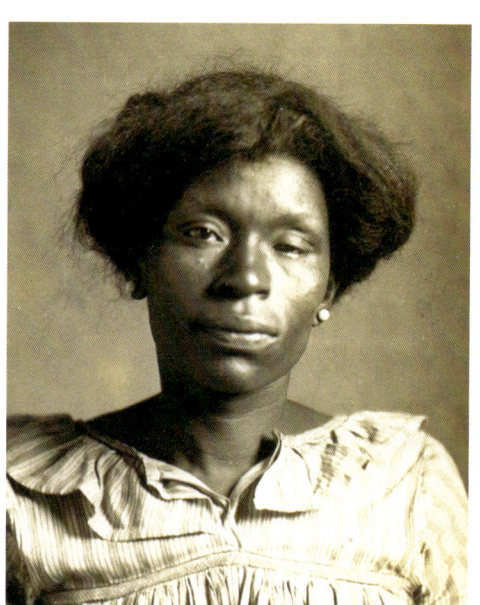

permitted advertisers to exaggerate, as if all their statements were placed within qualifying 'quotation marks,'"[6] as historian Roland Marchand discusses in his landmark book on the rise of modern advertising. Yet the claims of opulence for the premier bordellos made in the blue book ads were particularly extreme and over-the-top, almost as if to point out their own superfluity, given the obvious purpose of a visit.

To better understand this dynamic in the blue books we might briefly set them in the broader historical context of the Storyville era, with a focus on the development of a consumer society and the growth of the modern advertising industry. In the latter half of the nineteenth century, America experienced a revolution of sorts. Tremendous changes in the economy, such as mechanization in production, new organizational methods in business, and the growth of large corporations, transformed American society. As the historian William Leach puts it, "In the decades following the Civil War, American capitalism began to produce a distinct culture, unconnected to traditional family or community values, to religion in any conventional sense, or to political democracy. It was a secular business and market-oriented culture, with the exchange and circulation of money and goods at the foundation of its aesthetic life and of its moral sensibility." Its "cardinal features," according to Leach, were "acquisition and consumption as the means of achieving happiness; the cult of the new; the democratization of desire; and money value as the predominant measure of all value in society."[7]

Storyville flourished within these cultural transformations. The commercial sex district, both celebrated and maligned for its excesses of luxury and degradation, represented the epitome of the capitalist ethos, where *money* was the sole determinant of status and value.[8] Many Americans, however, had difficulty negotiating the transition to this modern world. One effect was what the historian Jackson Lears calls "weightlessness," a sense of being unmoored from reality. Generalized anxiety also bred a new disease of the nerves called neurasthenia, and created what scholars have described as a "crisis of masculinity." The lack of physical work and the effects of leisure among the developing middle and upper middle classes was leading, some feared, to "overcivilization," or a general condition of decadence that was unsuited to the American landscape and seemed to be a betrayal of the country's foundation in both Protestant religion and the rugged pioneer spirit. Lears argues that ministers, physicians, psychologists, intellectuals, and other self-proclaimed experts on the human condition developed a therapeutic ethos to soothe the psyches of the educated classes through intensely self-centered and entirely secular modes of self-improvement; meanwhile, ordinary men and women also looked for ways to cope with the dizzying new culture. Organized sport and a more "muscular" version of Christianity were thought to respond to these enervating trends.[9] Storyville, as a transgressive space, offered its own kind of escape from the pressures of the modern world. A district devoted to the sale of illicit sex, it could certainly be a place to find relief (and release) from anxiety about one's manhood. The blue books were oriented to this purpose.

Social unease might also be harnessed by capital. Having created a huge volume of mass-produced products, industry's bureaucratic corporations had to figure out how to transfer those goods from their factories into the homes of more and more people. This need created an imperative for business to generate, in Leach's words, a new "conception of paradise or some imaginative notion of what constitutes the good life," different from antebellum, agrarian conceptions of the American dream. Commercial capitalism thus wedded the notion of "the good life" to the purchase and possession of "goods," creating an aesthetic of longing and desire.[10]

Advertising played a crucial role. From the mid-1870s to 1900, the volume of advertising increased "more than tenfold, from 50 to 542 millions of dollars per year. Such an increase," writes cultural historian Alan Trachtenberg, "indicated not only an absolute expansion but a decisive change in the *function* of advertising."[11] Whereas before the 1880s print ads had served local merchants with informative text about specific products, after that time advertisers sought to facilitate the wider distribution of mass-produced goods to a national market. Corporate manufacturers began the practice of advertising not simply their products but their brands. As Trachtenberg explains, the earlier, informative mode of advertising "had swiftly given way to a mode in which information as such now fused with a message... about the potential consumer, that he or she *required* the product in order to satisfy a need incited and articulated by the advertisement itself."[12]

The advertiser's role became one "of coach and confidante," offering "the consumer advice and encouragement as together they faced the external challenge"—the challenge of transitioning to modern society, which the ads themselves elaborated.[13] It was crucially important in this anonymous urbanized milieu to make a good first impression, as ads for Aqua Velva, Camay soap, Listerine, and other brands emphasized.[14] Ads depicted scenes in which these particular brands rescued the innocent unknowing from the fatal gaffe—five o'clock shadow; rough, dry skin; bad breath; etc. Women especially faced new demands. Modern advertising reinforced middle-class gender roles and aspirations. Women were pictured as either society girls or housewives, and husbands were always *businessmen*, always portrayed in a suit and tie.[15]

Most of all, advertisers offered a vision of American society as a "democracy of goods," premised on the simultaneous acknowledgement of class difference and the denial that it mattered. "The wonders of modern mass production and distribution," writes Marchand, "enabled every person to enjoy the society's most significant pleasure, convenience, or benefit."[16] As one advertising magazine put it, Ward McAllister's register of "'The Four Hundred' had become 'the four million.'"[17] The "democracy of goods" redeemed the American promise of equality in an era of extreme wealth disparity. The advertising industry, and the businesses it served, prospered when the promise and fulfillment of the American dream moved from the realms of independent self-sufficiency and electoral choice to the realm of the marketplace, whose values had infiltrated every element of American life.[18]

The apotheosis of the advertising industry and consumer culture was the modern department store. Trachtenberg writes of their transformative effect: "Lavishly designed palaces of consumption, department stores tempted their customers (presumed to be shoppers entering from the street, requiring spectacular distraction to win their attention) with monumental neoclassical fronts, ornamental doorways, large window displays, and, inside...a rotunda with upper floors visible as galleries." Once inside, the shopper-cum-consumer was in a new world where everything "seemed magical and glamorous: not only a new world of goods but the world itself newly imagined as consisting of goods and their consumption."[19]

The authors of the blue books seem to have taken this vision as their paradigm, creating for their customers a fantasy world removed from the social realities of those who provided it. Consumption occupied its own realm, physically and ideationally distinct from production, which was made invisible—or "mystified"—by the dramatic displays and opulent ambience created by the merchants or, in the case of Storyville, by the madams or their agents. There is no reference to the factory in the department store, and there are no working class consumers in the advertisements, just as the bordello world of the blue books was all "high class."

Department store owners devised ingenious strategies to disassociate the shopping experience from the commercial world that made it possible. The stores became dazzling showplaces, spectacles in and of themselves. Merchants hired designers to make their stores look like "French salons, rose or apple-blossom festivals, cornucopias, 'the streets of Paris,' Japanese gardens, semitropical refuges in the middle of winter, or southern plantations."[20] The idea was to "eliminate the store by weaving through it some central ideas," as one decorator phrased it.[21] Some exploited the prevailing fascination with the "exotic East," making up their stores "in an indolent oriental atmosphere."[22] Merchants displayed works of fine art, culled from their own collections, on the walls of their establishments. They added live music to these magnificent displays, enveloping the customer in a sumptuous experience. The ethic was one of pure comfort and pleasure.[23] The reader of the present volume will see the same features represented in the blue books.

Along these lines, personalized service, too, became a hallmark of these grand emporia. As Leach writes, "To make customers feel welcome, merchants trained workers to treat them as 'special people' and as 'guests.'" The introduction of tipping in department store restaurants and cafes was also meant to make the customer or guest "feel at home and in the lap of luxury." Tipping "aristocratized consumption, integrating upper-class patterns of comfort into the middle-class lifestyle" and made the customer "feel like 'somebody,'"[24] much as the proprietors of bordellos such as Mahogany Hall promised. In attempting to put the consumer at ease and to immerse him or her within "an experience of total pleasure" completely removed from the world of work, merchants shielded clients from the discomfort and poverty of the service personnel. As Leach puts it, the separateness of the consumer world "tended to blot out the *human* contributions and sufferings involved in its creation."[25] The blue books echo this model of creating an entire world out of choosing and buying.

Storyville exemplified an aspect of the democratization of desire by promising access to a world of pleasure, where the "goods" included the company of beautiful and refined women. It is to be expected that the blue book ads ignored the social conditions and constraints that brought women into prostitution; what is surprising is that they also avoided all mention of sex.

> Like the Stars above, Miss Olive Russell, Of Customhouse St., has appeared before the better class of sporting gentlemen of this community and never has her reputation been other than a highly cultivated lady.…When out for a good time don't over-look her house, her ladies are of a like character.[26]

Like the ads in contemporary commercial culture, the blue book ads constituted the potential customer as middle class or better; congratulated him on ascending the social ladder; and rewarded him with access to sensual pleasure in a realm that was by definition exclusive. In the blue books, transgressive sex was converted into a rarefied privilege of class:

> If it's pretty women and a good time you are looking for—Miss Fisher's, 313 N. Basin St., is the place. Everyone of her ladies are entertainers, who sing, dance and converse; what more does a man want when out for a lark?
> 
> Miss Fisher also has one of the coziest places in the tenderloin. Her oil paintings are said to be worth thousands of dollars.[27]

The blue books flattered the reader as a member of the bourgeoisie, while making a mockery of the moral strictures of that class.

> Margaret Bradford has, without doubt, one of the finest equipped "CHATEAUS" in the Tenderloin District.
> 
> As for women, she has an unexcelled array, who aside from their beauty are all of high-class and culture.
> 
> There is always something new at the "BRADFORD" as the refined people call her mansion.[28]

Compared with most other ads, the blue book advertisements approach self-parody; they understood their purpose was to indicate things that could not be said. Storyville promised an escape from the busyness of the business world to an atmosphere of "fine furnishings" and "refined" women, but with a wink. Photographs and the reminiscences of musicians who worked in the District attest to the real grandeur of some of Storyville's top bordellos, but nonetheless one is struck by the repeated insistence on the costliness of the furniture:

> Miss [Hilma] Burt has been in our midst but a short while, and during that time she has spent a small fortune. When she first came to this city, she purchased the home of Miss Ray Owens, at a neat figure, (this has been less than a year ago) and her business improved such in that short period that she was compelled to seek another house, so she did with the purchasing of the Meeker home, which she gave nearly $20,000 (just for the contents) and since has spent thousands having same renovated.[29]

Like department stores and the advertising industry, the blue books obscured all labor, separating the luxurious world of consumption from the realities of power, class, gender, and race that made such luxury possible. In doing so, the blue books silenced genuine productive voices from within Storyville.

The blue books recognized and celebrated the modern commercial aesthetic in Storyville's burlesque of it. Yet they cannot completely be explained by the male gaze or the rise of the modern consumer. Their self-subversive and undermining humor makes them unique: in their insistence on class there is always an element of parody, and the extreme nature of their claims brings their discourse to the point of self-awareness. The very excesses of their descriptive language, the preposterousness in their claims to "refinement," and the jokiness and slang acknowledge the reader's doubts about their high-class claims, and thus let him "in" on things, which is itself a form of reassurance. Once he is brought into the joke, he can go "out on a lark" and enjoy himself without worry or hesitation. This particular method of salesmanship, this ironic knowingness, makes the blue books peculiarly, and recognizably, modern.

## NOTES

1. *Blue Book*, [1905], 1969.19.6, Williams Research Center, The Historic New Orleans Collection (hereafter THNOC).
2. Barthes, *Mythologies*, 75, 76.
3. See Haraway, "Teddy Bear Patriarchy," 237–91; Levine, *Highbrow/Lowbrow*; Nasaw, *Going Out*; Rydell, *All the World's a Fair*.
4. Mulvey, "Visual Pleasure and Narrative Cinema," 803–16.
5. Barthes, *Mythologies*, 51.
6. Spitzer, paraphrased in Marchand, *Advertising the American Dream*, 264.
7. Leach, *Land of Desire*, 3.
8. For more on Storyville's embrace of commercial values, see Landau, *Spectacular Wickedness*, 117–18.
9. Lears, "From Salvation to Self-Realization," 3–38. See also Agnew, "Consuming Vision of Henry James," 65–100.
10. Leach, *Land of Desire*, 8–9.
11. Trachtenberg, *Incorporation of America*, 136. My italics.
12. Ibid., 136–37.
13. Marchand, *Advertising the American Dream*, 13.
14. Ibid., 213.
15. Ibid., 186.
16. Ibid., 217–18.
17. *Delineator* magazine, qtd. in Marchand, *Advertising the American Dream*, 222.
18. Marchand, *Advertising the American Dream*, 234. See also Agnew, "Consuming Vision of Henry James."
19. Trachtenberg, *Incorporation of America*, 131–32.
20. Leach, *Land of Desire*, 81–83.
21. Jerome Koerber, qtd. in Leach, *Land of Desire*, 83.
22. Leach, *Land of Desire*, 83.
23. Ibid., 139, 142–43.
24. Leach, *Land of Desire*, 131–32.
25. Ibid., 150.
26. *Blue Book*, [1901], 1969.19.4, THNOC.
27. *Blue Book*, [1900], 94-092-RL, THNOC.
28. *Blue Book*, [1908], 1969.19.9, THNOC.
29. Ibid.

A boudoir in Hilma Burt's mansion, from No. 8

# INTRUDUCTION.

What is the good of living if you can't have a good time, or as the proverb goes. Live while you have a chance. You will be dead a long time.

Now the only way to get next to all the good things is to pay particular attention to what this PHAMPLET has to say.

Don't be misguided by touts or gold brick masons, but look for whatever you desire in this book.

This little book contains all the sporting houses in the tenderloin district, both Storyville and Anderson County.

Now to know you are in Storyville, we will give you the boundry, which is as follows:

N. Basin to N. Robertson, Customhouse to St. Louis. This is Storyville.

Anderson County (old tenderloin) is:

Customhouse street to St. Peter, Dauphine to Rampart streets.

The names in this book constitute the Tenderloin "400", one of the grandest sporting societies in existance to-day, including the popular ASTORIA and ARLINGTON.

## ATTENTION.

To tell a landlady from a boarder, their names have been printed in Capital Letters.

* The star on the side of a landlady's name indicates a first class house, where the finest of women and nothing but wine is sold.

The letter "B" on the side of a name indicates a house where beer is sold.

The "No. 69" is the sign of French house.

The Jew will be known by a "J."

Wishing you a good time while making your rounds, I remain yours

BILLY NEWS.

# INTRODUCTION
## STORYVILLE AND THE BLUE BOOKS

**M**uch of what has been written about prostitution over the centuries is either pious, judgmental diatribe or prurient, pornographic titillation. Recently, more scholarly interest in the subject has produced serious, in-depth analysis of many aspects of the business. This present work is neither a study of the history of prostitution in New Orleans nor an attempt at an exhaustive chronicle of the city's twenty-year experiment in confining the "world's oldest profession" to a designated area called Storyville, though some background information is given to set the scene. Instead, the focus centers on a group of guides and pamphlets, collectively called blue books, that served as the district's marketing tools.

Though the guides to Storyville have come to be called blue books, not all of them were published under that name. The most famous of these guides are editions of a publication titled *Blue Book*, but the term is also used to refer to other New Orleans prostitution guides such as *Hell-O*, *New Mahogany Hall*, and even *The Red Book*. Although hundreds of copies of each publication were probably printed, very few of the small, pocket-sized books have survived in libraries or other institutions, and therefore they are highly sought after by collectors. These guides were primarily directories of women working in Storyville but also included advertisements for individual establishments and luxury products printed alongside the listings. They promoted certain madams and their brothels as among the elite of such businesses anywhere. As one edition advised, "Read all the 'Ads', as all the best houses are advertised and are known as the 'Cream of Society.'"[1] Targeting a particular audience as New Orleans sought to present itself as a tourist and convention destination in the early twentieth century, these guidebooks suggested a glamorous, exciting, risqué New Orleans that men could be a part of by simply visiting these lavish houses. Indeed, the blue books promoted Storyville itself.[2] The continual marketing of Storyville in print during its existence has secured its legacy long after its posh bordellos were demolished.

The city's acquisition by the United States as the strategic focal point of the Louisiana Purchase, combined with the influx of émigrés from the Haitian Revolution, caused its population to balloon from approximately 8,500 in 1803 to over 17,000 by 1810, with more refugees and entrepreneurs continually flocking to New Orleans as the century progressed, eager to make their fortunes. Like many busy port cities, New Orleans witnessed an ever-changing influx of people and nationalities and attracted perhaps more than its share of prostitutes and underworld characters. Prostitution flourished uncontrolled throughout the antebellum period until, prompted by citizens' complaints, the New Orleans City Council passed "An Ordinance Concerning Lewd and Abandoned

Typography from introduction, from No. 1

Women," commonly called the Lorette ordinance, in 1857.[3] This law did not discourage prostitution per se but was intended to control it by encouraging prostitutes to ply their trade in less respectable areas of town. It required operators of brothels to purchase licenses, with the added benefit of providing revenue for the city. The short-lived Lorette law failed when landlords, who received substantial rents from prostitutes, pressured the Louisiana Supreme Court, made up of men of the same economic and social class as the landlords, to overturn the entire ordinance in 1859.[4]

A revised version of Lorette, also called "An Ordinance Concerning Lewd and Abandoned Women," was announced in the *Daily Picayune* on July 12, 1865. This new ordinance was similar to the original Lorette in that prostitution was essentially allowed to flourish unrestrained, as long as it remained in broadly defined, less savory areas of town. Again demonstrating the profitability of regulated prostitution to New Orleans, an annual license tax was collected by the city from prostitutes as well as from landlords who rented to them. Merging several earlier regulations regarding unacceptable behavior—public drunkenness, overt verbal or visual solicitation, creating a disturbance—into this ordinance allowed the city to collect numerous additional fines from women in the sex trade. There was no attempt at medical regulation in this revision; officials considered that removing prostitution to designated areas was enough to ensure public health, certainly a curious, head-in-the-sand attitude. Though the 1857 Lorette ordinance prohibited black and white prostitutes from working together in the same houses, racial distinctions were omitted entirely in the 1865 regulations. However, there is little evidence that racial segregation in local brothels was ever vigorously enforced. Even with this new ordinance, prostitution continued largely unchecked, aided by pervasive corruption throughout New Orleans's

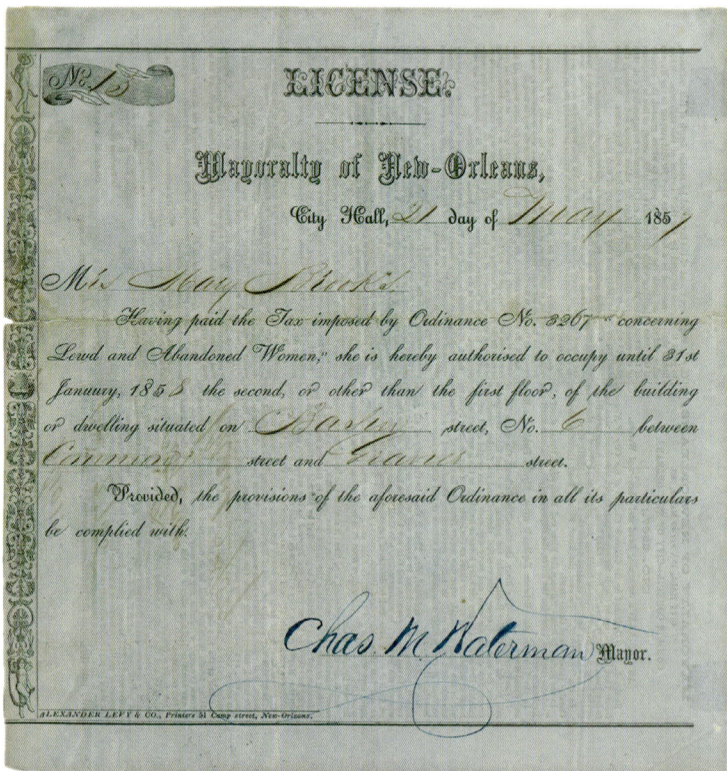

Prostitution license issued to Mary Brooks in 1857

INTRODUCTION | 28

Mug shot and arrest record for Rosie Gibson

Mug shot and arrest record for Jessie Knotts

criminal justice system and by some city leaders, all of whom profited in some way from the sex trade.[5]

Controlling prostitution in other American cities also proved to be a thorny problem. Just over ten years after the demise of the first Lorette ordinance in New Orleans, St. Louis was among the few cities to take extreme legal measures. Its "social evil ordinance," passed on July 5, 1870, began a four-year experiment in regulating the industry by licensing bordellos and by registering individual prostitutes and examining them for venereal disease on a regular basis. Power was given to the city's new board of health to oversee and enforce the ordinance, but this legislation also ran afoul of complex challenges and court cases disputing jurisdiction between city and state.[6]

The control and regulation of vice at the turn of the last century can be said to be a part of national progressive movements that included the regulation of alcohol consumption, attempts to eradicate venereal disease for the betterment of public health, concern for the welfare of children, and securing the right of women to vote. All of these were popular targets of reformers bent on improving society as a whole by identifying and calling public attention to these issues, while at the same time promoting solutions and societal change, often through legislation. Prostitution was not a crime but was considered a vice, a failure of morals. In order to discourage visible prostitution, laws were crafted to move prostitutes to less prominent areas of the city. "Lewd and abandoned women" were arrested not for selling sex but on public nuisance charges and were either jailed or fined and released. Men, without whom there would be no trade, faced no criminal consequences for engaging the prostitutes' services.[7] In an activity where both parties shared equally in perceived immorality, women at the turn of the last century bore the brunt of society's censure and punishment.

Years after the failure of the Lorette ordinance, and once again in response to public outcry regarding the proliferation of prostitutes throughout New Orleans, Alderman Sidney Story (1863–1937) prepared and sponsored legislation intended to regulate the activities of the city's "lewd and abandoned women" by denying them the use of housing for immoral purposes anywhere outside a designated area beginning January 1, 1898.[8] For the next twenty years, Storyville staked its claim as one of the nation's most notorious tenderloins.[9] Storyville encompassed an area just north of the French Quarter, from the uptown side of Customhouse (now Iberville) Street to the uptown side of St. Louis Street, and from the lake side of Basin Street to the river side of Robertson Street.[10] Story was incensed and embarrassed when his name became associated with the new red-light district, but nearly all of Storyville's inhabitants and habitués simply referred to it as the District.[11]

Many mistakenly believe that New Orleans was the first city in the United States to confine its prostitutes to a geographically prescribed area. That dubious honor may go to Virginia City, Nevada, on the Comstock Lode silver strike, which enacted a location ordinance restricting prostitution as early as 1865 and again in 1868, 1875, and 1878. In this frontier boomtown, however, these attempts were largely ignored.[12] In the late 1880s Omaha, Nebraska, followed by Waco and

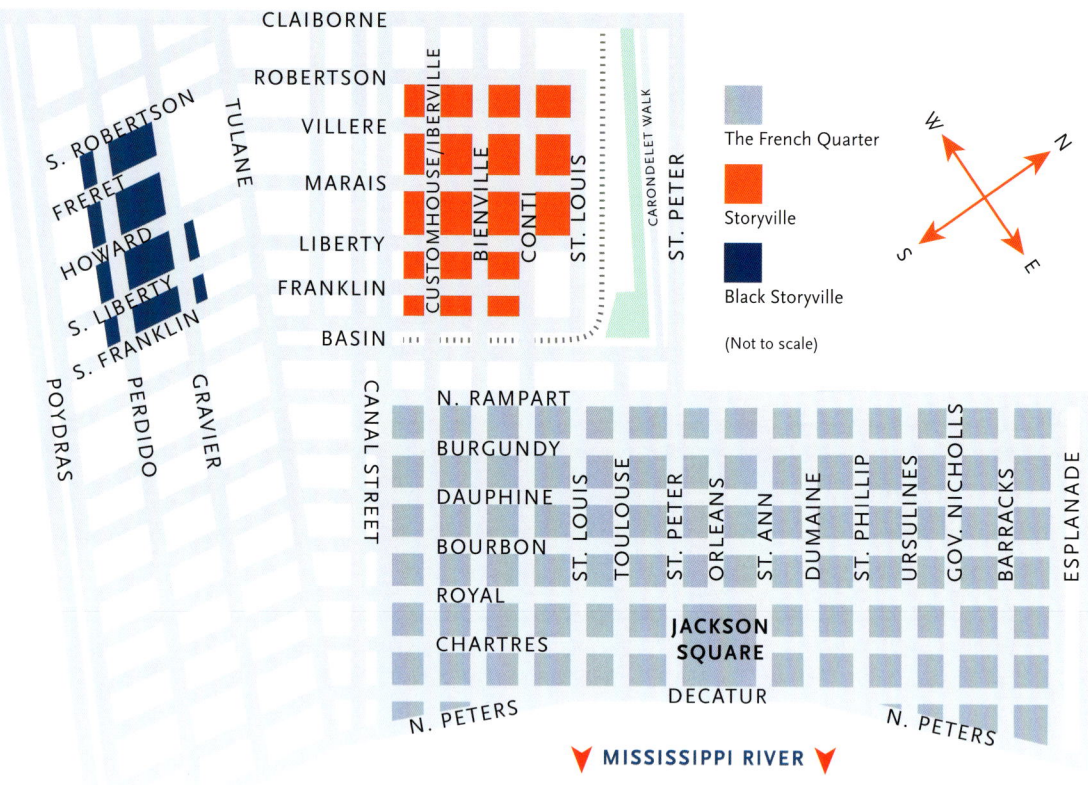

Relative locations of the French Quarter and the two vice districts in the Storyville era

San Antonio, Texas, also enacted similar legislation.[13] Notorious vice areas in other prominent American cities of the era, such as New York's Tenderloin, Chicago's Levee, San Francisco's Barbary Coast, and Fort Worth's Hell's Half Acre, as well as those in smaller towns, were not geographically defined by municipal ordinances, but had developed well before the late nineteenth and early twentieth centuries through years of tradition combined with governmental and police toleration. Even though Storyville was not the country's first legally established red-light district, nor New Orleans the only city with such legislation, its notoriety has lingered longer than most, adding a rosy-tinged hue of wickedness to the city's reputation. The madams' advertisements in the blue books, with their coy references to readily available sexual pleasure, cultivated this impression, creating a message so strongly tied into the city's self-promotion that it continues to define New Orleans as a good-time town to the present day.

Life in the District was more often than not far from rosy for many who made their living there. As author Craig L. Foster has noted, for some prostitutes plagued with venereal disease, alcoholism, or drug addiction, suicide was their last hope of release from a miserable existence.[14] Moralists and social reformers of the era decrying the evils of prostitution would have us believe that such was the inevitable end of all unrepentant "fallen" women. Closer to reality, most women who worked as prostitutes did so for a few years or part time, either to supplement their incomes during lean times, to achieve the means to start their own businesses, or to perhaps meet and eventually marry financially secure men. These short-term prostitutes hoped to better their situation and slip unnoticed back into general society.[15]

Foster's comparison of US census data from 1900 and 1910 gives some interesting insight into the changing demographics of the women

INTRODUCTION | 30

of Storyville. During this period, the median age of Storyville prostitutes crept up (twenty-four in 1900, twenty-six in 1910), and the women were much less likely to be married (17 percent married in 1900, about 1 percent married in 1910). Fewer Louisiana natives were working in Storyville at the end of the decade (45 percent in 1900, 35 percent in 1910). Numbers of African American prostitutes working in the District saw a similar decline (38 percent of the population of Storyville in 1900, 28 percent in 1910). The number of children of prostitutes living in the District decreased, from 197 in 1900 to 66 in 1910. Census data for the area also reveals that very often mothers and daughters, aunts and nieces, cousins, or sisters lived and worked together at the same address.[16]

Despite blue book ads' claims of highly accomplished, select, first-class ladies, not all women working in even the best of brothels were sophisticated, proper, or charming. Those with some degree of sophistication and charm certainly had a better chance of rising in the profession, however. Many were poor immigrants or were young women newly arrived from rural areas.[17] While the blue books promote gorgeously furnished houses staffed with beautiful women, all clever entertainers and charming young ladies, the local newspapers often went out of their way to report wild shenanigans and serious crimes involving these women.[18]

## BLUE BOOK ORIGINS

The term "blue book" has several meanings. A blue book is often a compilation of specialized information, such as a report or a registry published under governmental authorization; the phrase appears to come from English parliamentary records, which were bound in blue paper.[19] Perhaps the most familiar contemporary example, the *Kelley Blue Book* records the values of new and used vehicles for resale or insurance purposes. *Blue Guides* or *Guides Bleus*, highly detailed travel guidebooks first published in 1918 and still available for many destinations, were based on the popular nineteenth-century German series published by Baedeker (although Baedeker's guides usually had red covers). Visitors to the eastern Mexico coastal resort town of Cozumel since 1980 are probably familiar with its *Free Blue Guide*, also called *La Guía Azul*, which contains street maps; advertisements for restaurants, shops, and services; tourist tips; emergency numbers; and other useful information.

An air of the elite also suffuses the term "blue book." *Authentic Arabian Bloodstock, Volume I*, which contains pedigree listings relative to horse breeding, is often called "the blue book" by horse fanciers. In many cities during the late nineteenth and well into the mid-twentieth century, annually published society directories listed the addresses, some lineage information, and organizational affiliations of the wealthy and well-connected. *Soards' Blue Book of New Orleans* was published by the Soards Directory Company, which also printed city directories. These society directories often had dark blue covers and were referred to as blue books, perhaps also signifying the "blue bloods" listed within them. Central to the tone of the Storyville blue books was the implication that the prostitutes and madams listed inside were the crème of the demimonde, the elite of the scarlet sisterhood, the "Tenderloin 400"; use of the term "blue book" reinforced that aura of high society.[20] By 1908,

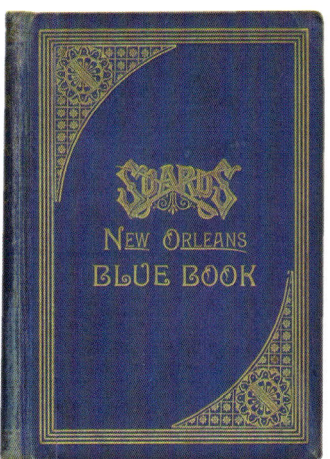

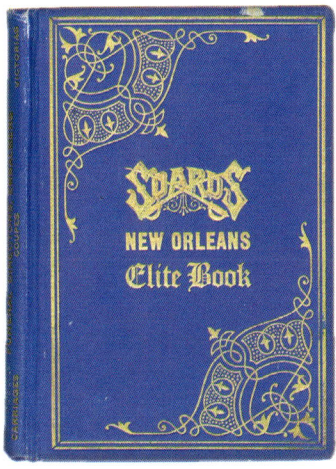

By 1908, the Soards Directory Company had dropped "Blue Book" from the title of its directories, replacing it with "Elite Book."

BLUE BOOK ORIGINS | 31

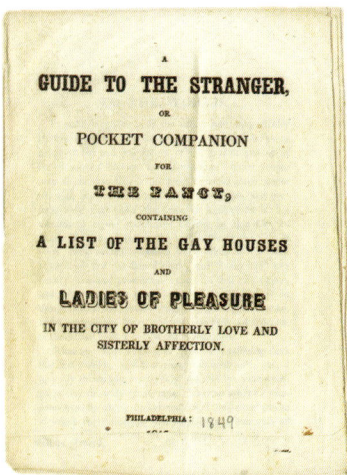

Philadelphia's 1849 *A Guide to the Stranger* contains reviews of brothels, unlike the Storyville guides.

Soards had changed the title of its directory to *Soards' Elite Book of New Orleans*—probably to eliminate any possibility of confusing these directories with New Orleans brothel guides.

New Orleans was not the only city whose centers of sinful pleasure had published guides. Such guides existed long before Storyville. Author Tony Perrottet describes *Il catalogo di tutte le principali et più honorate cortigiane di Venezia* (The catalog of all the principal and most honored courtesans of Venice), printed in 1565, as a listing of the names and addresses of 210 prostitutes with their prices for services, a feature lacking in most brothel guides, including New Orleans's blue books. Published annually between 1757 and 1795, *Harris's List of Covent-Garden Ladies*, which described and rated London's better class of harlots, has been attributed to Jack Harris, a pimp and waiter at the Shakespeare's Head pub.[21] In its Catalogue 155, issued in 2012, Charles B. Wood III Antiquarian Booksellers offered a copy for $1,500 of the twelfth annual edition (ca. 1875) of *Paris after Dark, Containing a Description of the Fast Women, Their Haunts, Habits, etc.* . . . The cover title of this guide, *Nocturnal Paris, An Indispensable Companion for the Stranger*, demonstrates that the audience for this publication, like that of the Storyville blue books, was largely tourists.[22]

In the United States, New York produced several guides over the years, among which were *Fast Man's Directory and Lovers' Guide to the Ladies of Fashion and Houses of Pleasure in New-York and Other Large Cities*, appearing in 1853, and *The Gentleman's Companion: New York City in 1870*, also titled *The Gentleman's Directory*. Oddly, 1859's *Directory to the Seraglios in New York, Philadelphia, Boston and All the Principal Cities in the Union* does not include entries for New Orleans, certainly a principal city at that time. In 1849 Philadelphia provided *A Guide to the Stranger, or Pocket Companion for the Fancy, Containing a List of the Gay Houses and Ladies of Pleasure in the City of Brotherly Love and Sisterly Affection*, certainly a descriptive and clever title.[23] Unlike the later blue books of Storyville, whose advertisements are nearly universally interchangeable in their praise of the madams' establishments, this Philadelphia publication actually performs as a true guide. Instead of simply directing the visitor to brothels and listing madams, it advises which houses are well managed, staffed with attractive prostitutes in pleasant surroundings, and safe for any gentleman to visit, and which houses are moderate to mediocre. It also bluntly cites those lowest dens that should be scrupulously avoided.

Many other American cities also produced brothel guides. There is the *Sporting and Club House Guide to Milwaukee: Containing a Complete List of All the First-Class Sporting and Club Houses in the City* and *The Sporting and Club House Directory, Chicago: Containing a Full and Complete List of All Strictly First-Class Club and Sporting Houses*, both published in 1889. Kansas City's *Little Black Book* appeared sometime in the 1880s or 1890s. A special guide to Louisville's prostitutes, *G. A. R. Souvenir Sporting Guide*, was produced for visitors to the 1895 encampment of the Grand Army of the Republic held in that city. *La Fiesta de Los Angeles Souvenir Sporting Guide* was published in 1897 to coincide with anticipated visitors to Los Angeles, California, during this event. An entire state is covered in *Traveler's Night Guide of Colorado*, with an unknown place of publication and publisher, but possibly released in 1893. These are but a few examples of the variety of brothel guides produced; there are undoubtedly numerous others.

## PROSTITUTION GUIDES OF NEW ORLEANS

I find it interesting that New Orleans, a city with a reputation of excessive prostitution activity during its long history, does not appear to have had a directory to its brothels until the Storyville era. In their books on the District, Charles F. Heartman (1883–1953) and Al Rose (1916–1993) both cite a brief paragraph in a locally published weekly scandal sheet that may herald the first appearance of a guide to madams and brothels of New Orleans.[24] The Society column of the February 2, 1895, issue of the *Mascot* announces:

> The society ladies of the city can now boast that they have a directory....Within the past week a little book, styled "The Green Book, or Gentlemen's Guide to New Orleans," has been freely distributed. In it are all the principal mansions de joie in the city (white and colored). The names of the madams of the houses are given, as also are those of all the angels, nymphs and fairies. The color and nationality of the darlings are stated. Twenty thousand copies of the guide will be distributed during Mardi Gras. The price is twenty-five cents. The publisher's name does not appear.[25]

Neither Heartman nor Rose was able to secure a copy of *The Green Book*. I join their ranks. I have not located a copy of this item in any repository and can only speculate that this little piece of ephemera may be lost forever, unless a copy exists in private hands.[26] Heartman was of the opinion that all copies were eventually destroyed; Rose suggests that the editors of the *Mascot* simply made up the story, but that does not seem likely. What purpose would such an announcement serve, if it were not true—perhaps to gauge the demand for such an item among the *Mascot*'s readership? This also seems unlikely.

The Storyville prostitution guides among The Historic New Orleans Collection's holdings were produced between 1898 and 1915. The

**No. 69 FRENCH RESORTS. F.**
ROSIE DELAIRE, French, 1018 Bienville.
Katie Weber, French, Marie Lewis, French, Angeline Besse, French, French, Marcelle Leo, French

"69" and "French" sex indicate fellatio, from No. 1.

majority of these have directory sections that list hundreds of women by address and race. There is no attempt at rating the houses or the services offered. In fact, the services are rarely mentioned other than references to "French" sex or "69" (both designating fellatio); further, no fees for such services are stated in any of the known, authentic blue books. Prices in the houses were likely established by the madams themselves and could be subject to economic as well as seasonal fluctuations. Advertisements printed in the guides—for brothels as well as saloons, liquor brands, and hangover cures—are among the most fascinating components of these publications, as they reveal how madams sought to portray their houses and offer a glimpse into what a night in Storyville would have been like. Spelling and grammar were not strengths of the genre, and along with errors in recording addresses, such mistakes can be seen in abundance throughout the majority of these guides. For example, 205 N. Basin is the stated address of Flo Meeker's establishment in her full-page advertisements over a number of years, but the directory sections in the same guides list her at 209 N. Basin, the correct address. In later editions, when management of the brothel changed from Meeker to Hilma Burt to Gertrude Dix, the inconsistency in address remained.

### BLUE BOOK AND BILLY STRUVE

The vast majority of the known guides to Storyville are editions of a publication called *Blue Book*, released more or less annually and so dominant that its title has been borrowed to describe the District's prostitution guides in general. The pseudonymous "Billy News" compiled *Blue Book*, which was released between 1900 and 1915. Though News's real identity is never revealed within the pages of *Blue Book*, the man behind the guides was William "Billy" Struve (1872?–1937), a police reporter for the New Orleans *Item*. Struve had both newspaper connections and intimate knowledge of the local underworld; his obituaries note that he was a widely known saloon and restaurant operator in New Orleans for more than a quarter of a century, and one definitively identifies him as the producer of the "once famous" guides.[27] He was a close friend and associate of Thomas C. "Tom" Anderson, businessman, state legislator, and the so-called Mayor of Storyville. Anderson, a frequent advertiser in *Blue Book*, probably also had a hand in producing it. In the 1900 and 1901 New Orleans city directories, Struve is listed as a "news dealer" and "reporter," respectively, but beginning in 1902 and for most of the Storyville years, his entry reads "mngr. T. C. Anderson, 201 N. Basin"— the address for Tom Anderson's Annex Cafe and Restaurant—and often notes that his residence is the same. This is probably where he compiled material for these guides.[28] Struve's real name sometimes appears in ads in *Blue Book* for Anderson's Annex.

It is very likely that madams paid Struve for the ostentatious descriptions given in their full-page advertisements, although the amount paid

Billy Struve

Tom Anderson

INTRODUCTION | 34

for these ads and any editorial input the madams may have had remains unknown. Heartman speculates that they were a "commercial proposition," and with fees from the madams and the other advertisers, Struve may have more than covered his production costs.[29]

Early editions of *Blue Book* were made using cheap paper on a letterpress printer and were probably produced by a local printer or stationer, or in the jobbing office—which handled commercial orders, or "jobs," as a sideline—of any number of local newspapers. In 1903, as more revenue from advertisers became available, especially those with nationally recognized brands, editions began sporting more expensive-looking and durable calendered paper. Graphic designer and stationer Nancy Sharon Collins observes that later illustrations and embellishments were most likely achieved with emerging cost-efficient printing technologies of the day, such as photomechanical processes (etched images in copper, magnesium, or zinc), magnesium or zinc line cuts, or possibly a stereotyping method.[30] Another printing feature called rubrication emphasized words, phrases, and design elements with red ink. Rubrication, often seen in medieval texts, had been enjoying a revival among avant-garde designers and publishers of some arts and literary magazines of the 1890s.[31] These influences can be seen in Storyville's *Blue Book*.

Beginning with the sixth edition of *Blue Book* (No. 4 in this bibliography), published in 1905, pages throughout the publication are randomly embellished with bold, whimsical figures and abstract designs called Mission Toys. This set of characters was created for American Type Founders (ATF) in 1904 by William H. Bradley (1868–1962), one of the American masters of typography and graphic design during the arts and crafts movement of the late nineteenth and early twentieth centuries. They were first made available to printers in the November 1904 issue of ATF's publication, the *American Chap-Book*. They could be purchased either singly or in a set of ten different designs in three point sizes, for a variety of decorative purposes.[32] It is interesting to note that nearly as soon as they were made available to printers, these Mission Toys appear in the pages of a New Orleans brothel guide.

I suspect that the *Sunday Sun*, a weekly New Orleans paper active before and during the Storyville years that reported happenings in the local sporting scene, may have had some involvement in *Blue Book*'s production. It has long been asserted that the guides were released in anticipation of the throngs of visitors to New Orleans during Carnival. A special Carnival edition of the *Sunday Sun* dated February 25, 1906, ran advertisements for prominent madams very similar in style to the full-page ads found throughout editions of *Blue Book*. For example:

Mission Toys, from Nos. 6 and 7

> Miss Brown has the honor of keeping one of the finest and most elaborately furnished establishments in the city, where beautiful women, good wine and sweet music reign supreme. Jessie is clever to every one and keeps one of the most refined houses in the Tenderloin. Miss Brown's number is 1542 Customhouse street. A royal time will be accorded all those visiting this up-to-date establishment. Jessie is a good fellow, full of fun, intelligent and as pretty as a doll. It is no wonder she is making so many friends.[33]

Many newspapers ran commercial print jobs as a lucrative sideline, and though the *Sunday Sun* is a strong candidate, it is not the only one. There were numerous printers and stationers in New Orleans at that time. Without further evidence, the printer or printers that produced various editions of *Blue Book* may remain unknown.

Because of the ephemeral nature of these publications, the lack of bibliographic information printed within them, and their poor survival rate, previous scholarship has found it difficult to verify their publication sequence. Of the ten known editions of *Blue Book*, only five are actually identified in their texts as "editions"—the sixth, seventh, eighth, ninth, and tenth editions (Nos. 4–8). Two of these are also dated: the seventh edition, 1906, and the eighth edition, 1907. In his book on the District, Al Rose disregards these facts, asserting that there were only five different editions of the publication ever produced, distinguished solely by their different cover designs (Nos. 1, 2, 4, 8, and 10) and erroneously claiming that all other editions were merely reprints.[34] I found that their organization, text, and entries are significantly different. Among the holdings of The Historic New Orleans Collection, there are four other editions of *Blue Book* not identified by Rose, each having different covers, which I consider distinct editions (Nos. 3, 5, 6, and 7), and another (No. 9) that he mentions in passing in a caption.[35]

Rose assigned a date to these guides by checking the addresses of prostitutes listed within against their addresses in New Orleans city directories and noting changes in street names.[36] Although this method can be useful in dating material, it is not entirely reliable, as older street names probably remained in common usage among locals for some time after an official change. Street names within the District that have changed include Customhouse, changed to Iberville in 1906; Franklin, changed to Crozat in 1924; and Liberty, changed to Treme in 1951. The portion of Basin Street that had been within the Storyville district was renamed Saratoga beginning in 1921—possibly to mask its notoriety—but reverted to its former name in 1945.

Both Heartman and Rose also overlooked an obvious and important source—advertisements for the French balls. These balls, described as "French" to indicate their bawdy nature, were held during the Carnival season, organized by Storyville's business owners, and attended by madams, prostitutes, and the men who frequented the District.[37] Many editions of *Blue Book* and one of the alternative guides contain advertisements and dates for these balls. The best-known of these Carnival gatherings of the demimonde were the balls given by the C. C. C. Club, always held on the Saturday evening prior to Mardi Gras, and by the Two Well-Known Gentlemen, always held on Mardi Gras night.[38] Although the advertisements for the French balls appearing in the 1900–1908 editions of *Blue Book* rarely state the year of the events, they do list the month and day. Since the balls were always held on the same days relative to Mardi Gras, consulting historical listings of Mardi Gras dates can supply the likely year of publication for these guides. Ads for the French balls in later editions of *Blue Book* do not supply dates at all. This could have been a cost- or time-saving measure, as the basic ad design and copy could be reprinted year after year without alteration. Unfortunately, it makes the later books more difficult to date with certainty.[39]

Advertisement for the French balls, from No. 3

The blue books frequently mention Carnival, suggesting that the release of these guides was tied to that season, from No. 12.

Further suggesting that *Blue Book* was released in anticipation of increased business during Carnival is a "Notice" that appears at the back of an early edition (No. 1): "Strangers need this book during the Carnival to steer proper." The inclusion of this warning, meant to protect the unwary carouser from disreputable establishments perhaps operating outside of the confines of the legally recognized district where he could be harmed, defrauded, or simply embarrassed by a sudden police raid, reveals that the books were produced with tourists in mind; it is repeated in the introductions of nearly all editions. The same page contains an offer to sell copies in bulk at a reduced rate to hotels and cafes, again showing that the publication was released in anticipation of an influx of visitors.[40]

Nearly all editions of *Blue Book* contain a warning that the little guides could not be mailed. The Comstock Law, passed by Congress in 1873, made it a crime to sell or distribute materials through the United States Postal Service that could be construed as corrupting to public morals. Named for its most vigorous proponent, Anthony Comstock (1844–1915), lobbyist for moral reform and head of the New York Society for the Suppression of Vice, the law prohibited mailing information about birth control, abortion, sexuality, or sexually transmitted diseases, or literature considered obscene or pornographic.[41] In promoting the sale of carnal pleasure, *Blue Book* certainly fell under this description.

These guides to the sporting scene—a world of sex, fraternal camaraderie, drinking, and gambling in New Orleans's male tourist mecca—allowed any white man to become an insider, sharing this knowledge with other white men and being a part of something bigger than himself.[42] Targeting a white male audience, Storyville guides offered access to sexually taboo attractions, most visibly the promise of sex with mixed-race women, or "octoroons." This desire was rooted in the fantasy of Southern antebellum planter aristocracy, when sexual power over light-complexioned black women—whether they were enslaved women purchased through the "fancy trade" or the relatively small number of free women of color who became contracted mistresses—was considered a status symbol.[43] At the time, a myth circulated that Jewish women, especially those having red hair, were extremely passionate, and some editions note the availability of Jewish prostitutes in Storyville.[44] A fascination with the exotic, particularly the perceived mysterious sensuality of the East, is revealed throughout editions of *Blue Book*—in photographs of the Arlington's lushly appointed Turkish Parlor and Chinese Parlor; in the name of another brothel, the Cairo, which features "Oriental Dancers"; in advertisements for the Alhambra Baths at 726 Gravier Street; and in the photograph and advertisement of Rita Walker, "The Oriental Danseuse."[45]

*Blue Book* was sold where men congregated—in barbershops, saloons, hotels, and railroad stations—and carried advertisements for other products and services of interest to men, such as liquor, cigars, restaurants, pawnshops, lawyers, and venereal disease "cures." An evening out in Storyville was more than simply a visit to a brothel. It could contain an entire slate of the male-centric activities reflected in the publication's advertisements, but the main attraction and purpose of the guide was to promote the District's top-of-the-line brothels and madams.

Advertisement for Rita Walker, "The Oriental Danseuse," from No. 10

## ALTERNATIVE STORYVILLE GUIDES

Editions of *Blue Book* may be the most well-known publications related to Storyville, but they do not present the full spectrum of the area's prostitution guides. This bibliography contains five alternative guides, all quite distinct from editions of *Blue Book*, that exhibit some overlap in content, language, and intent. There is evidence of at least one rival to that more famous publication in *The Red Book* of 1901 (No. 12), which also has a comprehensive directory section, but far superior production values. *Sporting Guide, of the Tenderloin-District of New Orleans, LA.* (No. 13) contains advertisements similar to those in *Blue Book*, but no directory section other than a short phone list of madams and advertisers. Two smaller guides, *Hell-O* (No. 14) and *"The Lid"* (No. 15), are just a few centimeters tall and have only eight pages each. These include simplified listings of madams and advertise Tom Anderson's establishments exclusively. Lulu White produced her own guides and souvenir booklets advertising her brothel, including *New Mahogany Hall* (No. 11), and there certainly could have been other enterprising women who promoted their own versions of the Storyville experience. Al Rose mentions these five alternative guides in his book on the District.

Cover of the alternative guide *Hell-O*, from No. 14

## BROTHEL ADVERTISEMENTS

A successful madam possesses a considerable degree of business sense and management skills, as well as a thorough knowledge of her trade and the tastes of her clientele. Most houses in Storyville were well-run operations under their landladies' iron hands, while others appear in police reports and newspapers with accusations of thievery between the women as well as from their clients, and boisterous fights.[46] In most instances, the madams' full-page advertisements in the blue books—among the guides' most important and interesting features—provide little real information about these sexual entrepreneurs and almost no physical descriptions. Promoting the pleasures of wine, women, and song in florid language that in itself is amusing, the advertisements for the "better" brothels are suggestive rather than explicit, written in relatively demure terms. Every madam or landlady is glorified as a queen among queens, keeping the most elaborate and costly establishment

> She never wears stays, and she loves to show her tremendous, white, heaving globes, surmounted by rich strawberry nipples. There is something masculine in her manner and temperament. She often scours the low haunts of our city, to pick up fledglings for her private diversions, which are those of a thorough tribade.

A fake blue book published in 1963 contains explicit language not seen in genuine editions, from No. 18.

> Grace is regarded as an all-round jolly good fellow, saying nothing about her beauty. She regards life as life and not as a money-making space of time.

*The phrase "jolly good fellow" appears throughout the blue books, from No. 10.*

where "fun is the watchword" and "good times reign supreme." Certain phrases and indicators present the aura the most successful madams attempted to project and the clientele they hoped to attract to their establishments.

Though some of the madams' advertisements are suggestive, graphic descriptions of services offered or sexual proclivities of the madams never appear in any of the genuine Storyville-era prostitution guides that I have examined. A 1963 souvenir reprint based on the 1908 *Blue Book* (No. 18) has perhaps contributed to the myth that these books were explicit. This souvenir contains fifteen fake advertisements that do not appear in the edition of *Blue Book* it otherwise replicates, featuring phrases like "firm, globular, heaving breasts of abundant size": language far more descriptive and explicit than that in the genuine publications.[47] Perhaps the producer of this cut-and-paste reprint felt that the tame ads present in the genuine copy needed some spice to entice mid-twentieth-century purchasers. In his book on Storyville guides, Heartman states that he'd seen fragments of pamphlets containing explicit photographs of nude women, and a small book promoting Lulu White's brothel containing tickets illustrated with various sexual positions that "entitled the bearer to the service depicted."[48] He includes mention of these so as not to be accused of "carelessness and ignorance," although he feels that "they [did] not deserve to be investigated" in his bibliography.[49] Heartman thought enough of Storyville's blue books to produce his bibliography as a guide for the curious collector (albeit under a pseudonym), but his descriptions of the guides are casually dismissive, projecting an attitude that indicates that he thought they were beneath the dignity of the serious book enthusiast.

In the genuine guides, the language in the ads is largely interchangeable from madam to madam and from edition to edition. One can imagine the reactions of W. O. Barrera and Jessie Brown when they saw their ads on facing pages in a later *Blue Book* (No. 10); except for their names, the ads read almost exactly the same.[50] Despite their lack of concrete information, the madams' ads are still entertaining in their extravagant promises of an elite and costly environment where white men "in the know" could share a sense of non-competitive camaraderie.[51] Flora Randella's full-page advertisement for the Cairo from the 1913–15 *Blue Book* contains many of the typical elements that can be found throughout these ads.

*Flora Randella, who is better known as "Snooks," the Italian beauty, is one woman among the fair sex who is regarded as an all-round jolly good fellow.*

BROTHEL ADVERTISEMENTS | 39

Josie Arlington's mirrored ballroom, from No. 4

> Nothing is too good for "Snooks," and she regards the word "Fun" as it should be, and not as a money-making word. She is a good fellow to all who come in contact with her.
>
> "Snooks" has the distinction of keeping one of the liveliest and most elaborately furnished establishments in the city, where an array of beautiful women and good times reign supreme.
>
> A visit will teach more than pen can describe.
>
> "Snooks" also has an array of beautiful girls, who are everlastingly on the alert for a good time, and her Oriental dancers are among our cleverest entertainers.[52]

She is a "jolly good fellow," a popular phrase intimating her standing and acceptance in the underworld of male entertainment that appears in numerous blue book ads.[53] The claims of an "elaborately furnished establishment," staffed by beautiful, fun-loving women, and the promise of risqué good times are repeated throughout nearly all of the madams' ads. "Oriental dancers" imply something foreign and exotic. The teasing sentence "A visit will teach more than pen can describe" is repeated through several editions, in ads for the houses of Bessie Cummings, Como Lines, Vivian DeWitt, May Tuckerman, and Grace Lloyd.

Many ads emphasize the luxuriousness of the brothel, its exclusivity, or its reputation as a discreet, refined, well-managed establishment. Some brothels are described in their ads as so lavishly appointed with costly and unique furnishings that a visit could be considered a not-to-be-missed educational experience much like attending an art museum—with the added attraction of commercial sex. Such ads suggest that men from all social strata might better themselves simply by visiting these sporting palaces, although in promoting their brothels as elite and discriminating, madams were also targeting the class of men they wanted as customers. Lillian Irwin's advertisement from the 1905 *Blue Book* provides a good example of this. In addition to emphasis on the vouched-for elegance of her establishment, the statement that she is a favorite of the "club boys" implies, and therefore aims to attract, an upper class clientele.

Josie Arlington's Japanese Parlor, from No. 3

INTRODUCTION | 40

> Miss Irwin has the distinction of conducting about one of the best establishments in the Tenderloin District, where swell men can be socially entertained by an array of swell ladies. As for beauty, her home has been pronounced extremely gorgeous by people who are in a position to know costly finery, cut glass and oil paintings, foreign draperies, etc.
>
> Miss Irwin, while very young, is very charming, and, above all things, a favorite with the boys—what one might say, those of the clubs.
>
> Lillian, as the club boys commonly call her, has never less than fifteen beautiful ladies—from all parts of this great and glorious country.[54]

Josie Arlington's and Flo Meeker's 1905 advertisements in *Blue Book* also consistently emphasize the costliness of their mansions by naming luxurious features and cultural references intended to resonate with their desired clientele. Both women evidently had on display souvenir items from the Louisiana Purchase Exposition, an international event held in St. Louis over several months in 1904 that commemorated the centennial of the Louisiana Purchase and was a subject of interest at this time. Arlington's ad specifically calls attention to her international art collection, and Meeker's, to her taste in interior design, as approved by bon vivants and connoisseurs (whether she actually designed her furnishings is unknown). Meeker's mirrored ballroom also warrants a mention; music rooms with mirrored walls and ceilings were features of the Arlington and of Lulu White's Mahogany Hall as well.

> Nowhere in this country will you find a more complete and thorough sporting establishment than the Arlington.
>
> Absolutely and unquestionably the most decorative and costly fitted out sporting palace ever placed before the American public.
>
> The wonderful originality of everything that goes to fit out a mansion makes it the most attractive ever seen in this and the old country.
>
> Miss Arlington recently went to an expense of nearly $5,000 in having her mansion renovated and replenished.
>
> Within the great walls of the Arlington will be found the work of great artists from Europe and America. Many articles from the Louisiana Purchase Exposition will also be seen.[55]

Drawing of Josie Arlington's brothel, from No. 10

> Without a doubt [Flo Meeker] has one of the most gorgeously fitted-out establishments in Storyville.
>
> *Bon vivants* and connoisseurs pronounce her mansion the Acme of Perfection. Her furniture and fittings were all made to order from her own designs; many of the articles in her domicile, such as paintings and cut-glasses, came from Paris and Germany and the late St. Louis Exposition. Her new mirror dance hall, recently put in at great expense, is the talk of the town. See it.
>
> Don't fail to form Miss Meeker's acquaintance. She is clever, and her coterie of ladies are of a like disposition—always ready for a joyous time.[56]

Discretion—certainly of interest to some men out for a night in Storyville—is stressed in advertisements in *Blue Book* for the brothels of madams Dorothy Denning (1901) and Frances Morris (1913–15). Both

BROTHEL ADVERTISEMENTS | 41

state that visitors can come and go "without being seen," although it is a mystery how anyone could reach Morris's brothel, a prominent two-story building that stood on the uptown-river corner of Conti and Liberty (now Treme) Streets, without detection. Morris further stresses that her brothel is "select"; in stating that men "must be of some importance" to patronize her establishment, she flatters every man who walks through the door.

> Miss Denning has the honor of keeping one of the quietest and most elaborately furnished establishments in the city where beautiful women, good wine and sweet music reign supreme. Miss Denning while clever to everyone has the distinction of keeping one of the most refined houses in the Tenderloin, where one can have enjoyment unmolested and without being seen.[57]

> This place [Frances Morris's] is one of the few gorgeously furnished places in the Storyville District, located so that the most particular person in the world can reach it without being seen by anyone.
> The mansion is under the sole direction of Frances Morris, who is one of the handsomest landladies in the District and is a princess. Her ladies are of like type.
> The success and reputation enjoyed by this establishment in the past is more than surpassed under the able management of Miss Morris, who has not overlooked anything that goes to make a place famous and select.
> You make no mistake in visiting 1320. Everybody must be of some importance, otherwise he cannot gain admittance.[58]

Other madams avoided the superfluous verbiage present in so many of the typical advertisements and came right to the point. Sometimes less really is more. The entirety of Grace Simpson's ad in the 1908 *Blue Book* reads, "House full of pretty and clever women."[59] The Phoenix, under Fanny Lambert's direction in 1906, advertises "Wine and Beer. House Full of Jolly and Pretty Ladies."[60] Mary Smith's ad from 1905, after a short list of "entertainers," simply states, "A pleasant time for the boys."[61]

To further entice the visitor and promote the District's facade of sophisticated elegance, several editions of *Blue Book* contain photographs of luxurious interiors: mirrored music rooms or ballrooms, sumptuously appointed parlors, dining rooms, boudoirs, and dens decorated in exotic themes labeled "Turkish" or "Japanese." Typical of the inconsistencies of this publication, often the same photograph reprinted in various editions will have a different caption from one edition to the next; the image of Josie Arlington's Chinese Parlor in the 1901 edition is identified as the Japanese Parlor in the 1903 edition. Photographs of only three brothels' interiors are printed in genuine editions of *Blue Book*: Arlington's (225 N. Basin), Ray Owens's Star Mansion (1517 Iberville), and Hilma Burt's (209 N. Basin). The majority of the photographs are from the Arlington, suggesting that Josie Arlington, and to a lesser extent Owens and Burt, funded *Blue Book* significantly beyond the cost of their individual full-page advertisements. To the modern eye, these photographs depict the fussy, over-decorated, domestic interiors typical of middle and upper

A boudoir in Hilma Burt's mansion, from No. 8

"The beautiful Estelle Russell," from No. 11

class late-Victorian houses—except few residences contained mirrored ballrooms. To the typical reader during the Storyville era, these photographs projected an aura of the elite. They provide more immediate and concrete evidence of the lavishness of these brothels than the written claims of the madams' advertisements.[62] Though none of the alternative guides in The Historic New Orleans Collection's holdings contain photographs of brothel interiors, some do feature photographs of famous Storyville figures, and *New Mahogany Hall* prominently features photographs of a number of Lulu White's "boarders."

## DIRECTORIES OF PROSTITUTES

Not every madam in Storyville had her own full-page advertisement in *Blue Book*. Visitors to the District could locate specific women using a directory section, present in every edition of this publication, which lists the women who were living or working in Storyville. Some of the alternative guides also have directory sections, but they are typically less comprehensive. Madams' names are often set either in all capitals or in boldface to distinguish them from prostitutes. Within these directories, women are listed sometimes geographically, by the streets of the District; sometimes alphabetically, by surname; and sometimes by race. Starting with the edition published in 1903 (No. 3), a woman's race—"white," "colored," or "octoroon"—is always indicated in *Blue Book*, and Jewish women and those specializing in fellatio are occasionally identified. The alternative guides typically do not include notations on the women's races. Beginning with the tenth edition of *Blue Book*, likely published in 1909 (No. 8), white prostitutes are listed first, followed by those of color. When the directory is organized geographically, it becomes apparent that, at least in many of the less pretentious houses, white and black prostitutes did work from the same address. It also reveals that some women worked as independent operators from their own addresses. The earliest editions of *Blue Book* also include a separate list of women who were in charge of houses but were not necessarily madams; they managed houses of assignation, where rooms could be rented on a short-term basis for the purpose of sex. Although this feature does not appear after the first couple of editions, it is no indication that such houses were no longer in demand or available.

Tracing the names of specific women through the directory listings and advertisements in the Storyville guides over a number of years reveals

| Color. | Name. | Location. |
|---|---|---|
| W | Ashley, Midget | " |
| C | ROBERTSON, EMMA | 326 Marais ** |
| C | MOORE, MARY | 328 Marais ** |
| W | HAWKINS, GUSSIE | 332 Marais * |
| W | Ray, Minnie | " |
| C | JACKSON, IDA | 334 Marais * |
| W | Thomas, Josie | " |
| C | Gedrick, Victoria | " |
| C | Wilson, Rosie | " |
| C | BURRELL, OLIVIA | 336 Marais * |
| C | Jones, Lottie | " |
| C | Williams, Alice | " |

Directory excerpt, from No. 3

Sadie Reed worked for Lulu White in the late 1890s, from No. 11.

| Color. | Name. | Address. |
|---|---|---|
| W. | MOORE, MARIE | 1408 St. Louis |
| W. | Herbert, Alice | " |
| C. | KLEIN, CARRIE | 1410 St. Louis |
| C. | Segur, Thelma | 1410 St. Louis |
| C. | SHAY, ROSIE | 1412 St. Louis |
| W. | McKnight, Lillian | " |
| C. | REED, SADIE | 1416 St. Louis |
| C. | JOHNSON, Mary | 1420 St. Louis |
| C. | SMITH, ELIZA | 1426 St. Louis |
| W. | Diamond, Annie | " |
| W. | Sullivan, Mamie | " |
| W. | JACOBS, ALICE | 1430 St. Louis |
| W. | BLACK, DELLA | 1510 St. Louis |
| C. | CORDELL, SARAH | 1518 St. Louis |

By 1906, Reed was running her own brothel on St. Louis Street, from No. 5.

that advancement was possible for business-savvy prostitutes. Women listed as a member of a landlady's parlor house in early publications sometimes appear as madams themselves in later ones. The opportunity for advancement as reflected in blue book listings during the District's existence deserves intensive study beyond the few examples that follow. It should be noted that it can be a challenge to trace women listed in these directories in other resources because prostitutes often worked using pseudonyms to reinvent themselves or to shield from shame families they left behind. Prostitute Mary Deubler, for example, went by the names Josie Alton, Josie Lobrano, and, most famously, Josie Arlington.[63]

Como Lines, one of Grace Simpson's women at 1022 Customhouse in 1900, is included in a short list of "Those Who Are Still Alive But On The Q. T." in 1901; was back with Grace Simpson at 223 N. Basin in 1905; was in charge of her own house at 1565 Iberville in 1906; then moved her operation to 1552 Iberville Street by 1907.[64] May Spencer, who worked for Flo Meeker at 211 N. Basin in 1901, was madam of her own establishment at 315 N. Basin by 1912.[65] Nina Jackson, a member of Dorothy Denning's house at 132 Burgundy near Customhouse in 1900, was the landlady of 1418 Conti in 1903.[66] One of Nina Jackson's women in that 1903 *Blue Book* listing, Claudie Sparks, worked for Lillian Irwin at swanky 313 N. Basin in 1905 and was the madam of 327 N. Franklin in 1907.[67] The same Lillian Irwin was previously another of Dorothy Denning's "fair ones" at 333 N. Basin in 1901.[68] Ray Owens worked for Josie Arlington in 1900; is listed at the Cottage, a two-person operation at 1306 Conti, in 1901; was the landlady of the Cottage and in charge of its five women in 1903; and became the madam of the fabulous Star Mansion at 1517 Iberville in 1905.[69] The enterprising Eunice Deering appears to have worked at both the Arlington and Flo Meeker's, according to the 1901 *Blue Book*; she then became a Basin Street landlady herself, presiding over 341 N. Basin in 1905.[70] "Prettie Sadie Reed," one of Lulu White's octoroon women pictured in her special souvenir booklet *New Mahogany Hall* of 1898 or 1899, was the proprietress of 1416 St. Louis in 1906.[71]

There was a dizzying degree of fluidity in the District as landladies and prostitutes came and went. It was almost like a game of musical chairs, with some madams changing venues from one year to the next. Many addresses saw frequent changes in proprietorship because the majority of madams in New Orleans did not own their houses, but rented them. Even famous brothels saw a series of madams, as an examination of the management of the Star Mansion reveals. Ray Owens, who was running the Star Mansion in 1905, was no longer listed as its madam in the 1906 *Blue Book*;[72] Hilma Burt, newly arrived from St. Louis, took over the reins for the next few years. While running the Star Mansion, Burt also took charge of Flo Meeker's at 209 N. Basin, according to the 1907 *Blue Book*, though she was replaced at that address by Gertrude Dix in the edition of 1913–15.[73] Annie Ross, madam at 210 Marais in 1909, presided over the Star Mansion by 1912.[74] Although Meeker appears at first glance to have moved frequently—she is listed as madam of 1025 Customhouse, 211 N. Basin, 209 N. Basin, and then 205 N. Basin between the years 1900 and 1906[75]—these last three addresses all likely identify the same structure.

The Star Mansion, from No. 5

On the other side of the coin, some women seem to have fallen from the ranks of landladies or simply left town for better opportunities in fresher venues. The euphonious Trilby O'Ferrell, "a refined and clever entertainer . . . noted for fun . . . the country over" and madam of 936 Customhouse in the 1900 *Blue Book*, appears on a list of those "on the Q. T." in 1901, and subsequently drops out of sight.[76] Lottie Fisher who "has one of the coziest places in the tenderloin" at 313 N. Basin in 1900, also described as a "first-class and very magnificently fitted up place" in 1901, is replaced as madam at that address by Dorothy Denning in the 1902 *Sporting Guide* and is not included in later brothel guides. After 1903, Denning vanishes for a few editions, reappearing in 1908 at 337 N. Basin, only to disappear again.[77] Some of these women may have left New Orleans; some may simply have died.

A few madams managed to reign somewhat serenely over a single mansion for the entire span of Storyville's existence, but these were few, indeed. Most notable, perhaps, was Lulu White. She owned the successful Mahogany Hall at 235 N. Basin, which was celebrated by her nephew, Spencer Williams, in the jazz piece "Mahogany Hall Stomp."[78] Willie V. Piazza, "the Countess," an elegant and well-read woman, also owned her house at 317 N. Basin and continued to live there long after Storyville's demise, until her death in 1932.[79] Emma Johnson, the "Parisian Queen of America" notorious for sexual "circuses" she presented in her "House of All Nations," was associated with the big double mansion at 331–33 N. Basin Street for most of the Storyville years. The Arlington, at 225 N. Basin, continued to operate under Josie Arlington's name after she retired in October 1906 to a substantial residence at 2721 Esplanade, leaving the fabled bordello under the management of her longtime associate, Anna (or Annie) Casey.[80] Prominent madams were even included in New Orleans city directory listings. For example, in the 1901 *Soards' New Orleans City Directory*, "house" is added to the entries for Josie Arlington and Willie V. Piazza, while "New Mahogany Hall" is listed by Lulu White's name.[81]

While Storyville guides are usually associated with gaudy Basin Street mansions, their directory sections also record working-class brothels and the women who worked in them. Sanborn Insurance Maps indicate brothels with the letters "F. B.," meaning female boarding. Most addresses within Storyville are shown in the 1908 Sanborn maps to be modest buildings, rather than mansions along the lines of the Arlington. The maps identify another class of venue: cribs—narrow, one-story structures—eleven of which are shown between 1559½ and 1579 on Bienville Street near Robertson. The women who worked from these cribs are not listed in the 1908 *Blue Book*. In marketing the promise of erotic adventures among the elite entertainers of New Orleans's fabulous Storyville, the District's promoters were not interested in including prostitutes who did not contribute to the desired glamorous image.[82] "Crib girls," who worked in shifts and were a more itinerant segment of the District's prostitutes, were not usually listed in *Blue Book*.[83]

A further systematic and comparative study of names from New Orleans city directories, federal census data for the Storyville area, and the blue books, even with all their flaws, would provide a more

Josie Arlington in 1908

Willie Piazza, from No. 13

Emma Johnson's, from No. 8

DIRECTORIES OF PROSTITUTES | 45

comprehensive documentation of the movements of madams and prostitutes among these addresses.

## MUSIC IN THE BLUE BOOKS

A man out for a night in the District, while interested in wine and women, might also look in a blue book for brothels offering music as a part of the evening's fun. Parlor houses considered among the better class would have live music; those establishments with fewer resources might have just a piano, or a coin-operated mechanical player piano, or a hand-cranked gramophone. The infectiously syncopated sound of ragtime had captivated the nation by the 1890s, and the form's dominance coincidentally parallels the years of Storyville's existence. Jazz, too, has long been associated with Storyville. Though jazz was not born in the District, many musicians who later gained fame as its pioneers were employed there. Rock-and-roll historian Robert Palmer observed that new developments in popular culture often come from the margins of society.[84] Many musicians who were employed in the brothels of Storyville came from those margins themselves, and certainly society looked upon prostitutes and madams, even those in the most elaborate brothels, as unsavory fringe elements. Musicians were not typically playing jazz in the brothels; extemporaneous experimentation with the new sound occurred in cabarets and clubs. But the two worlds were undoubtedly linked—the last known edition of *Blue Book* (No. 10) includes a list of nine cabarets.[85]

Customers frequently wanted to hear popular tunes from Broadway shows of the day such as *The Belle of New York*, *Florodora*, *Little Johnny Jones*, and the Ziegfeld Follies; songs from opera and operetta; and ragtime hits from the prolific music publishing houses of New York's Tin Pan Alley.[86] Bawdy lyrics sometimes replaced the actual words to these songs, often sung by the madam herself or some of her women. The best bordellos had musicians who worked mostly for tips, and swells out for a good time were encouraged to be generous with their money. Musicians had to be prepared to play anything the customer wanted to hear. Early-jazz historian William "Bill" Russell recorded some of Manuel "Fess" Manetta's reminiscences about his employment at Countess Willie

Directory excerpt, from No. 10

Hilma Burt's mirrored ballroom, between 1907 and 1913

INTRODUCTION | 46

Piazza's and at Lulu White's Mahogany Hall during Storyville's heyday.[87] Manetta said that the brothel inhabitants would often go to the stores on Canal Street to buy sheet music, and that they would sing and play piano in the parlor when not otherwise occupied with company. In another resource, Manetta recalled that some of White's residents had good singing voices and were capable of performing light classical songs.[88] Ferdinand Joseph LaMothe, more commonly known as Jelly Roll Morton, played in the parlors of the Countess, Hilma Burt, and Emma Johnson. Another piano great, Tony Jackson, also played in the brothels and clubs of the District, and often accompanied madam Antonia Gonzales when he was working in her mansion.[89] Names of individual musicians or ensembles, however, do not typically appear in the Storyville guides.

Gonzales was apparently an accomplished musician in her own right; music is mentioned in all of her ads. Descriptions of her talent range from the simple—"Miss Antonia herself plays the Cornet and Violin"—to the extravagant—"first Octoroon Lady Cornetist before the public in the world . . . playing cornet since she was twelve years of age."[90] In a later advertisement, Gonzales is said to have "the distinction of being the only classical Singer and Female Cornetist in the United States. . . . For rag-time singing and clever dancing, and fun generally, Antonia stands in a class all alone."[91] Music is mentioned in many other madams' ads; clearly it was one of Storyville's main attractions. The same recycling of language seen throughout the blue books occurs here as well: Bertha Golden is said to have "the distinction of being the only classical Singer and Salome dancer in the Southern States. . . . For rag-time singing and clever dancing, and fun generally, Bertha stands in a class all alone."[92] May Evans ran a house "where beautiful women, good wine and sweet music reign supreme"; and, not to be outdone, Lulu White's ad boasts that "there are always ten entertainers who get paid to do nothing but sing and dance."[93] Willie Piazza's was the place to visit for "anything new in the singing and dancing line."[94] Hilma Burt had "an orchestra in her ballroom that should be heard—all talent"; while in the next edition Gertrude Dix, who had taken over at Burt's former address, also had "an orchestra in her ballroom that should be heard—all talented singers and dancers."[95] Advertisements for Tom Anderson's Annex, located at the corner of Iberville and Basin Streets, usually mention "music nightly" or "orchestra nightly."[96] One ad for Anderson's Annex goes further, stating, "All the Latest Musical Selections Nightly, Rendered by a Typical Southern Darky Orchestra."[97]

That music is mentioned in so many advertisements reveals that this form of entertainment was a major draw for visitors to Storyville. Other evidence suggests that locals were also reading the ads. Piano tuner C. D. Walton, "King of Piano Tuners," had a shop at 1405 Canal Street near the District and offered electric pianos, violin and piano harps, and banjos. His ad in a later *Blue Book* boasted "No Instrument too Difficult for Walton. Ask Billy Struve at Anderson's Annex, He Knows."[98] This ad's presence underscores the importance of music in Storyville, as well as throughout New Orleans. A tourist would probably not need the services of a piano tuner; this notice was most likely directed at madams, musicians, and other locals.

Miss Antonia P. Gonzales

CORNER VILLERE AND IBERVILLE STREETS

CORNETIST    SONGSTRESS

Antonia Gonzales's ads always contain musical references, from No. 4.

Jelly Roll Morton ca. 1906

## ADVERTISEMENTS FOR OTHER GOODS AND SERVICES

Other advertisements in the blue books create a revealing snapshot of what a visitor to the District could expect to encounter. Since most of the ads address the needs and desires of men out for an evening of wine, women, and song in the red-light district, it is not surprising that, by far, the majority of advertisements are for alcoholic potables—liquor, champagne, and beer. What may surprise contemporary readers is the fact that many major national and international companies were promoted in these small, locally produced brothel guides. Unfortunately, there are no known records indicating how much these companies were paying for their advertisements. Many of the brands advertised in *Blue Book* are still available, while others have faded away. Liquor brands still in existence today include I. W. Harper, George A. Dickel and Co., Black and White, Dewar's, and Burnett's. Among the champagnes are Krug and Co., Moët and Chandon, G. H. Mumm, Piper-Heidsieck, and Veuve Clicquot. Beers are represented by Anheuser-Busch's Budweiser ("America's Favorite Drink To-Day"[99]), Falstaff, Pabst Blue Ribbon, and Schlitz.[100] Several local importers and distributors, including F. Hollander and Co. and the Ned Palfrey Co.,[101] appear, and at least two New York firms, Geo. A. Kessler and Co. and E. A. Rosenham Co., are represented.[102] Ads also appear for Abita Water, sourced from Abita Springs, located on the north shore of Lake Pontchartrain and known for its mineral water as well as the supposedly healthy qualities of its ozone-heavy fresh air. They tout its usefulness both on a night out and as a remedy for such, stating that it "adds zest to all mixed Drinks,"[103] in addition to making "one feel new after a large night"[104] and relieving "that tight hat band feeling."[105]

Advertisements reveal that cigars were also an essential component of the discriminating gentleman's big night in the District. Tom Anderson's establishments advertised their "high-class . . . cigars" and "Complete Stock of High-Class Turkish Cigarettes," further advising patrons, "Don't be ashamed to name the cigar you like—We Have 'Em."[106] Though most cigar advertisements are from manufacturers in Key West, Florida, there are advertisements for a few local cigar makers. Elias Aaron and Bro. at 543–45–47 Magazine Street proudly proclaimed their El Albert as "The cigar that made Havana envious."[107] Alisa Havana Cigars—"they have no equal"—were advertised by "A. Falk, maker, New Orleans."[108] Tadema cigars were made by Charles Meyer and Co. at Canal and Royal Streets.[109] Unlike the alcoholic beverages promoted in the pages of the blue books, most of the cigar brands are unfamiliar today.

Other companies that frequently advertised in the blue books naturally included restaurants, saloons, and cafes in and around the District. The establishments that advertised most regularly were those belonging to Storyville fixtures Tom Anderson (owner of the Stag, the Arlington, and the Annex) and Frank Lamothe (of Lamothe's Restaurant). Other restaurants advertised in these guides include the Waldorf Café, the Unexpected Saloon and Restaurant, Frank Toro's New Monte Carlo Café and Restaurant, the Olympic Saloon, and the Milwaukee Saloon.[110]

Whiskey advertisement, from No. 10

Advertisement for Budweiser beer, from No. 6

Advertisement for Tom Anderson's restaurants, from No. 5

Ads for other goods and services appeared less frequently but help round out a portrait of a visit to the District; among these are ads for transportation services such as the Renault Taxi Service[111] and Cooke's Taxis;[112] the Alhambra Baths at 726 Gravier Street;[113] local, "made last night" Jacobs Candies;[114] and the American Laundry at 123 N. Liberty (now Treme) Street.[115] Jeweler Joe Traverse, at 131 St. Charles Street, advertised in several editions of *Blue Book*,[116] and there is an ad for a pawn shop, the New Orleans Loan and Pledge Co., 1037 Canal, near Rampart,[117] which is perhaps to be expected near a large vice district.

For those who encountered legal "trouble while on a lark in the Tenderloin,"[118] Paul Louis Fourchy, attorney and counselor-at-law, advertised that he practiced in all courts, and ensured that potential clients would be able to find him by providing his office hours, phone number, and address (806 Gravier), as well as his home phone number and address (1448 N. Rocheblave, near Kerlerec). Fourchy was the only lawyer who advertised in *Blue Book*, and he has an ad in nearly every edition, noting his changes of address. An advertisement for Smith's Private Detective Agency at 309 St. Charles also hints at the darker side of Storyville.[119]

A mere hangover was not as serious a consequence of an evening in Storyville as the possibility of contracting venereal disease. A popular saying at the time was "a night with Venus; a lifetime with Mercury." Prior to the widespread use of penicillin in the 1940s, venereal diseases were treated—but not cured—with mercury or mercuric compounds. Should a visitor notice symptoms such as "crawlers" or "gleet," he could find ads in early editions of *Blue Book* directing him to drugstores selling the Famous Number Seven Specifics,[120] Anti-Crab Lotion, Bailey's Sure Injection, and "Hellmann's No. 206 Mixture, A sure cure in a short time.... Remember you won't be away from your girl long if you use No. 206."[121] Dr. Miles' No. 150 Specific-Mixture, which also "guaranteed a sure cure," was prepared by druggist Charles G. Peter, at the corner of Baronne and Poydras Streets.[122]

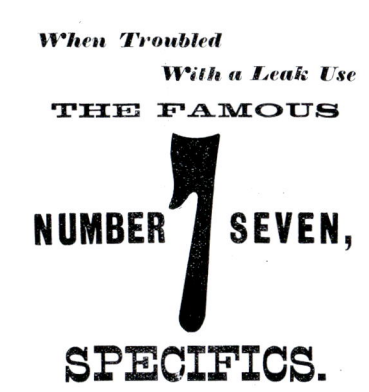

Though these advertisements for pawn shops, lawyers, and venereal disease cures might have put a damper on the sense of fun promoted in the Storyville guides, perhaps none did so more than ads for A. E. Ravain, funeral director and embalmer, located at 302–4 N. Rampart, at the corner of Bienville. Illustrated with a photograph of one of his fine carriages for hire in front of his establishment, Ravain's ad appears in only the first two editions of *Blue Book*.[123] Perhaps by later editions Billy Struve decided that ads that forced a visitor to contemplate mortality while out carousing were unappealing at best and a deterrent at worst.

But not all the advertisements address the immediate needs of a man out on the town. Considering the mirrors and fancy etched glass that adorned the more elegant brothels and saloons, it is not surprising to find an ad for the Central Glass Co., 518–22 Bienville Street, manufacturers of "French mirror plates, figure windows, art glass ... and window glass."[124] Another local business that advertised in *Blue Book* was the Loubat Glassware and Cork Company, founded in 1874 and located at 510–16 Bienville Street, next to the Central Glass Company. Loubat, claiming to be the "Largest Glassware & Crockery House in the South,"

Advertisement for venereal disease cure, from No. 1

Advertisement for laundry services, from No. 10

ADVERTISEMENTS FOR OTHER GOODS AND SERVICES | 49

probably supplied many of the saloons, restaurants, and brothels that appear in the pages of the Storyville guides.[125] Advertisements for manufacturers or suppliers of restaurant and house goods indicate that madams, restauranteurs, bartenders, and other locals were also among the audience for the blue books.

## INFLUENCE AND DECLINE

By 1911 New Orleans's *Blue Book* had become so well known to sporting men visiting the Crescent City that it influenced at least one similar publication in another city. An entrepreneur in San Antonio—which claimed to have the largest red-light district in Texas, ranked third in the nation behind Storyville and San Francisco's Barbary Coast—produced that city's own guide for visitors looking for salacious amusement. *The Blue Book for Visitors, Tourists and Those Seeking a Good Time While in San Antonio, Texas* took its title and some elements of its tone and format from the infamous *Blue Book* of New Orleans. The cover of this guide states "Published Annually," but only this single edition, for 1911–12, which lists 106 prostitutes and sporting houses along with other local businesses, is known.[126]

When the United States entered World War I in 1917, the federal government prohibited open prostitution within five miles of any military installation and, consequently, forced closures of red-light districts across the nation. In New Orleans, the curtain fell on November 12, 1917. Short-lived legal recognition of the separate red-light district catering to African American men also ended.[127] Located blocks away from Storyville proper, in the area encompassed by Gravier, Perdido, South Franklin, and Locust Streets (near today's city hall), this so-called Black Storyville was an impoverished neighborhood, largely neglected by city officials. Black Storyville does not appear to have produced its own guidebooks, and the women who worked there are not included in the Storyville blue books.

Storyville was already in a state of decline as many younger men found more sport in the pursuit of respectable but adventurous young women than in sex trade professionals. "The country club girls are ruining my business!" Countess Willie Piazza supposedly claimed, as the number of brothels and prostitutes in the District dwindled.[128] On the sociopolitical stage, as Emily Epstein Landau notes, "By 1917 the segregation of the races had been nearly completed in public conveyances, spaces, and institutions, such as education and marriage, and the segregation of vice had run its course. The 'modern' viewpoint held that red-light districts were ineffective."[129] The war merely hastened the end of the restricted vice district, as a new generation of progressives, moralists, and the American middle class condemned this failed social experiment, seeking to eradicate rather than merely control prostitution. The Middle French phrase "honi soit qui mal y pense" (shame on him who thinks evil of it) appeared prominently in *Blue Book* beginning with the seventh edition in 1906 (No. 5); perhaps it was a small gesture against this rising tide of moralists and reformers. Their allure fading, Storyville's famous mansions were becoming frayed around the edges. The last known prostitution guide was printed between 1913 and 1915

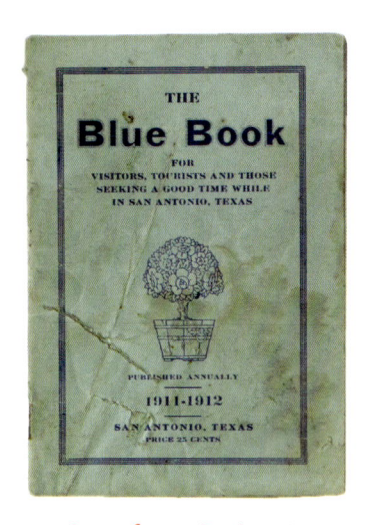

Cover of a 1911 San Antonio brothel guide

Cartoon published the day after Storyville closed

(No. 10), a couple of years before this end. After the District's demise, prostitution was again an illicit industry, and there was no place for this kind of published advertising for visiting men-about-town. With the changing times, word of mouth and a surreptitious nod and wink replaced printed guides.

Storyville's blue books promoted New Orleans's emporiums of sex without attempting to rate or rank them, as earlier guides to Philadelphia's and New York's brothels had. I have never seen actual sexual services explicitly described or a list of fees in any genuine Storyville-era guide. These books provided an introduction to the District for visitor and local alike, uniformly implying promises of a carnival of sexual experiences as well as the opportunity to rub shoulders with the worldly and sophisticated. Blue books marketed a fantasy of sex—glamorous, exotic, and taboo—but most of the women listed in their directory pages lived and worked in Storyville's lower-class houses or semi-independently; their reality was neither glamorous nor exotic. Except for a few top-of-the-line sporting palaces, mainly clustered along or near Basin Street, most of the District's houses were unpretentious.

The blue books are ephemeral mementos of a rowdy time and place striving to lend a veneer of elegance and class to the tawdry business of sex. Much is unknown—and may never be known—about the Storyville brothel guides. Regardless, they have a captivating charm that fascinates the bibliophile.

Cover of 1919 pamphlet condemning red-light districts

## NOTES

1. *Blue Book*, [1903], 2006.0237, Williams Research Center, The Historic New Orleans Collection (hereafter THNOC). Because most of the Storyville guides in THNOC's holdings are not paginated, notes citing these guides do not contain page numbers.
2. Mir, "Marketplace of Desire," 74.
3. Mackey, "Red Lights Out," 174–75.
4. Schafer, *Brothels, Depravity, and Abandoned Women*, 157. See also Chapter 9, "An Ordinance Concerning Lewd and Abandoned Women," 145–54. "Lorette" in the underworld terminology of the day indicated a prostitute. The term is associated with a neighborhood in Paris around the cathedral of Notre Dame de Lorette.
5. Smith, "Southern Sirens," 30–50.
6. Mackey, "Red Lights Out," 144.
7. Flexner, *Prostitution in Europe*, 107–10.
8. Mackey, "Red Lights Out," 176–77. Ordinance No. 13,032, Council Series, was passed on January 29, 1897, but was modified on July 6 to become effective January 1, 1898.
9. Use of the term "tenderloin" to refer to an area of concentrated prostitution activity is attributed to New York police inspector Alexander "Clubber" Williams (1839–1917). When he was promoted to take charge of the burgeoning vice district along Broadway in 1876, he remarked "I've been living on rump steak since I been on the force; now I'm going to have a bit of Tenderloin." Zacks, *Island of Vice*, 88. Williams's implication was that he would now be receiving substantial income from bribes and payoffs, making the pricier cut of meat easily affordable. The term, also suggesting fleshly pleasure, quickly caught on.
10. The French Quarter itself had been the scene of prostitution activity before and would be again after the demise of Storyville. Anderson County, nicknamed for sporting man, entrepreneur, and political figure Thomas C. "Tom" Anderson (1858–1931), was an unofficial pre-Storyville vice area bounded by Customhouse (now Iberville), St. Peter, Dauphine, and Rampart Streets.
11. Following the success of the Storyville model, in 1903 Shreveport, Louisiana, enacted a similar ordinance that confined prostitutes to an area near the Red River known as St. Paul's Bottoms. A few years later, in 1909, Crowley became the third city in Louisiana to legally designate a zone in which prostitution was allowed without criminal penalty. See Brock, *Red Light*, 8, 37; also Corrales, "Prurience, Prostitution, and Progressive Improvements," 40–43.
12. Goldman, *Gold Diggers*, 147–48.
13. Kent Biffle, "Waco was 1st to Reserve Area for Brothels," Kent Biffle's Texana, *Dallas Morning News*, November 30, 1997, 45A–46A; Bernstein, *First Waco Horror*, 13.
14. Foster, "Tarnished Angels," 393. "Found Dead in the Tenderloin. Annie Seymann's End Due to Dissipation—Death Was Attributed to Alcoholism," *Daily States*, August 14, 1907, p. 9, col. 5. Also see "Hazards of the Game" in Goldman, *Gold Diggers*, 124–35.
15. Topping, "Fact and Fiction Regarding Prostitution," 8–9. The seasonal ebb and flow of the business and the existence of the occasional prostitute is also discussed in Flexner, *Prostitution in Europe*, 19–24 and 84–85; and in Landau, *Spectacular Wickedness*, 151.
16. Foster, "Tarnished Angels," 388–90.
17. Ibid., 396. See also Longstreet, *Nell Kimball*, 6, 58–62. This book, presented as a genuine memoir of a famous madam, is entertaining, but appears to have been largely invented, with its undocumented protagonist and whole sections paraphrased from the works of Herbert Asbury (1889–1963), an American author of popular urban crime and vice histories. See a review by James L. Wunsch discussing the work in *Journal of Social History*. A contemporaneous study of the social, educational, and occupational backgrounds of prostitutes appears in Flexner, *Prostitution in Europe*, 63–70.
18. See, for example, "A Battle in a Bagnio," *Daily Picayune*, August 19, 1895, p. 6, c. 5; "Bit Her Hand and Blood Poising [sic] Set in as a Result. Eva Mill, the Victim, Is, However, Convalescent—Jennie Donahue Did the Mischief," *Daily States*, October 6, 1900, p. 1, c. 4; and "Redlight Murder Winds Up a Spree," *Daily Picayune*, September 27, 1904, p. 4, c. 1.
19. *Oxford English Dictionary*, s.v. "blue book." For more information on the blue books produced by the British Parliament, see Temperley and Penson, *A Century of*

*Diplomatic Blue Books*.

20. "Tenderloin 400" actually appears on and within some blue books. The origin of the signifier "the four hundred" is attributed to Ward McAllister, social observer and advisor to Mrs. William Backhouse Astor Jr., the empress of New York society during the late nineteenth century. He claimed that there were only four hundred persons who composed the truly elite, coincidentally the number of people who could be accommodated in Astor's ballroom. See O'Connor, *The Golden Summers*, 57.

21. Tony Perrottet, "Guidebooks to Babylon," *New York Times Book Review*, January 22, 2012, 31. Perrottet describes several other such guides.

22. Charles B. Wood III, *One Hundred Rare Books*, 48–49.

23. One may view the entire guidebook at the Library Company of Philadelphia's online exhibition *Capitalism by Gaslight*.

24. Heartman, "*Blue Book*," 36–38; Rose, *Storyville*, 136. The *Mascot* had ceased publication by the time Storyville was established.

25. Quoted in Heartman, "*Blue Book*," 37–38. Herbert Asbury repeats much of this basic information, stating that *The Green Book* was published in January 1895, but in an edition of only two thousand copies, which were quickly sold at twenty-five cents each. Asbury, *French Quarter*, 442.

26. In her book *Gold Diggers and Silver Miners*, Marion S. Goldman gives a full bibliographic citation of *The Green Book*, but it is not clear whether she consulted an actual copy or found the information in another source. See Goldman, *Gold Diggers*, 58 and 187.

27. The birth date on Struve's World War I draft card is given as September 19, 1872. One obituary, however, implies that 1875 was his birth year. "William Struve, 62, Saloon Keeper Dies," *Times-Picayune*, October 22, 1937, p. 2, col. 7. His obituary in the *Item* states that he published *Blue Book*. "Billy Struve of Night Life Fame Passes," *Item*, October 21, 1937, p. 1, col. 2.

28. It has long been conjectured that Struve kept an office on the second floor of Lulu White's saloon, a two-story structure built in 1908 or 1909 on the corner of Basin and Bienville Streets next to her celebrated brothel, Mahogany Hall. This building still stands at 237 Basin Street, although its second story was heavily damaged and removed in 1965 following Hurricane Betsy. It now houses a convenience store. Rose, *Storyville*, 82. New Orleans city directory listings for William Struve during the era, however, do not corroborate this kernel of Storyville legend.

29. Heartman, "*Blue Book*," 54.

30. Calendering is a finishing step in the commercial paper-making process that smooths the surface, much as burnishing or polishing smooths the surface of metal. Nancy Sharon Collins, email to author, December 26, 2012. In printing, stereotyping involves setting an entire page of copy, with any other decorative elements, then taking an impression of the type to make a mold. The metal plate cast from this mold—known as a stereotype plate—is sturdier than the composed page of type by itself and can be reused. *Encyclopaedia Britannica Online*, s. v. "stereotype," accessed February 15, 2014, http://www.britannica.com/EBchecked/topic/565675/stereotype.

31. For more on the use of rubrication in publications of the 1890s, see MacLeod, *American Little Magazines*.

32. Nancy Sharon Collins, email to author, January 1, 2013. Also see *American Chap-Book* 1, no. 3 (November 1904), 29.

33. Rose, *Storyville*, 207.

34. Ibid., 142.

35. Ibid.

36. Rose's use of street name changes did not always prove accurate. For a discussion of how he dated the Storyville guides, including *The Red Book*, see *Storyville*, 135.

37. For further discussion of the French balls held in New Orleans during Carnival, see Leathem, "'A Carnival,'" 183–91.

38. Tom Anderson and Frank Lamothe, the "two well-known gentlemen," were regular advertisers in the Storyville guides, and tickets for these events were usually available for sale at Anderson's saloons and at Lamothe's Restaurant.

39. The Carnival season officially begins on January 6, which is Twelfth Night or the Feast of the Epiphany, and ends on Mardi Gras. Mardi Gras, French for "Fat Tuesday," is the last day before the penitent season of Lent and is a movable date occurring forty-seven days before Easter, as established by the Catholic Church. Mardi Gras can be as early as February 3 or as late as March 9. See Hardy, *Mardi Gras in New Orleans*, 6.

40. *Blue Book*, [1900], 94-092-RL, THNOC. This offer does not appear in subsequent editions.

41. *West's Encyclopedia of American Law* (2005), s.v. "Comstock Law of 1873," http://www.encyclopedia.com/doc/1G2-3437701022.html. The Comstock Law was seriously weakened in 1936, in a federal case involving birth control and women's rights advocate Margaret Sanger.

42. Landau, "'Spectacular Wickedness,'" 145.

43. Ibid., 106. For further study of the marketing of women of color in Storyville, see Long, "'As Rare as White Blackbirds,'" in *Great Southern Babylon*, 191–224; and Landau, "Where the Light and Dark Folks Meet," in *Spectacular Wickedness*, 109–31. For an examination of the marketing of women of color during the antebellum period, whether enslaved or free, see Clark, "Selling the Quadroon," in *Strange History*, 162–87.

44. Herbert Asbury mentions a myth of the era that red-haired prostitutes were especially passionate, but none more so than a red-haired Jewish prostitute. Asbury, *Barbary Coast*, 259. This myth was picked up in Longstreet, *Nell Kimball*, 223, 229, and has been subsequently repeated in various books and internet sources.

45. Mir, "Marketplace of Desire," 77.

46. Foster, "Tarnished Angels," 396–97. Examples include "Negress' Finger Was in the Mouth of the White Woman," *Daily States*, October 6, 1900, p. 10, c. 4; "A Redlight Row in Which Women Accuse Each Other of Larceny," *Daily Picayune*, July 29, 1904, p. 4, c. 5; and "Ada Hayes Jailed on a Story of a Redlight Robbery, Which Accuser Afterwards Denied," *Daily Picayune*, May 25, 1905, p. 16, c. 4.

47. For the original study that misidentified the 1963 souvenir reprint as a genuine Storyville-era publication, see Mir, "Marketplace of Desire," 77–78. The "facsimile" reprints discussed are Nos. 18 and 19 in this bibliography. The genuine ads appearing in those reprints were taken from the ninth edition, *Blue Book*, [1908], 1969.19.9, THNOC.

48. Heartman, "*Blue Book*," 74–75.

49. Ibid., 74.

50. *Blue Book*, [1913–15], 1969.19.11, THNOC.

51. Landau, "'Spectacular Wickedness,'" 104.

52. *Blue Book*, [1913–15], 1969.19.11, THNOC.

53. For a definition of this phrase in eighteenth- and nineteenth-century America, see Stott, *Jolly Fellows*, 8. For understanding the term in the Storyville era, the chapter "Sporting Men," 214–47, is especially useful.

54. *Blue Book*, [1905], 1969.19.6, THNOC.

55. Ibid.

56. Ibid.

57. *Blue Book*, [1901], 1969.19.4, THNOC.

58. *Blue Book*, [1913–15], 1969.19.11, THNOC.

59. *Blue Book*, [1908], 1969.19.9, THNOC.

60. *Blue Book*, 1906, 1969.19.7, THNOC.

61. *Blue Book*, [1905], 1969.19.6, THNOC.

62. Although the photographer who supplied these images has not been identified, and any number of active commercial photographers of the era could have taken these interiors, it is possible that Ernest J. Bellocq (1873–1949), now known for his photographs of Storyville's prostitutes, took them.

63. Rose, *Storyville*, 47–48; Long, *Great Southern Babylon*, 151, 155.

64. *Blue Book*, [1900], 94-092-RL, THNOC; *Blue Book*, [1901], 1969.19.4, THNOC; *Blue Book*, [1905], 1969.19.6, THNOC; *Blue Book*, 1906, 1969.19.7, THNOC; *Blue Book*, 1907, 1969.19.8, THNOC.

65. *Blue Book*, [1901], 1969.19.4, THNOC; *Blue Book*, [1912], 2012.0141.1, THNOC.

66. *Blue Book*, [1900], 94-092-RL, THNOC; *Blue Book*, [1903], 2006.0237, THNOC.

67. *Blue Book*, [1903], 2006.0237, THNOC; *Blue Book*, [1905], 1969.19.6, THNOC; *Blue Book*, 1907, 1969.19.8, THNOC.

68. *Blue Book*, [1901], 1969.19.4, THNOC.

69. *Blue Book*, [1900], 94-092-RL, THNOC; *Blue Book*, [1901], 1969.19.4, THNOC; *Blue Book*, [1903], 2006.0237, THNOC; *Blue Book*, [1905], 1969.19.6, THNOC.

70. *Blue Book*, [1901], 1969.19.4, THNOC; *Blue Book*, [1905], 1969.19.6, THNOC.

71. *New Mahogany Hall*, [1898–99], 56-15, THNOC; *Blue Book*, 1906, 1969.19.7, THNOC.

72. *Blue Book*, [1905], 1969.19.6, THNOC; *Blue Book*, 1906, 1969.19.7, THNOC.

73. *Blue Book*, 1907, 1969.19.8, THNOC; *Blue Book*, [1913–15], 1969.19.11, THNOC.

74. *Blue Book*, [1909], 1969.19.10, THNOC; *Blue Book*, [1912], 2012.0141.1, THNOC.

75. *Blue Book*, [1900], 94-092-RL, THNOC; *Blue Book*, [1901], 1969.19.4, THNOC; *Blue Book*, [1903], 2006.237, THNOC; "The Lid," [1906], 1969.19.1, THNOC.

76. *Blue Book*, [1900], 94-092-RL, THNOC; *Blue Book*, [1901], 1969.19.4, THNOC. This madam likely lifted her name from the title character of *Trilby*, a phenomenally popular 1895 novel by George du Maurier, an example of how women in the sex trade often took pseudonyms. The correct spelling of the namesake (O'Ferrall) does not appear in any of the blue books.

77. *Blue Book*, [1900], 94-092-RL, THNOC; *Blue Book*, [1901], 1969.19.4, THNOC; *Sporting Guide*, [1902], 1969.19.3, THNOC; *Blue Book*, [1903], 2006.0237, THNOC; *Blue Book*, [1908], 1969.19.9, THNOC.

78. Rose, *Storyville*, 81.

79. Long, *Great Southern Babylon*, 223.

80. Ibid., 178. The house at 2721 Esplanade was moved to its current location, 2863 Grand Route St. John, around 1922 when the school board purchased the property for the construction of McDonogh No. 28. J. E. Bourgoyne, "Famous Madam Slept Here?" *Times-Picayune*, June 25, 1978, sect. 5, 25.

81. *Soards' New Orleans City Directory*, 1901, 80, 690, 905.

82. Mir, "Marketplace of Desire," 80.

83. Sanborn Map Company, *Insurance Maps of New Orleans*, plates 129, 130, 134, 135; *Blue Book*, [1908], 1969.19.9, THNOC. Landlords owning property in the District could also partition their larger houses into cribs. An article published in 1917 in the *Times-Picayune* gives an example: "a house of six rooms was partitioned off into three 'cribs,' of two rooms each, and the usual rental was $3 or $4 per night. The rent usually was collected nightly and in advance." "City Will Control Segregated Area Under New System," *Times-Picayune*, January 24, 1917, p. 4, c. 5–6.

84. Palmer, *Rock and Roll*, 16.

85. *Blue Book*, [1913–15], 1969.19.11, THNOC.

86. For more on ragtime, a popular precursor to jazz, see Blesh and Janis, *They All Played Ragtime*.

87. These oral histories are now in the holdings of The Historic New Orleans Collection. See the William Russell Oral Histories, especially MSS 530.2.18, .2.30, .2.40, .2.46, .2.68.

88. Collins, *New Orleans Jazz*, 215.

89. Rose, *Storyville*, 111.

90. *Sporting Guide*, [1902], 1969.19.3, THNOC; *Blue Book*, [1903], 2006.0237, THNOC.

91. *Blue Book*, 1907, 1969.19.8, THNOC.

92. *Blue Book*, [1909], 1969.19.10, THNOC.

93. *Blue Book*, [1909], 1969.19.10, THNOC; *Blue Book*, [1905], 1969.19.6, THNOC.

94. *Blue Book*, 1907, 1969.19.8, THNOC.

95. *Blue Book*, [1912], 2012.0141.1, THNOC; *Blue Book*, [1913–15], 1969.19.11, THNOC.

96. For examples, see *Blue Book*, 1906, 1969.19.7, THNOC; *Blue Book*, [1909], 1969.19.10, THNOC.

97. *Blue Book*, [1913–15], 1969.19.11, THNOC.

98. Ibid.

99. *Blue Book*, [1905], 1969.19.6, THNOC.

100. In most of her full-page advertisements, Countess Willie Piazza informs her visitors that "while her maison joie is peerless in every respect, she only serves the 'amber fluid.'" *Blue Book*, [1905], 1969.19.6, THNOC. Americans in the early twentieth century would be familiar with this slang term for beer.

101. *Blue Book*, 1906, 1969.19.7, THNOC.

102. *Blue Book*, [1905], 1969.19.6, THNOC; *Blue Book*, [1908], 1969.19.9, THNOC.

103. *Blue Book*, [1905], 1969.19.6, THNOC.

104. Ibid.

105. *Blue Book*, [1908], 1969.19.9, THNOC.

106. *Blue Book*, [1912], 2012.0141.1, THNOC.

107. *Blue Book*, 1906, 1969.19.7, THNOC.

108. Ibid.

109. *Blue Book*, [1909], 1969.19.10, THNOC.

110. *Blue Book*, [1900], 94-092-RL, THNOC.

111. *Blue Book*, [1909], 1969.19.10, THNOC.

112. *Blue Book*, [1913–15], 1969.19.11, THNOC.

113. Ibid.

114. Ibid.

115. Ibid.

116. *Blue Book*, 1906, 1969.19.7, THNOC.

117. *Blue Book*, [1900], 94-092-RL, THNOC.

118. *Blue Book*, [1903], 2006.0237, THNOC.

119. *Blue Book*, 1906, 1969.19.7, THNOC.

120. *Blue Book*, [1901], 1969.19.4, THNOC.

121. *Blue Book*, [1900], 94-092-RL, THNOC.

122. Ibid. Charles G. Peter, druggist, appears in the 1900 New Orleans city directory at 901 Poydras, this same corner.

123. *Blue Book*, [1900], 94-092-RL, THNOC; *Blue Book*, [1901], 1969.19.4, THNOC.

124. *Blue Book*, 1906, 1969.19.7, THNOC.

125. *Blue Book*, [1909], 1969.19.10, THNOC. A well-established firm patronized by generations of New Orleanians, Loubat was purchased by Denver-based FoodServiceWarehouse.com in 2013.

126. Morgan, "San Antonio Blue Book," 1–3. The San Antonio guide was perhaps produced by former policeman Billy Keilman, a colorful figure who owned the Beauty Saloon, which also housed a brothel.

127. Rose, *Storyville*, 38–39, 193–94. The original Storyville ordinance allowed for a separate red-light district for African American men, but this provision was not included in the 1897 ordinance that was enacted. The area, which had previously been a site of prostitution, continued to operate quasi-legally. An ordinance passed in February 1917, only months before all prostitution in New Orleans was made illegal, reinstated legal recognition of the African American red-light district, in an attempt to fully segregate prostitution. See Long, *Great Southern Babylon*, 216–20; and Landau, *Spectacular Wickedness*, 157–59.

128. Asbury, *French Quarter*, 455; quoted in Long, *Great Southern Babylon*, 231.

129. Landau, *Spectacular Wickedness*, 204. For further discussion of Storyville's decline, see pages 175–91, as well as Krist, *Empire of Sin*, 152, 226–38. Flexner, *Prostitution in Europe*, 175–79, presents a contemporaneous view of the futility of segregated red-light districts as a means of controlling prostitution. In 1919 a pamphlet completely refuting all arguments supporting such districts was issued, drawing some of its points from Flexner's work. See American Social Hygiene Association, *Why Let It Burn?*

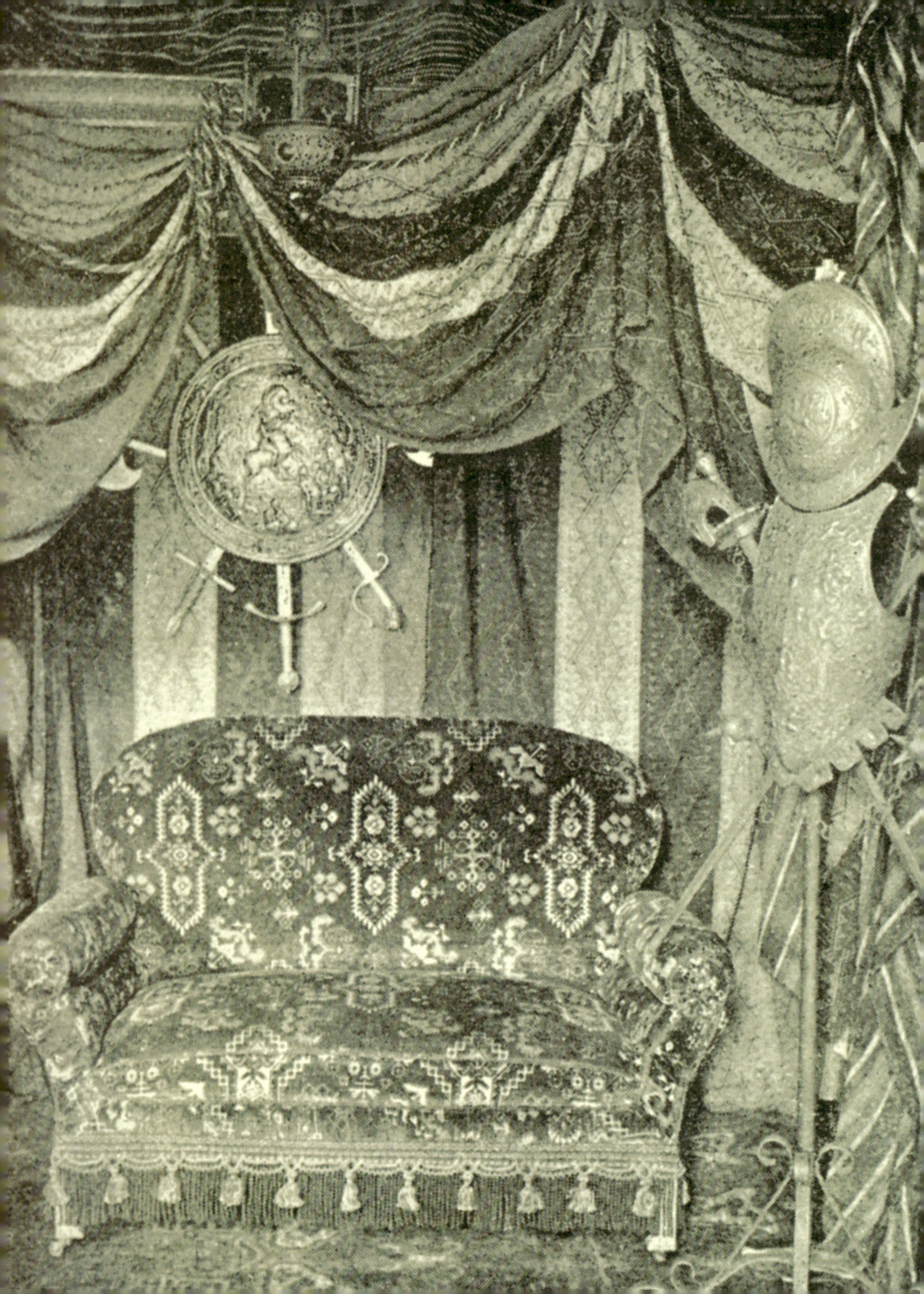

# PROVENANCE

## THE HISTORIC NEW ORLEANS COLLECTION'S STORYVILLE GUIDES

Storyville's blue books have long excited the interest of collectors familiar with this glamorously sordid side of New Orleans history, but authentic examples—especially those in good condition—have been difficult to come by. Original owners may have been embarrassed to have such souvenirs found by loved ones and discarded them themselves. Upon discovering copies among a recently deceased relative's effects, loved ones and descendants may have disposed of this evidence, not wanting his sterling character tarnished. When individual Storyville-era guides appear in rare-book dealers' catalogs, they can be listed in the thousands of dollars, depending upon the scarcity and the condition of the item. For example, the William Reese Company listed a copy of *Blue Book* (identical to No. 9 in this bibliography) for $3,500 in one of its 2006 catalogs, and in 2012 offered a copy of the last known edition of that publication (identical to No. 10) for $2,500, noting that "all *Blue Book* guides are extremely rare."[1] In several instances, the copy held by The Historic New Orleans Collection is the only example of a particular edition I have ever seen anywhere.

Twelve of THNOC's authentic Storyville-era prostitution guides are the exact copies Charles F. Heartman wrote about in his privately printed 1936 bibliography, *The "Blue Book."* How did Heartman acquire them, and how did they come to The Historic New Orleans Collection? This story involves four important collectors—Simon J. Shwartz, Heartman, Thomas W. Streeter, and L. Kemper Williams—three of whom were closely associated with New Orleans. These men were pivotal in keeping this group of ephemeral directories, small souvenirs from a brief, bawdy segment of New Orleans history, together.[2]

### SIMON JAMES SHWARTZ

Simon James Shwartz (1867–1936) was a New Orleans businessman, civic leader, and philanthropist, and a collector of rare books, documents, and art. As a young man, he was employed by his family's mercantile firm, A. Shwartz and Son, remaining with the company when it became Maison Blanche department store in 1897. The Maison Blanche building at 921 Canal Street, now the Ritz-Carlton Hotel, was constructed between 1906 and 1908, during his tenure as president of the store. While he was president of the Louisiana Commission for the Blind, Shwartz conceived and established the Lighthouse for the Blind in New Orleans (now Lighthouse Louisiana), a training and work facility. It was partially because of this philanthropic endeavor that Shwartz was awarded the *Times-Picayune* Loving Cup in 1928. He died in 1936 in his house at 3803 St. Charles Avenue of a heart ailment that had plagued him for some time.

A den in Josie Arlington's mansion, from No. 4

Simon James Shwartz

His obituary remarks that he had a national reputation as a collector, and that ten years prior to his death, "he disposed of the entire collection of rare documents, art and records he had spent a lifetime gathering."[3] The Anderson Galleries of New York administered the auction of Shwartz's collection in a series of five sessions held on November 8 through 12, 1926. They issued two auction catalogs devoted to this sale. The foreword of the first describes Shwartz's library of "Books, Broadsides, Autograph Letters and Documents relating to the Louisiana Territory, the Mississippi Valley, and the Development of the West" as "in all probability the largest and most important which has ever appeared for sale by public auction" and the "most complete, covering the early days of discovery…down to the present time."[4] Though we know Shwartz collected Storyville-era prostitution guides, none appear in these auction catalogs.

Heartman stated that the thirteen blue books documented in his own bibliography were acquired from Shwartz, whose advice and assistance had been essential in Heartman's study of the guides, but he doesn't describe how Shwartz came to possess the collection.[5] Noted bookman and dealer Bailey Bishop observed that Heartman was in Perth Amboy, New Jersey, at the time of the Shwartz auction and would have attended the sales. In his bibliography, Heartman reports that Shwartz's collection was "unmercifully butchered…at auction," that is, badly described or lotted.[6] Bishop goes a bit further, speculating that the blue books were probably "lotted up with other pamphlets or books because they were considered improper or not worth enough to be cataloged alone. Perhaps they weren't even itemized, and were sold in some miscellaneous lot."[7] Shwartz's Storyville guides may not have been included in this auction at all; it is possible that he gave or sold this group of curiosities to Heartman directly.

## CHARLES FREDERICK HEARTMAN

Charles Frederick Heartman (1883–1953), a noted rare book dealer, editor, and publisher, was a native of Hanover, Germany, who came to America in 1911.[8] A book collector from his youth, he owned bookstores in New York and Vermont and lived for many years in Metuchen, New Jersey, where he often held book auctions from his house. Heartman moved to New Orleans in 1935 with his wife and daughter and continued publishing the annotated and detailed bibliographies and reprints that make up the seventy-seven titles in his Heartman's Historical Series.[9]

Heartman was also interested in the idea of establishing a utopian colony of artists, writers, and intellectuals where creativity could flourish without the interference of economic and political reality. To this end, he purchased roughly four hundred acres of wooded hills outside of Hattiesburg, Mississippi, which contained several buildings, a pond, a stream, pecan trees, and a power plant. He called it the Book Farm, and he lived and worked there between 1937 and 1945, while making frequent book-buying trips to New Orleans. Although the Book Farm did not become the intellectual utopia he envisioned, Heartman was indeed one of the leading bibliophiles of the twentieth century, which

Charles Frederick Heartman

is evident in his numerous publications and extensive correspondence with business associates in the rare book trade, scholars, collectors, and librarians.[10] After a few years in Biloxi, Mississippi, and New Braunfels, Texas, Heartman returned to New Orleans, where he died in 1953 of a heart attack in his house at 3646 Camp Street.

Heartman released a prospectus for his publication on the Shwartz collection of blue books in 1936, noting that the bibliography would be published as a limited edition and that not many more copies than orders received would be printed. Five dollars sent to Mayco Press, at 754 East 222nd Street in New York, would secure a copy. The prospectus, titled "An Exciting Bibliographical Adventure," also states that a special edition, printed on handmade paper and bound in half morocco, would be available for fifteen dollars.[11] Exactly how many regular copies of Heartman's Historical Series No. 50—bound in dark navy-blue cloth—were printed is unknown. The verso of the title page states that fifteen copies of the special edition were produced, but neither I nor collectors of Heartman's publications with whom I have corresponded have seen an edition bound in half morocco.[12]

Prior to publication, it seemed as though Heartman's bibliography would succumb to the same postal restrictions as those that had controlled the Storyville guides themselves. Fellow bookman Harry B. Weiss, who was very familiar with Heartman's career, made this tantalizing observation: "The story of the difficulties in getting this book out cannot yet be told."[13] On August 3, 1936, C. A. Battles, US post office inspector in New York, instructed personnel with Mayco Press to appear two days later for an "official interview relating to the advertising that you are sending through the U.S. Mails, describing the Blue Book that you are offering for sale."[14] An official of the US attorney's office had commented on the lewd nature of a couple of passages in the prospectus, and Battles requested that a copy of the book be made available for examination. The book was not quite ready, so a set of page proofs with illustrations was presented at the meeting.

When informed of this snag, Heartman quickly sent a heated defense of the project to Battles. He pointed out that any lewd or obscene passages are "merely illustrations to support the underlying reformatory tendencies as developed in my book. New Orleans is a cesspool and in order to bring the assertion home it was necessary to make a few drastic quotations. After all, my booklet is not intended for the general public but for serious minded people."[15] Heartman does seem to have been genuinely interested in informing "serious minded people" of New Orleans's low moral character, as he expands upon this observation at length in the introduction of his bibliography. Positing "that New Orleans and prostitution are synonymous," Heartman claims that the city's reputation for nearly unrestricted prostitution is among the main attractions for visitors and is instrumental in drawing many conventions vital to the local economy, an opinion that, while extreme, may not be entirely untrue. Heartman then launches into a brief history of "the low moral condition of the growing city" and describes the current state of its degeneracy: "New Orleans is the cancer in the body of the United States. Luckily, because nowhere else will such fertile ground be found, this gangrene will remain a localized affair."[16]

Title page of Heartman's *The "Blue Book"*

In a letter, Inspector Battles reassured Heartman that he had not personally raised objections to the book, and that "the sole purpose of the investigation is to determine whether or not the book is obscene within the meaning of the statute governing the advertising and sale of obscene literature."[17] Apparently it was not, because Heartman's Historical Series No. 50, entitled *The "Blue Book": A Bibliographical Attempt to Describe the Guide Books to the Houses of Ill Fame in New Orleans as They Were Published There. Together with Some Pertinent and Illuminating Remarks Pertaining to the Establishments and Courtesans as Well as to Harlotry in General in New Orleans*, was published in the fall of 1936, bearing the pseudonym Semper Idem (Latin for "always the same") on the title page and in the preface. Heartman occasionally used other pseudonyms, but this is the only appearance of Semper Idem in his publications.[18]

For the purposes of his bibliography, Heartman placed the thirteen Storyville guides he had acquired from Shwartz in as close a chronological order as he could determine and assigned a Roman numeral to each, which he penciled on the front cover of each book; Heartman used these numbers as shorthand to refer to the books in his bibliography. After completing his research, Heartman sold the entire group in July 1936 to a distinguished collector and bibliographer of Americana, Thomas W. Streeter.

Heartman's marks appear on the covers of the blue books he owned.

## THOMAS WINTHROP STREETER

Thomas Winthrop Streeter (1883–1965), born in Concord, New Hampshire, was a lawyer and banker in Boston and New York City before his passions turned to book collecting. He graduated from Dartmouth College in 1904 and Harvard Law School in 1907. After moving to New York, in 1917, he served in executive positions with various companies and amassed a fortune by the time he retired in 1939, at the age of fifty-six. By his late thirties, in 1920, Streeter had developed an interest in rare books and attended an auction at the Anderson Galleries,[19] the same New York auction firm that would handle the sale of the Shwartz collection in November 1926. Upon retirement he moved to Morristown, New Jersey, having the means and leisure to pursue his lifelong interest in American history and books.[20] Streeter served as president of the American Antiquarian Society and the Bibliographical Society of America as well as treasurer of the New-York Historical Society; was a fellow in both the California Historical Society and the Texas State Historical Association; and was active in several scholarly societies. He was acknowledged as "the foremost collector of Americana in the 20th century."[21]

The strength of Streeter's remarkable library lay in its original publications carrying the first reports of exploration and development of areas throughout North America, as well as significant examples of early printing as this technology followed pioneers across the frontier. Ultimately, his massive collection included books, pamphlets, broadsides, and maps from New England to San Francisco and from the Gulf of Mexico to Canada. During his tenure as chairman of the board for Simms Petroleum Corporation, he had frequently traveled to Texas, fueling a fascination with the state's early history. Streeter published

Thomas Winthrop Streeter

several scholarly bibliographies based on his private collections, including *Americana—Beginnings* (1952), *Texas Imprints* (1955), *Mexican Imprints Relating to Texas* (1956), and *United States and European Imprints Relating to Texas* (1960), the last three titles forming the important *Bibliography of Texas, 1795–1845*. After completing his documentation of publications on early Texas in 1960, he sold that portion of his collection, some 2,000 volumes, to Yale University.[22]

Upon his death on June 12, 1965, Streeter's remaining Americana collection of approximately 5,000 volumes was sold in a series of seven auctions in twenty-one sessions from October 1966 to October 1969 by Parke-Bernet Galleries in New York.[23] The sale ultimately fetched $3,104,892, called "the highest dollar total ever realized by any sale of printed books in the United States up to that time,"[24] and prices of individual items profoundly influenced the market in printed Americana for years to come. *The Celebrated Collection of Americana Formed by the Late Thomas Winthrop Streeter*, the catalog of the sale, composed of seven volumes and a carefully organized index volume, is considered by bibliophiles to be an important reference tool in the study of Americana.

The collection of New Orleans blue books that Streeter had acquired from Charles F. Heartman in 1936 was presented near the end of this important series of auctions. The books Streeter owned are easily distinguished from other blue books—upon acquisition, he penciled Heartman's initials and "July 1936" in each, typically on the first page. Among his holdings, Streeter also had a copy of the prospectus and of the standard navy-cloth-covered edition of Heartman's bibliography, personally signed by the author to him on the front flyleaf with the inscription, "At last I have 5 copies Send you this one C. F. H."[25] He also had acquired a copy of Thurman W. Reeves's 1951 publication *From the Scarlet Past of Fabulous New Orleans* (No. 16 in this bibliography). These items, along with an 1857 brothel license and a receipt for payment for the license, were part of lot 4290 at the twentieth session of the auction of Streeter's massive collection on October 21, 1969.[26] The description of this lot in volume 7 of the catalog of the Streeter sale states, "collection of twelve of the thirteen guide books to the houses of ill repute in New Orleans," but actually lists only eleven.[27] Though it was not listed, the copy of *Blue Book* Heartman identified as VI (No. 4 in this bibliography) arrived with the rest of the lot.[28] Heartman's XI—the same edition as No. 9 in this bibliography—was not included in the sale and seems to have vanished. If Streeter had acquired all thirteen of Heartman's Storyville guides, but only twelve were sold at the Streeter sale in 1969, what happened to the thirteenth one? Still bearing the penciled notations of Heartman and Streeter, this artifact may be in private hands.

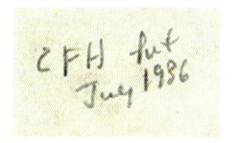

Streeter's marks typically appear on the first page of the blue books he owned.

## LEWIS KEMPER WILLIAMS

Lewis Kemper Williams (1887–1971) was born in Patterson, Louisiana, the third of four sons of lumber industrialist Francis Bennett Williams and his wife, Emily Seyburn Williams. He attended public school in Patterson before going to the Lawrenceville School in New Jersey, then the University of the South in Sewanee, Tennessee, graduating in 1908. Maintaining an interest in his alma mater throughout his life, he became

Lewis Kemper Williams

a regent of the university in 1949 and later served as chairman of the board of regents. He was a major in the United States Army during World War I, then a reserve officer during World War II, taking an active duty assignment with the War Department in Washington, DC, and attaining the rank of brigadier general.[29]

Williams took a prominent role in the business, civic, cultural, and military life of New Orleans, serving as an officer in numerous organizations. Among these were his family's business, the F. B. Williams Cypress Company, as well as the National Bank of Commerce, International Trade Mart, Louisiana Civil Service League, the Audubon Park Commission, and the New Orleans Philharmonic Society. He was also a longtime member of the *Times-Picayune* Doll and Toy Fund. Like his father, who received this honor in 1924, Williams was awarded the *Times-Picayune* Loving Cup in 1937, for his "outstanding service as chairman of the New Orleans Housing Authority."[30] He was also a member of the Sons of the American Revolution, the Society of the Cincinnati, the Mayflower Society, and several prominent clubs including the Boston Club, the Louisiana Club, the Plimsoll Club, and New Orleans Country Club. At the time of his death, he was also serving as honorary consul general of Monaco.

Williams married Leila Moore (1901–1966) of New Orleans in New London, Connecticut, in 1920. Like her husband, she was actively engaged in many social, cultural, and philanthropic interests throughout her life, including the Junior League of New Orleans, the Orleans Club, the New Orleans Symphony, and the Altar Guild of Christ Church Cathedral.[31] Together, the couple amassed an incredible collection of Louisiana-related items. They created and endowed The Historic New Orleans Collection shortly before Leila Williams's death, in 1966, through the establishment of the Kemper and Leila Williams Foundation. Their goals were to preserve their collection, to enable further acquisition of appropriate items about the history and culture of the area in order to enhance and strengthen this core collection, and to make the material available for public study and enjoyment. The Historic New Orleans Collection was first opened to the public on a limited schedule in 1970 and has tremendously expanded its holdings, exhibitions, services, and staff since then. Williams acquired a copy of Lulu White's promotional booklet, *New Mahogany Hall* (No. 11), in 1956. It appears that no other Storyville-era prostitution guides were collected until the Streeter sale, which occurred after Leila Williams's death.

Following the Streeter sale, the *Times-Picayune* announced, "N.O. Guidebooks Are Auctioned" in a brief article dated October 23, 1969, noting that "the books were sold to the Goodspeed Bookshop of Boston, who was bidding for a private client."[32] Michael J. Walsh and Bailey Bishop of Goodspeed's represented the client—L. Kemper Williams—who had previously purchased other Louisiana- and New Orleans–related books from the Streeter auctions for The Historic New Orleans Collection. Williams wrote in his diary on October 24, 1969, "I have been anxious to acquire these little books for several years. They are very rare and much sought after by collectors."[33]

When the Storyville guides acquired through the Streeter sale arrived at The Historic New Orleans Collection, they were carefully identified,

White patches with Heartman's numbers were applied to the back covers of the blue books when they were acquired by THNOC.

housed in a series of acid-free mats specially cut to accommodate each book, and put in an archival print case. In the lower left corner of the outside back cover of each item was affixed a small white square patch printed with the Roman numeral Heartman had assigned to it for his published bibliography. These small white patches, along with Heartman's and Streeter's penciled notations on the covers and inside each book, clearly identify the copies that belonged to Shwartz, then Heartman, then Streeter, and, finally, Williams.[34] Other blue books acquired after this group purchase from the Streeter collection were simply assigned accession numbers, which were penciled on their inside back covers, and housed together in a second archival print case.

### ACCESSING THE HISTORIC NEW ORLEANS COLLECTION'S STORYVILLE GUIDES

In 1999 Yale University doctoral candidate Emily Epstein Landau received a fellowship from the Social Science Research Council under its Sexuality Fellowship Research Program, funded by the Ford Foundation. The fellowship provided funds for her first year of writing her dissertation, "'Spectacular Wickedness': New Orleans, Prostitution, and the Politics of Sex, 1897–1917."[35] As much of her research involved extensive use of THNOC's collection of fragile blue books, Landau used a portion of the fellowship to have them microfilmed. In 2000 one copy of each of the thirteen Storyville-era guides then owned by THNOC was microfilmed along with my revised article, which had appeared in *The Historic New Orleans Collection Quarterly*.[36] None of the fakes or facsimiles was microfilmed for this project. Two copies were made: One is available for use by researchers at the Williams Research Center of The Historic New Orleans Collection, while the other was given by Landau to Yale University.[37] Since the 2000 microfilming project, only three other genuine blue books have been acquired: No. 3 in 2006, No. 10 in 2011, and No. 9 in 2012.

In anticipation of the publication of this book, we have digitized the collection of Storyville-era prostitution guides at THNOC, with the desire that all of these extremely fragile little books be made available online to researchers and the curious bibliophile.

### NOTES

1. William Reese Company, *Catalogue Two Hundred Ninety-Seven*, item 142.
2. Other additions to THNOC's collection of blue books were donated or purchased from individuals and dealers. Only one authentic Storyville guide was found in the William Russell Jazz Collection (see No. 10), which contains approximately 16,000 items relating to early jazz music and musicians of New Orleans collected by historian, musician, and enthusiast William Russell (1905–1992); this collection was acquired by THNOC in 1992.
3. "Simon J. Shwartz, Collector of Art, Civic Leader, Dies," *Times-Picayune*, February 8, 1936, p. 2, col. 3.
4. Foreword to Anderson Galleries, *Library of Mr. Simon J. Shwartz...Part One*, n.p.
5. Heartman, "*Blue Book*," 40, 8. Heartman does not relate how or when Shwartz acquired them.
6. Heartman, "*Blue Book*," 40.
7. Bailey Bishop, email to author, October 21, 2011.
8. "Noted Rare Book Dealer, 70, Dies," *Times-Picayune*, May 9, 1953, p. 2, cols. 1–2, 6.
9. According to Bishop, although the final title in Heartman's Historical Series is numbered 78, there are actually only 77 in the series. There are no numbers 51, 55, or 72, and both numbers 15 and 53 are repeated. Bailey Bishop, email to author, October 22, 2011.
10. Price, "The Book Farm."

11. Heartman, "Exciting Bibliographical Adventure," cover.

12. Though no half morocco edition has surfaced, in 2011 dealer Bill Grady of Hughes Books offered an edition bound in a "light blue washed-looking cloth" and printed on paper of a better quality than the standard, for $450. Hughes Books, *Catalog 44*, item 69; Bill Grady, email to author, September 10, 2015. THNOC has copies of both the navy blue and the light blue clothbound editions.

13. Weiss privately printed an annotated bibliography of his colleague Heartman's body of work through 1938 along with a brief biographical sketch. In this work, he also confirmed Heartman as the link between Shwartz and Streeter. "The collection of 'Blue Books' described, was formerly the property of the late J. S. [sic] Shwartz of New Orleans, and is now in the possession of Thomas W. Streeter." Weiss, *Bibliographical, Editorial, and Other Activities*, 20.

14. Battles to Mayco Press, August 3, 1936, Heartman (Charles F.) Papers, M94, series 2, box 6, folder 10, McCain Library and Archives, University of Southern Mississippi, Hattiesburg, MS (hereafter Heartman Papers).

15. Heartman to Battles, August 10, 1936, Heartman Papers.

16. Heartman, *"Blue Book,"* 13–32.

17. Battles to Heartman, August 17, 1936, Heartman Papers.

18. His other pseudonyms include Stefan Stumpf, Steven Stump, and Heinrich Hartman. Finding aid for Heartman Papers, accessed October 5, 2011, http://www.lib.usm.edu/legacy/archives/m094.htm.

19. Lawrence C. Wroth, introduction, in Parke-Bernet Galleries, *Celebrated Collection*, vol. 1, n.p.

20. Hewes, "Thomas W. Streeter."

21. "A note," in William Reese Company, *Catalogue Two Hundred Fifty-Seven*, n.p.

22. Streeter, "Streeter, Thomas Winthrop."

23. Ibid.

24. "A note," in William Reese Company, *Catalogue Two Hundred Fifty-Seven*, n.p.

25. Streeter's copy of Heartman's *The "Blue Book,"* 1969.19.13, THNOC.

26. The 1857 New Orleans brothel license authorized a Mary Brooks to occupy a specific building, in accordance with Ordinance No. 3267 regarding "lewd and abandoned women," and the receipt was for payment of the license. Similar documents are described and pictured in Heartman's bibliography. Prostitution license, May 21, 1857, 69-19-L.10, THNOC; receipt for payment for prostitution license, May 21, 1857, 69-19-L.9, THNOC.

27. Parke-Bernet Galleries, *Celebrated Collection*, vol. 7, no. 4290. THNOC's copy of volume 7 of the Streeter sale catalog is packaged with a list that details the final bids for each lot, revealing that the top bid for lot 4290 was $1,700.

28. Bailey Bishop, who examined this lot while appraising Streeter's library for Boston's Goodspeed's Book Shop, confirmed that there were twelve. Bailey Bishop, email to author, May 10, 2011.

29. "Gen. Williams Taken by Death," *Times-Picayune*, November 18, 1971, p. 1, col. 4; cont. p. 20, col. 1–5.

30. "Gen. Williams Dies; Was Civic Leader," *States-Item*, November 18, 1971, p. 4, col. 7–8.

31. "Mrs. Williams Taken by Death," *Times-Picayune*, December 14, 1966, p. 3, col. 3–4.

32. The correct name of the store was Goodspeed's Book Shop. "N.O. Guidebooks Are Auctioned," *Times-Picayune*, October 23, 1969, sect. 1, p. 4, col. 6.

33. L. Kemper Williams diary, October 24, 1969, L. Kemper Williams and Leila Hardie Moore Williams Papers, 97-63-L, series 2, subseries 11, box 346, folder 3546, THNOC.

34. This processing was executed perhaps by the Williamses' close friend Alvyk Boyd Cruise, the first director of The Historic New Orleans Collection; his colleague and partner, Harold Schilke; or someone else associated with THNOC.

35. Landau, "'Spectacular Wickedness,'" ix. The same grant also funded in part the New Orleans Public Library's 2008 exhibition *Hidden from History: Unknown New Orleanians*, curated by Landau. This exhibition may be viewed online at http://nutrias.org/exhibits/hidden/hiddenfromhistory_intro.htm (accessed October 12, 2012).

36. Arceneaux, "Storyville's Blue Books," 8–9.

37. Landau, *Spectacular Wickedness*, 268.

**Fan light over the door of Lulu White's Mahogany Hall**

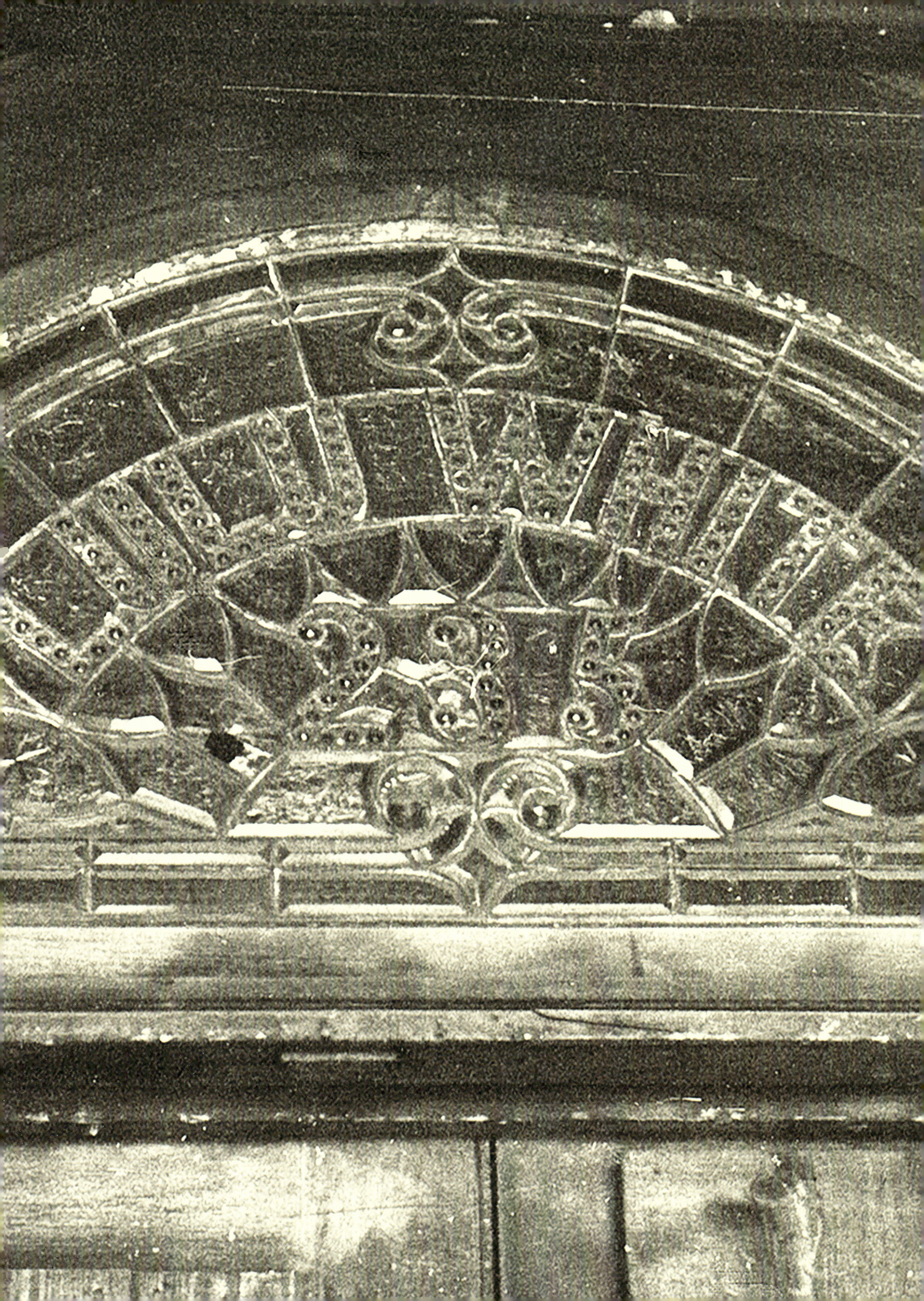

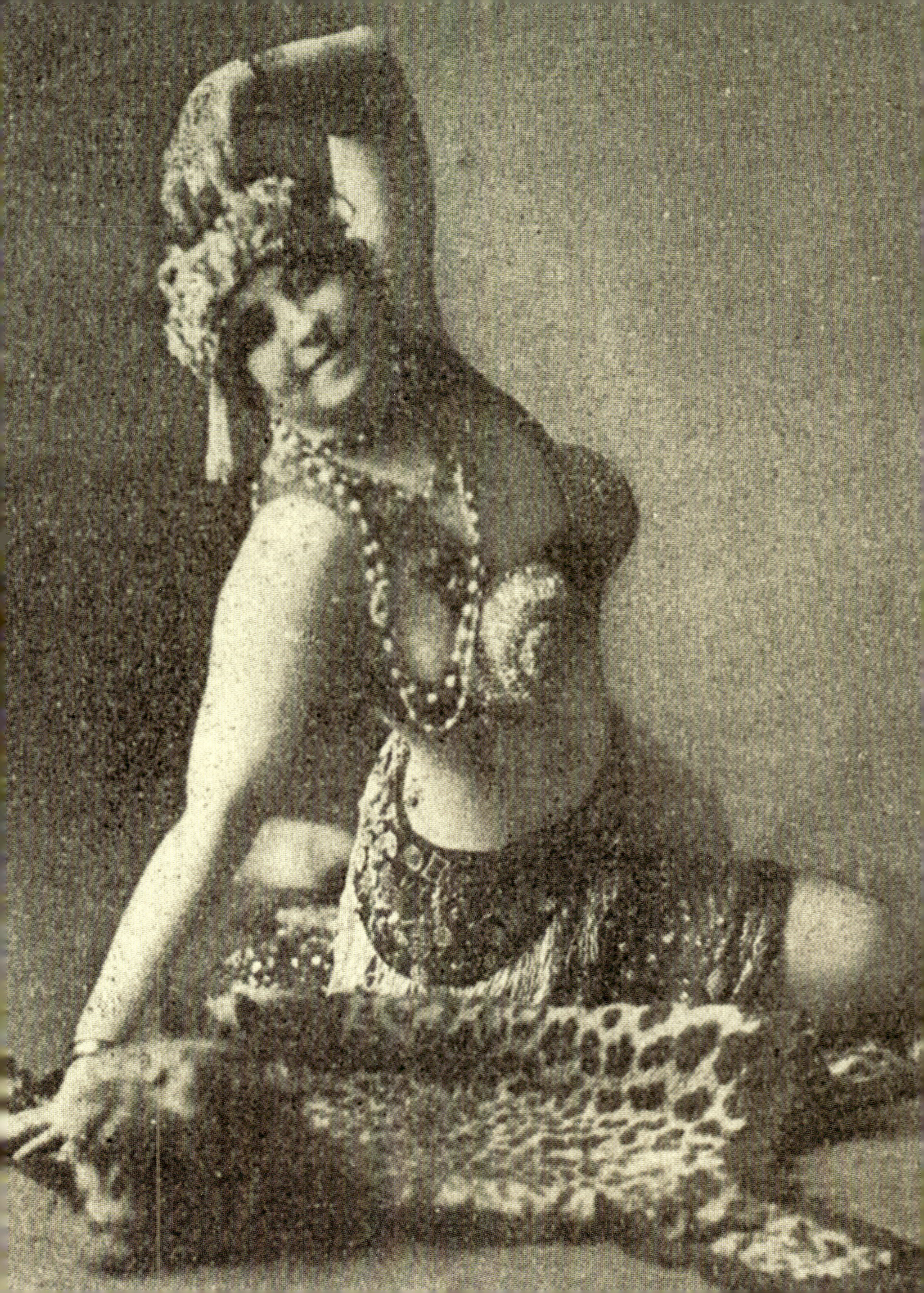

# BIBLIOGRAPHY OF PROSTITUTION GUIDES

For the purposes of this bibliography, I have divided The Historic New Orleans Collection's various prostitution-related directories into three groups. The first contains editions of an authentic Storyville-era publication titled *Blue Book* that are somewhat consistent in their content and physical appearance and were published by Billy Struve, a reporter and saloon manager. The second contains authentic Storyville-era prostitution guides with varying titles, sizes, and origins; I call these publications the alternative guides. A third group contains fakes and facsimiles that were produced for the post-Storyville tourist market, trading on the District's cachet well after its demise. A few of these facsimiles or partial reproductions were issued as party favors for special events. Some are outright fakes, with new content spliced in alongside facsimile pages from original blue books.

As of this writing, THNOC has in its holdings twenty-four authentic Storyville-era prostitution guides representing fifteen different editions, and sixteen post-Storyville fakes and facsimiles representing ten different editions. Occasionally in this bibliography I describe other New Orleans prostitution directories that I have examined but that are not among the holdings of The Historic New Orleans Collection.

A photograph of the publication's cover accompanies each bibliographic entry, to which I have assigned a number. Each entry contains the edition, when stated, and publication date. When the date appears in brackets, this is the date I deduced and assigned to the book based upon clues noted within it. THNOC owns multiple copies of some editions; in these cases, the best artifact is featured, but every copy is listed, with its measurements, accession number, and donor credit, where applicable. If the item was described in Charles F. Heartman's 1936 bibliography, the number he assigned to the item is also noted.

Produced during the early twentieth century, these prostitution guides employ the then-common terms "colored" and "octoroon" when describing African American women. I also use these archaic terms in describing and analyzing the contents of these guides, in the service of maintaining a consistency with the source material.

**EDITIONS OF BLUE BOOK**

Nos. 1–10

**ALTERNATIVE STORYVILLE-ERA GUIDES**

Nos. 11–15

**FAKES AND FACSIMILES**

Nos. 16–25

Advertisement for Rita Walker, "The Oriental Danseuse," from No. 10

EDITIONS OF *BLUE BOOK*

# No. 1
## Blue Book | *TENDERLOIN* | "400."

Cover printed in red ink on medium green paper; interior printed in black ink on plain paper.
No edition number, undated [1900]. 36 unnumbered pages.

14.7 cm × 9.8 cm, THNOC, 94-092-RL

iiiiiiiiiiiiiiiiiiiiiiiii

This very copy, showing a fashionably dressed young woman holding a partly opened fan, with its obvious creases caused by folding, is the one extensively photographed and reproduced in Al Rose's *Storyville, New Orleans* (pp. 136, 137, 140, 141, and 142). The back cover advertises the French balls for the Carnival season, giving the date of Mardi Gras night as February 27, which fell on that date in 1900 and in 1906. THNOC has a copy of *Blue Book* dated 1906 (No. 5 in this bibliography) that also contains an advertisement for the French balls on the same dates. In comparison with the 1906 edition, this one contains simpler telephone exchanges and appears more crudely produced, using a cheaper paper, which leads me to believe that this edition was published for the 1900 Carnival season. This ad for the French balls also features a saucy drawing of a scantily clad woman with a man in evening clothes in the

BIBLIOGRAPHY | 66

background—the reversed signature of Billy News suggests that the image has been flipped. This drawing also appears in ads for the French balls in Nos. 2 and 3.

This edition was unknown to Charles F. Heartman, and Rose believed it was the earliest of the extant New Orleans prostitution guides, assigning a date of 1898 to it, possibly based on wording in the "Intruduction" by Billy News giving the boundaries of Storyville and indicating that the District had been recently established. This introduction makes a distinction between Storyville and Anderson County, a pre-Storyville vice area located in the French Quarter, nicknamed for sporting man, entrepreneur, and political figure Thomas C. Anderson. The introduction also contains some valuable philosophical advice: "What is the good of living if you can't have a good time, or as the proverb goes. Live while you have a chance. You will be dead a long time."

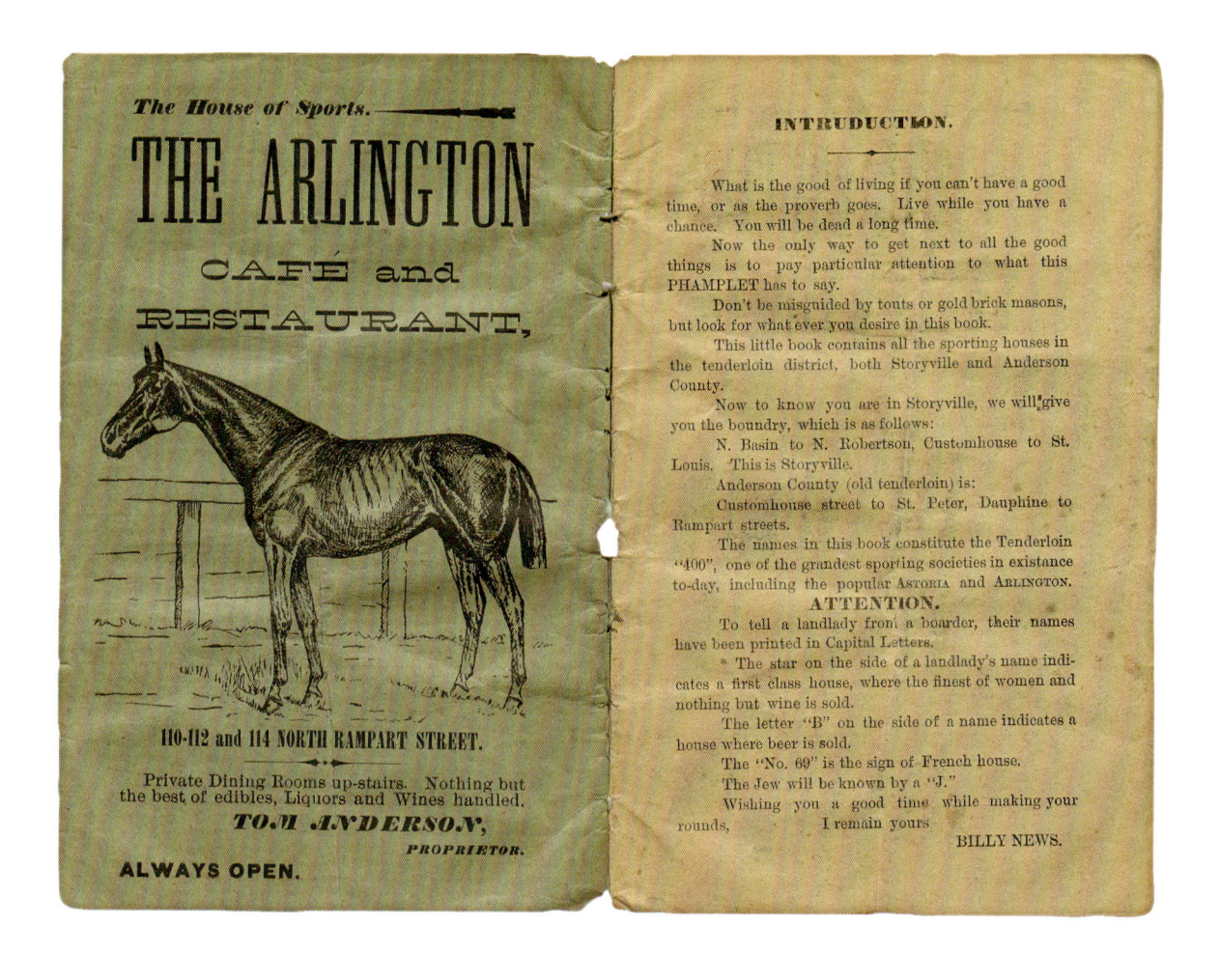

Overall, 432 women's names appear in the directory, organized very loosely by address within certain categories. A section of the introduction provides a key to decoding the shorthand used throughout the directory. Names of madams are in capital letters. An asterisk indicates "wine castles," "where the finest of women and nothing but wine is sold," and the letter "B" indicates "beer houses." "No. 69" designates "French houses" or "French resorts," which featured fellatio. Unlike in later editions, the races of white and black individuals are not noted, although some racial notations are made: "J" identifies an area along the 800 and 900 blocks of Bienville Street offering prostitutes who were Jewish, called "The Jew Colony," and though they are not discussed in the introduction, a small section lists octoroon establishments. In total, six octoroon houses are listed, along with twenty assignation houses, nineteen wine castles, thirty-seven beer houses, nine French resorts, fourteen Jewish brothels, and fifty-three "miscellaneous houses."

Notable advertisements in this book include a full-page ad with a photograph of a horse-drawn open carriage (perhaps a victoria) outside the establishment of A. E. Ravain, Funeral Director and Embalmer, located at 302–4 N. Rampart, corner Bienville. There are four advertisements for different pharmacies that offered venereal disease cures. Frank P. Custer, proprietor of the Olympic Saloon at Canal and Basin Streets, "can boast of having one of the finest and most complete lot of nude photograph reproductions of famous women. He has in all about 800 photos, among the number some of the leading actresses." There are only seven full-page brothel ads. This early *Blue Book* contains an advertisement for Josie Arlington's four-story, turreted mansion at 225 N. Basin Street, featuring an architectural rendering of the mansion's facade, an image that appears in most subsequent editions.

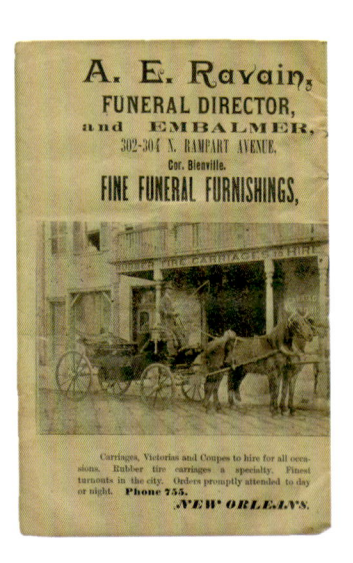

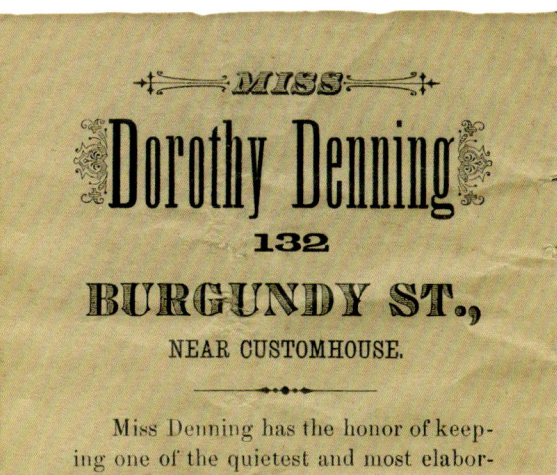

## MISS
# Dorothy Denning
## 132
## BURGUNDY ST.,
### NEAR CUSTOMHOUSE.

Miss Denning has the honor of keeping one of the quietest and most elaborately furnished establishments in the city where beautiful women, good wine and sweet music reign supreme. Miss Denning while clever to everyone has the distinction of keeping one of the most refined houses in the tenderloin, where one can have enjoyment unmolested and without being seen.

The following are the names of her ladies': Misses Florence Davis, Alice Knoll, Bertha Knight, Nina Jackson, Vivin Stetson and several others whose name can not be published.

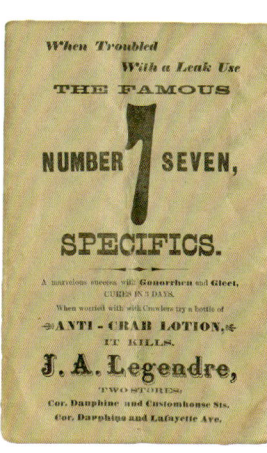

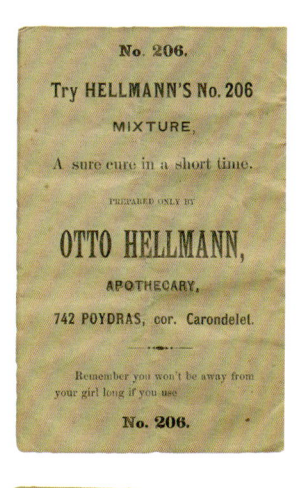

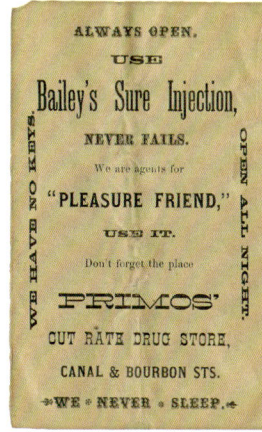

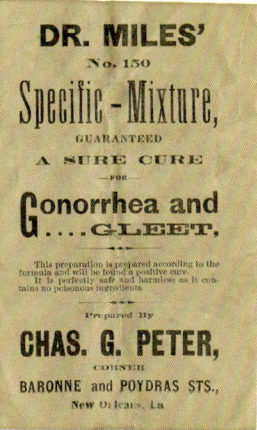

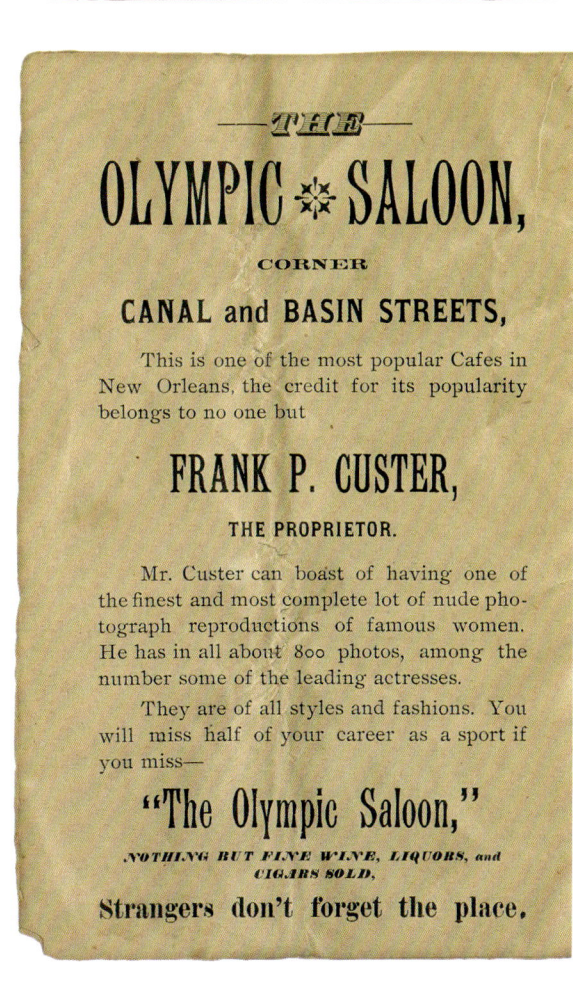

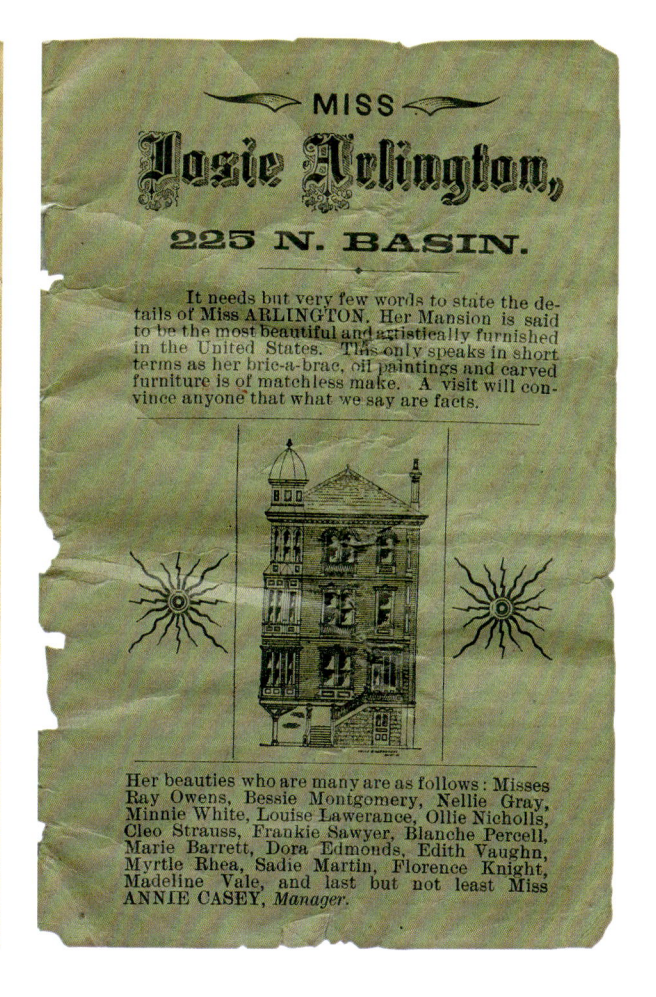

---

**When Troubled With a Leak Use THE FAMOUS NUMBER SEVEN SPECIFICS.**

A marvelous success. All Gonorrhea and Gleet. CURES IN 3 DAYS.
When worried with sick Crabbers try a bottle of
**ANTI-CRAB LOTION,**
IT KILLS.
**J. A. Legendre,**
TWO STORES.
Cor. Dauphine and Customhouse Sts.
Cor. Dauphine and Lafayette Ave.

---

**No. 206.**
Try HELLMANN'S No. 206
MIXTURE.
A sure cure in a short time.
PREPARED ONLY BY
**OTTO HELLMANN,**
APOTHECARY,
742 POYDRAS, cor. Carondelet.

Remember you won't be away from your girl long if you use
**No. 206.**

---

**ALWAYS OPEN.**
USE
**Bailey's Sure Injection,**
NEVER FAILS.
We are agents for
**"PLEASURE FRIEND,"**
USE IT.
Don't forget the place
**PRIMOS'**
CUT RATE DRUG STORE,
CANAL & BOURBON STS.
WE NEVER SLEEP.
WE MAKE ON KEYS. OPEN ALL NIGHT.

---

**DR. MILES'**
No. 150
**Specific-Mixture,**
GUARANTEED
A SURE CURE
FOR
**Gonorrhea and GLEET,**
This preparation is prepared according to the formula and will be found a positive cure. It is perfectly safe and harmless as it contains no poisonous ingredients.
Prepared By
**CHAS. G. PETER,**
CORNER
BARONNE and POYDRAS STS.,
New Orleans, La.

---

## THE
# OLYMPIC ✦ SALOON,
### CORNER
### CANAL and BASIN STREETS,

This is one of the most popular Cafes in New Orleans, the credit for its popularity belongs to no one but

### FRANK P. CUSTER,
#### THE PROPRIETOR.

Mr. Custer can boast of having one of the finest and most complete lot of nude photograph reproductions of famous women. He has in all about 800 photos, among the number some of the leading actresses.

They are of all styles and fashions. You will miss half of your career as a sport if you miss—

### "The Olympic Saloon,"
NOTHING BUT FINE WINE, LIQUORS, and CIGARS SOLD,

**Strangers don't forget the place.**

---

## MISS
# Josie Arlington,
## 225 N. BASIN.

It needs but very few words to state the details of Miss ARLINGTON. Her Mansion is said to be the most beautiful and artistically furnished in the United States. This only speaks in short terms as her bric-a-brac, oil paintings and carved furniture is of matchless make. A visit will convince anyone that what we say are facts.

Her beauties who are many are as follows: Misses Ray Owens, Bessie Montgomery, Nellie Gray, Minnie White, Louise Lawerance, Ollie Nicholls, Cleo Strauss, Frankie Sawyer, Blanche Percell, Marie Barrett, Dora Edmonds, Edith Vaughn, Myrtle Rhea, Sadie Martin, Florence Knight, Madeline Vale, and last but not least Miss ANNIE CASEY, Manager.

## EDITIONS OF *BLUE BOOK*

# No. 2
## BLUE BOOK | *TENDERLOIN 400.*

Cover printed in black ink on sage-green paper; interior printed in black ink on plain paper.
No edition number, undated [1901]. 40 unnumbered pages.

14.8 cm x 10.2 cm, THNOC, 1969.19.4 (Heartman IV)

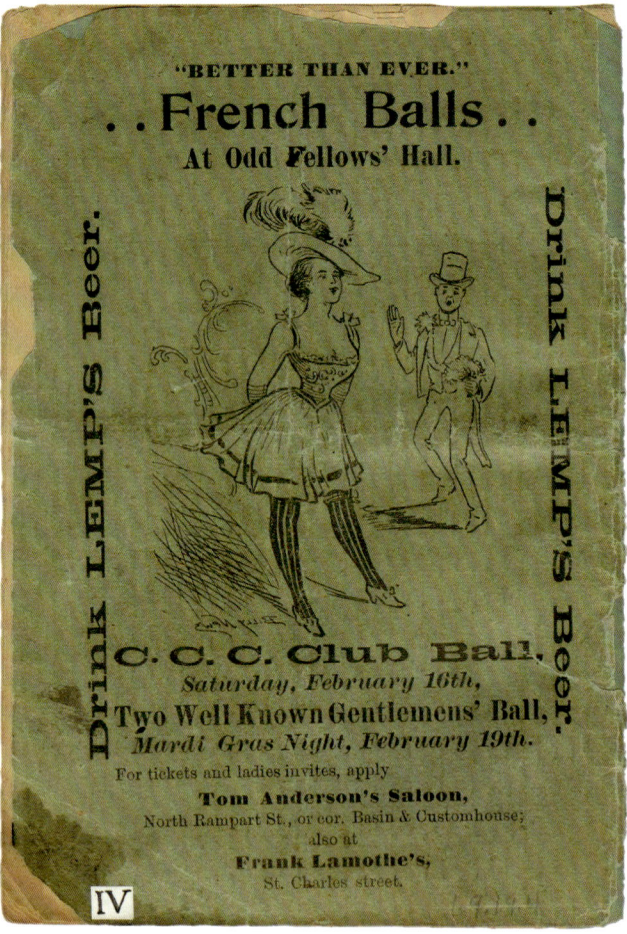

With its Charles Dana Gibson–style illustration of an elegant woman in a dark evening gown, surrounded by fainter images of women and a girl in earlier clothing styles, all holding stemmed glasses, this is one of the most striking editions of *Blue Book*. The inclusion of the little girl in the foreground gives one pause and serves as a sobering reminder that children, especially young girls, were a part of the District's milieu.[1] An advertisement for the French balls on the back cover gives the date of the ball given by the Two Well-Known Gentlemen, always held on Mardi Gras night, as February 19. Mardi Gras fell on February 19 in 1901. The drawing by Billy News from No. 1 is repeated in the ad. Heartman penciled "1895"—a pre-Storyville date—on the lower right corner of the cover. The book has deteriorated since 1936, and part of this date is no longer visible, but it can be seen in the photograph of the cover he included on page 47 of his bibliography (an interior spread is also reproduced on page 49 of Heartman's book). Heartman's entry for this book has a question mark by this date and states that the "attribution of the date is given to me by an old timer. Others disagree."[2] The advertisement for the French balls disproves this earlier date.

The introduction, titled "How to be Wise," does not have a byline but does contain certain lines repeated in most subsequent editions of *Blue Book*, such as "The contents of this book are facts and not dreams from a 'hop joint.'" This is a reference to smoking opium (hop) in dens, usually located in the Chinatown section of many large cities at this time. New Orleans's Chinatown, along Common Street, was only a few blocks away from the red-light district. The introduction gives the location of Storyville but incorrectly states that it is synonymous with Anderson County (this earlier vice district was located in the French Quarter). This edition appears to contain the first use of the warning "This Book not Mailable" in the Storyville guides, in compliance with the Comstock Law of 1873, regulating the sending of pornographic materials via the United States Postal Service. Similar notices are repeated in most subsequent editions of *Blue Book*.

The directory is broken into sections: a mix of specialties on offer ("French 69" and "Beer Houses"), specific brothels (including Mahogany Hall, the Crescent, the Arlington, the Studio, and the Club), and more mysterious categories ("Speak Easy Houses" and "Those Who Are Still Alive but on the Q. T."). Within these categories, the women are listed loosely by address. Though black and white prostitutes are not identified as such, there is a section listing twenty-one octoroon women, and five Jewish prostitutes are identified by the letter "J." Overall, some 387 women's names appear here, and nearly all are set in full capitals. There are seven full-page ads for individual brothels.

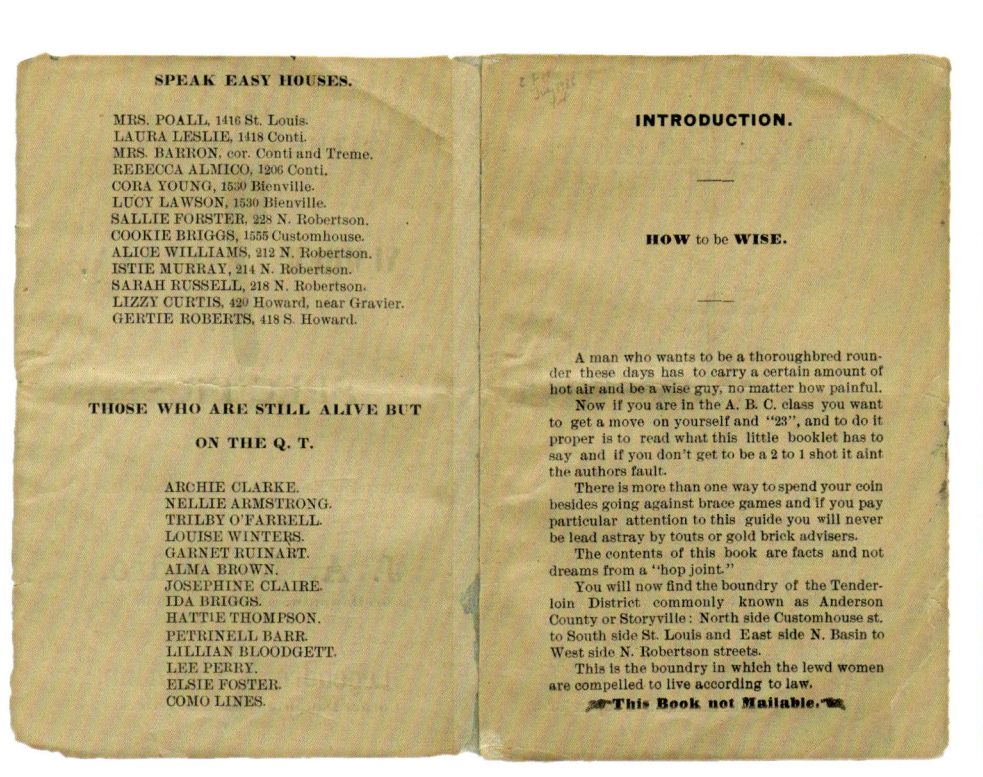

> Don't forget to pay a visit to the well-known
>
> **UNEXSPECTED SALOON,**
>
> 340 Marais, Cor. Conti Sts.
>
> You can't find a better fellow in the sporting district than the proprietor, Mr. F. Briant, he is of a jovial disposition and always ready to add on a new friend.
>
> Open day and night. Peoples Phone 1961; Cumberland 2241-21. Private rooms.

> MISS
>
> **Nellie McDowell,**
>
> 221 N. Basin Street
>
> has a most worthy name for being the mistress over one of the foremost sporting palace in the Tenderloin District where swell men can be socially entertained by clever and as well a beautiful array of ladies who know how to entertain the most tedious gentleman.
>
> Miss McDowell is ever willing to increase her friends, so don't be backwards in paying her a call. The ladies are named as follows: Missess Gladys Harris, Josie Howard, Mona Desmond, Magie Roe, Gloria Ely and 3 who recently arrived from the East — Telephone 1663.

> If its a jolly good time and pretty women you are in search for you, don't want to forget
>
> —MISS—
>
> **Lottie Fisher,**
>
> 313 N. Basin St.
>
> This is a first-class and very magnificently fitted up place, and if you can't be entertained by Mrs. Fisher's ladies in a Royal style, then you are no "sport". The names of her ladies are Marie Gates, Etta Ross, May Howard, Ethel Bothick, Nettie Nelson, Effie Russell, and 3 awful pretty and refined girls who ask not to be made known but they can be seen nevertheless.

This edition contains the same advertisement for the funeral parlor of A. E. Ravain as No. 1, although in a different typeface. Josie Arlington's ad states, "No pen can describe the beauty and magnifiance [*sic*] that reign supreme within the walls of Miss Arlington's Mansion." To ensure that this grandeur was appropriately comprehended, seven photographs of the interior of her 225 N. Basin Street brothel were interspersed throughout the book. These include a corner of her private boudoir, an unnamed parlor, the Turkish Parlor, a corner of the Chinese Parlor, a "den" in the Turkish Parlor, the American Parlor, and the Vienna Parlor. Often reproduced in subsequent editions of *Blue Book*, these photographs convey an idea of what was expected and considered elegant at a top-flight establishment of the era.

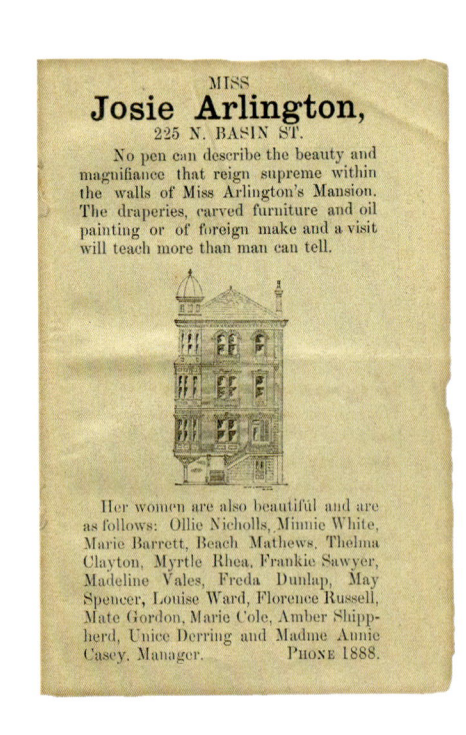

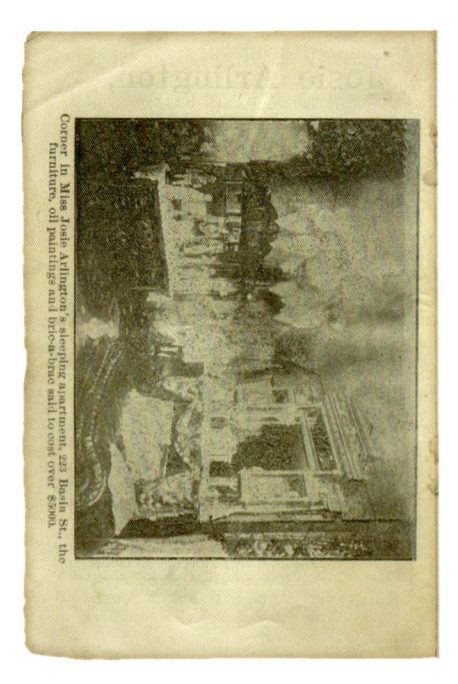

> MISS
> **Josie Arlington,**
> 225 N. Basin St.
>
> No pen can describe the beauty and magnifiance that reign supreme within the walls of Miss Arlington's Mansion. The draperies, carved furniture and oil painting or of foreign make and a visit will teach more than man can tell.
>
> Her women are also beautiful and are as follows: Ollie Nicholls, Minnie White, Marie Barrett, Beach Mathews, Thelma Clayton, Myrtle Rhea, Frankie Sawyer, Madeline Vales, Freda Dunlap, May Spencer, Louise Ward, Florence Russell, Mate Gordon, Marie Cole, Amber Shippherd, Unice Derring and Madme Annie Casey, Manager.      Phone 1888.

> Corner in Miss Josie Arlington's sleeping apartment, 225 Basin St, the furniture, oil paintings and bric-à-brac said to cost over $3000.

BIBLIOGRAPHY | 72

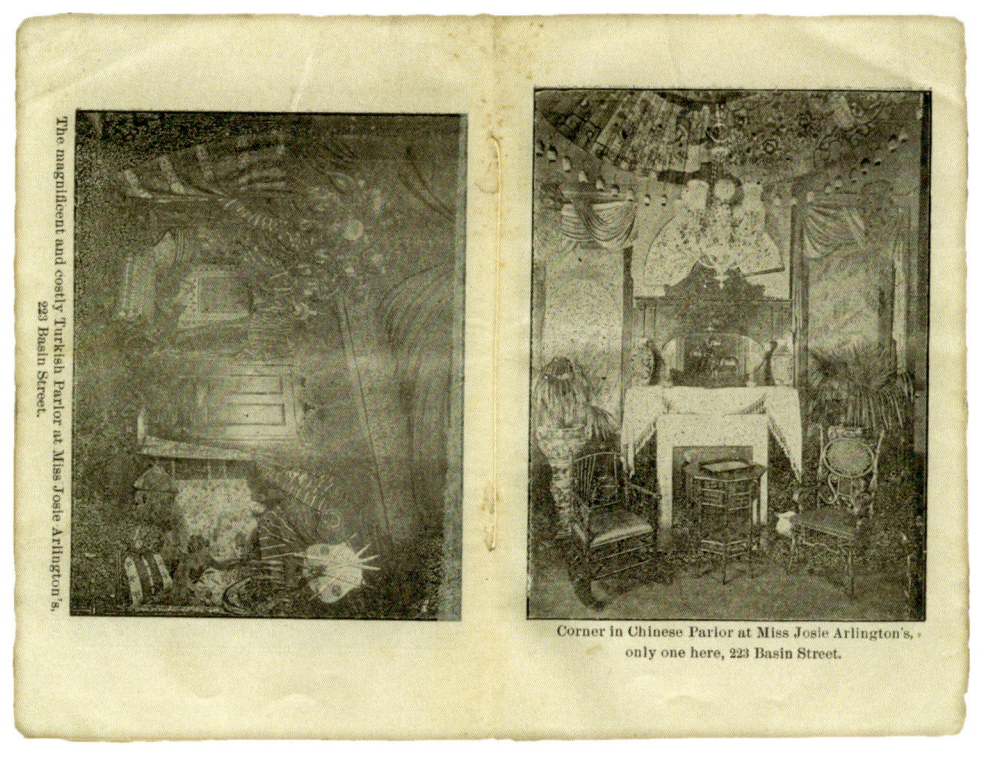

The magnificent and costly Turkish Parlor at Miss Josie Arlington's, 223 Basin Street.

Corner in Chinese Parlor at Miss Josie Arlington's, only one here, 223 Basin Street.

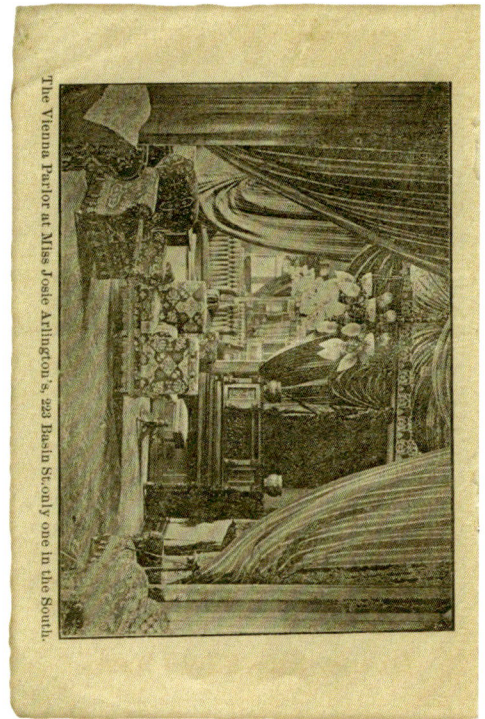

The Vienna Parlor at Miss Josie Arlington's, 223 Basin St., only one in the South.

One of the gorgeous "dens" in Miss Josie Arlington's costly Turkish Parlor, 223 Basin Street.

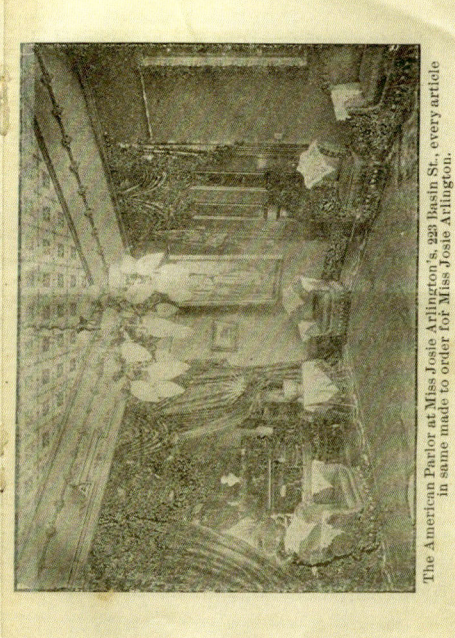

The American Parlor at Miss Josie Arlington's, 223 Basin St., every article in same made to order for Miss Josie Arlington.

One of the many parlors at Miss Josie Arlington's 223 Basin Street.

EDITIONS OF *BLUE BOOK*

# No. 3

## Blue Book

Cover printed in red-orange ink on blue-gray paper; interior printed in black ink on calendered paper.
No edition number, undated [1903]. 64 unnumbered pages.

14.4 cm × 9.8 cm, *THNOC*, 2006.0237

### PREFACE

*"Don't be a noax all"*

It's bad know to much sometimes; there is not a day to pass that some wise guy doesnot go to the "high brush" with his bad information on all he *knows* about Race Horses.

It's the same way with the fast women of the tenderloin, while they are not classed as bangtails, some of 'em hang a new record out every day—Fast!! Well 'eh! wish you'd hush.

You'll hear some wise guys tell his girl not to this or that—now do you think they listen? If he'd said nothing she might have listened, but he "knew all."

Now it's the same way with people who try to tell you the best place to go to spend your money (not his.)

This book is on it's fourth year and is noted for it's fairness as a directory for strangers who see fit to visit the tenderloin.

---

"This book is on it's [sic] fourth year and is noted for it's [sic] fairness as a directory for strangers who see fit to visit the tenderloin." So says Little Willie, perhaps another of Billy Struve's aliases, in the introductory pages of this guide. This statement tantalizes the reader with the idea that a third edition of *Blue Book* was produced in 1902 but has not surfaced; however, it is possible that Little Willie miscounted, as errors abound throughout these publications. There are two advertisements for the French balls ("Better Than Ever"), held Saturday, February 21, and Mardi Gras night, February 24, which reveal that this guide was published in anticipation of the 1903 Carnival season. The first of the two ads features the same illustration signed "Billy News" that appears in Nos. 1 and 2. There is also a reference in Flo Meeker's ad to the "late

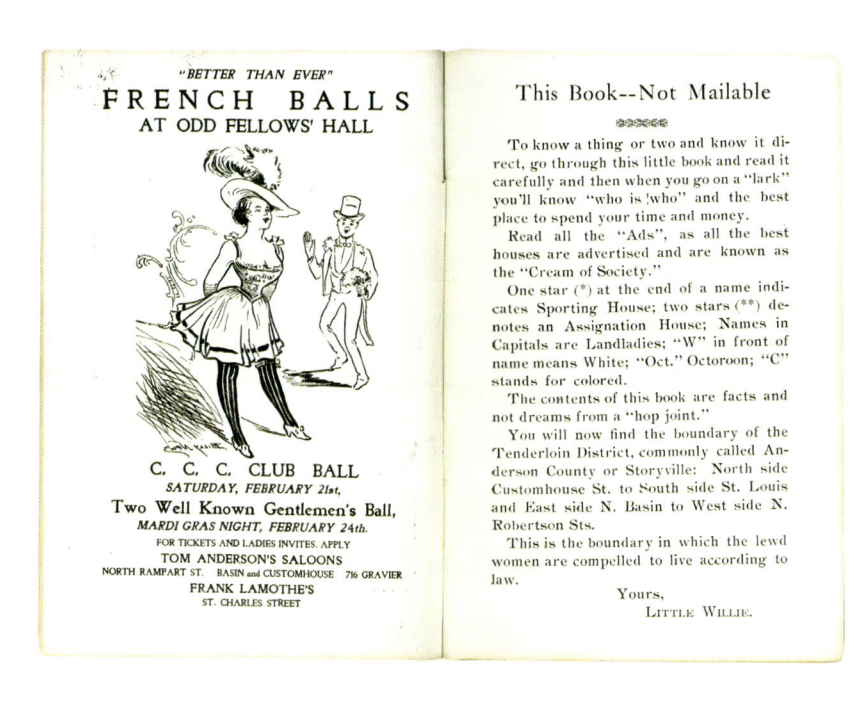

Paris Exposition," which was held in 1900. This edition, not discussed by Heartman or Rose, was acquired by THNOC in 2006.

The directory section is titled "Names Storyville '400'" and within it, women are listed geographically by address, beginning with parallel streets Basin, Franklin (now Crozat), Liberty (now Treme), Marais, Villere, and Robertson, then Customhouse (now Iberville), Bienville, Conti, and St. Louis. As the introduction notes, brothels are identified by a single asterisk; two asterisks denote an assignation house; madams' names are set in full capitals; and for the first time in *Blue Book*, all women's races are indicated: "W" for white; "C" for colored; and "Oct." for octoroon. There are 651 women listed in the directory section, of which 419 are white, 196 are colored, and 36 are octoroon. Of these, 163 are white madams, 116 are colored madams, and 6 are octoroon madams.

Between this arrangement by street and address, and the racial identification of the landladies and prostitutes, one can make some interesting observations. Many of the names given in capital letters are listed as the

**MISS JOSIE FRIEDMAN**
1318 BIENVILLE, CORNER LIBERTY

Miss Friedman is a jewish by birth, but that has nothing to do with to-day or yesterday, Josie came to this city from New York, where she has wealthy relations, to have a good time and she is going to have it while she lasts. Her house has been fitted at a cost second to none in the United States so you can judge for yourself its magnificence.

A visit will tell the whole story.

The ladies who are at this beautiful mirror mazed house are:

Minnie Howard,
Lilly Mallory,
Inez Moore,
Laura Gilmore,
Hamazelle West,
Sybil Shelton,
Alma Bush,
Lydia Sterling,
Paula Baily,
Grace Everet,
Ruth Wallace,
Zetta Kennedy,
Lola Danel,
Louise Roebrick,
Mable De Angelis,
Dove De War,
Stella Marton,
Edith Nichols

---

**FLORENCE MANTLEY**
215 333 BASIN STREET

Has always been a head-liner among those who keep first-class octoroons. She also has the distinction of being the only Singer of Opera in the tenderloin. She has had offers after offers to leave her present business and take the stage but her vast business has kept her among her friends.

Any person out for fun among a lot of pretty creole damsels, here is the place to have it.

Remember the number—215 Basin

Her ladies are:

Augie Osella
Ida Wren
Alice Hart
Loretta
Blanche Irwin
Vera Pedros

And three handsome girls who ask that their name be kept private.

Don't forget to call on
FLORENCE.

---

DON'T FAIL TO SEE
**BERTHA GOLDEN**
213 BASIN STREET

IN HER NEW
...PARISIAN DANCE...

As a dancer she has no equal and is known the world over as the Parisian Muscle dancer of the age. Her first appearance in this country was on the Midway at Chicago during the World's Fair. She also appeared on the public stage all over America.

Bertha also has one of the coziest lot of creole girls in the Tenderloin who are also clever at dancing and singing. Remember if you pass up Bertha Golden's house, you are way back in life.

Here are her Creole Belles;

Geraldine Codot,        Violet Smith,
Carrie Smith,           Olga Banks,
Clara Fars,             Ollie Burke Wilson,
Lucille Whitton,        Pearl Worth,
Thelma Rothschilds,     Blanche Gould,
Alma Littlefield,       Flossie Dupree,
Nellie Howard,          Bessie D. Silva,
Stella Ways,            Alicia Hart,
Elenora Peoples,        Vanita Vandonhoff,
Alma Maxwell,           Mamie Cline.

---

sole occupants of their addresses, indicating that these women worked for themselves. Though many believe that black and white prostitutes were not allowed by law to work out of the same house, there are numerous instances listed here where a landlady with a "W" by her name is followed by several women at the same address with the letter "C" by their names. Also, there are colored landladies whose directory listings reveal that they managed both black and white women at the same address. Many of these listings are found along Franklin and Liberty Streets. Another loosely defined area—the 1300 and 1400 blocks of Customhouse Street—is identified as "Sheenie Town," employing a derogatory slang term for Jews. This is the term's only appearance in the Storyville guides.

The book contains an advertisement for P. L. Fourchy, Attorney and Counsellor-at-Law, advising that visitors who "get in trouble while on a lark in the Tenderloin" give him a call. Fourchy would advertise in many future editions of *Blue Book*. There are sixteen full-page brothel ads. Ten photographs of the interiors of Josie Arlington's mansion—the seven listed in No. 2 and three new images of a dining room, a boudoir, and the Mirror and Music Hall—are distributed throughout the guide. The Chinese Parlor is now captioned "Japanese Parlor." There is also a photograph of the magnificent bar at Tom Anderson's Annex, identified as the "swellest fitted out cafe in the South." Though all of the interior printing is in black ink, the ad for Florence Mantley's brothel on Basin Street contains an address correction: a red ink block covers the number 333, and 215 is stamped in red beside it.

Following the list of "beautiful women" at the end of Nellie McDowell's ad is this interesting statement: "and several pretty girls who ask that their names be with held from publication." Perhaps a woman's anonymity in Storyville could be protected, just as one can choose not to be listed in a telephone directory.

---

If you get in trouble while on a lark in the Tenderloin, call up

**P. L. FOURCHY**
ATTORNEY AND
COUNSELLOR-AT-LAW

OFFICE
806 GRAVIER ST. COR. CARONDELET

RESIDENCE
1448 N. ROCHEBLAVE ST., NEAR KERLEREC

AT RESIDENCE          AT OFFICE
CUMB. PHONE 2060-22   PEOPLE'S PHONE 1533
PEOPLE'S PHONE 2519   CUMB. PHONE

OFFICE HOURS
8 to 10 A. M.
3 to 4 P. M.

NEW ORLEANS — LOUISIANA

---

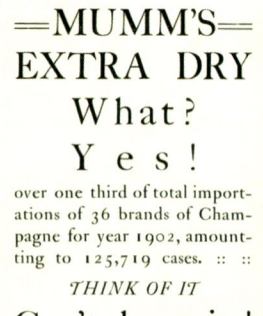

=MUMM'S=
EXTRA DRY
What?
Yes!

over one third of total importations of 36 brands of Champagne for year 1902, amounting to 125,719 cases. :: ::

*THINK OF IT*

Can't beat it!
Why?

Because it is always the same---The Best

## LULU WHITE

### CORNER BASIN AND BIENVILLE STS.

Much has been said and written locally and abroad about this distinguished personage, but no one could ever be made more satisfied until they have met her and her array of beautiful Southern octoroons.

Aside from her handsome women her mansion possesses some of the most costly oil paintings in the Southern country. Her mirror parlor is also a dream.

There's always something new at Lulu White's that will interest you. "Good time" her motto.

The following are her Belles:
Corinne Valery,
Thelma Seegar,
Sadie Reed,
Belle Liard,
Emma Hayes,
Cleo Marcellus,
Flora Lee Collins,
Celona Meagee,
Lillian Russell,
Carrie Kline,
Stella Mayo.

Aside from the above named women, there are ten entertainers who get paid to do nothing but singing and dancing.

---

Miss
Olive Russell
1559
Customhouse Street

with able assistants is now back at the old stand—Guests of the house are:
Miss Adele Ritchie
Inez Russell
Grace Taylor
Virginia Cornell
and others

Cumberland Telephone
1024

---

**TOM ANDERSON'S ANNEX**
CORNER BASIN AND CUSTOMHOUSE STREETS
SWELLEST FITTED OUT CAFE IN THE SOUTH

---

Costly dining-room in Miss Arlington's, 225 Basin Street. Panels in Wall and Wood Carpet put in at a great expense.

---

Never before has a more complete and grander Mirror and Music Hall been seen anywhere than the one at MISS ARLINGTON'S, 225 BASIN STREET

---

A boudoir in Miss Arlington's, 225 Basin Street. Everything being the best that money could purchase.

EDITIONS OF *BLUE BOOK*

# No. 4

## Blue Book

Cover printed in dark blue ink on gray paper; interior printed in black and red ink on calendered paper.
Sixth edition, undated [1905]. 92 unnumbered pages.

14 cm × 10.1 cm, THNOC, 1969.19.6 (Heartman VI)

14.2 cm × 10.3 cm, THNOC, *gift of Henry Alcus, 81-050-RL*

The first page of this edition is an advertisement for two French balls ("Fun Galore!!") giving the dates only as "March 4th and Mardi-Gras Night." March 4 was the Saturday before Mardi Gras in 1905, allowing us to date this book to that year. References in Josie Arlington's ad to the Louisiana Purchase Exposition, which was held in St. Louis, Missouri, the previous year, also support a publication date of 1905 for this edition.

Like many of the Storyville guides, this edition contains a preface. Under the phrase "A word to the wise" is a statement touting the author's authority on the subject. Along with these introductory remarks, Billy News gives two reasons "Why New Orleans Should Have This

BIBLIOGRAPHY | 78

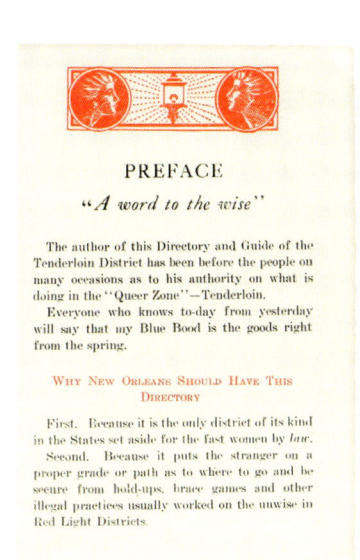

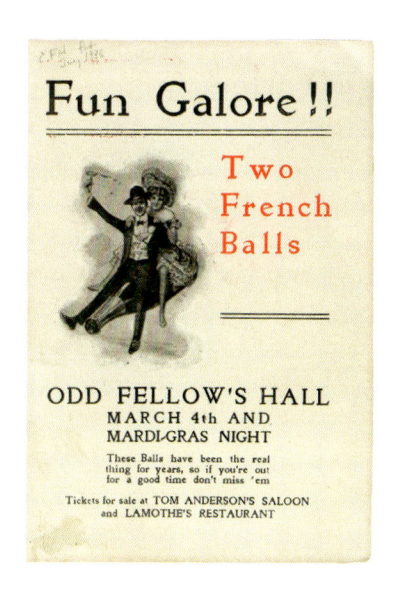

Directory," namely that Storyville was "the only district of its kind in the States" and that *Blue Book* "puts the stranger on a proper grade or path as to where to go and be secure." This justification suggests to the visitor that all names and houses listed within are reputable establishments, implying that other women and houses in the District should be avoided. This warning was not likely to have been true, but not everyone in the District was listed in *Blue Book*. The list of justifications for *Blue Book* is a feature expanded upon in future editions.

This edition is the first one assigned a specific edition number by its compiler, and it is the first two-color guide, printed in black with red highlights. It also contains numerous illustrations and whimsical printers' devices and uses a distinctive header on the directory pages—two women in profile, facing each other, separated by a glowing lamp—all printed in red. This header appears again in later editions. Near the beginning of the book is a full-page image of a female jester with a white cat upon her shoulder, superimposed on a large red heart.

The directory section in this edition has been simplified. Entries are organized geographically by street, then by address, as in No. 3.

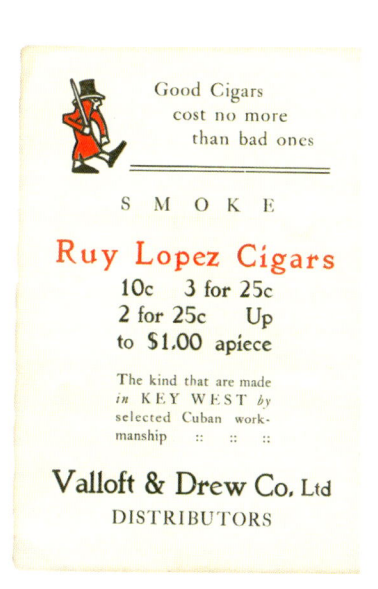

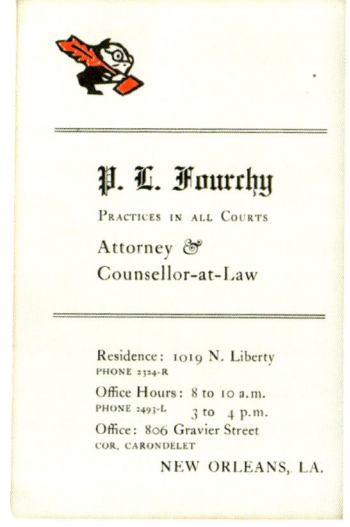

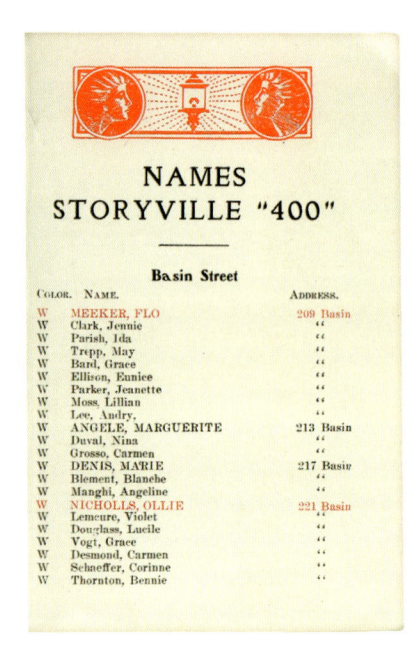

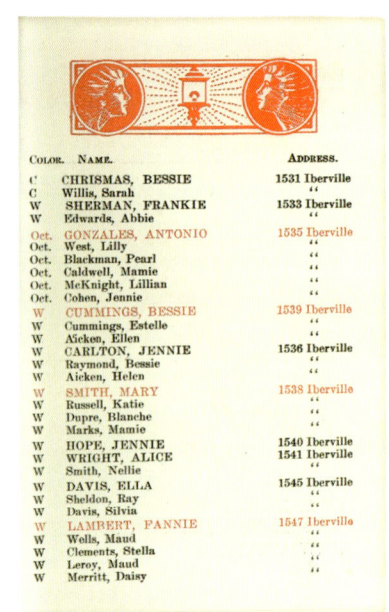

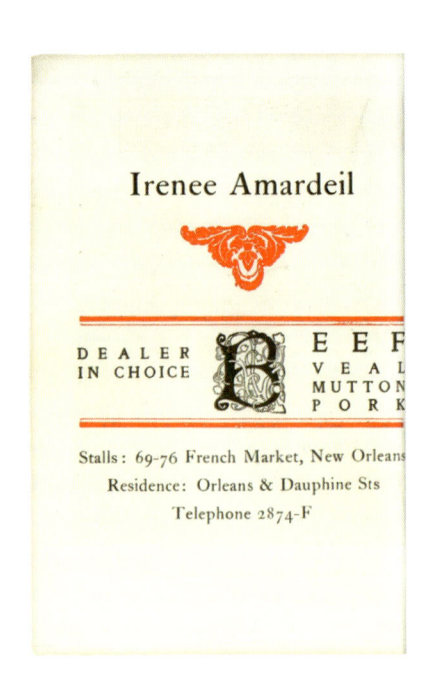

Madams' names are set in full capitals, and red ink denotes which madams have full-page descriptive advertisements in the book; following the precedent set in No. 3, "W," "C," and "Oct." indicate the races of the women listed. Two hundred fifty-seven madams or women occupying individual addresses are listed, with 189 designated white, 65 colored, and 3 octoroon. Overall, 568 women's names are listed in the directory section, here titled "Names Storyville '400'"—433 white, 109 colored, and 26 octoroon.

There are nineteen full-page brothel ads. This edition contains exterior photographs of Ray Owens's Star Mansion at 1517 Iberville Street, with its distinctive carving of a woman's head above the entrance, and Emma Johnson's two-and-a-half-story, symmetrical duplex at 331–33 Basin Street. The ten familiar photographs of interiors at Josie Arlington's are reprinted here, along with four interior views—Turkish Room, Ball Room, Dining Room, and Colonial Room—of the Star Mansion.

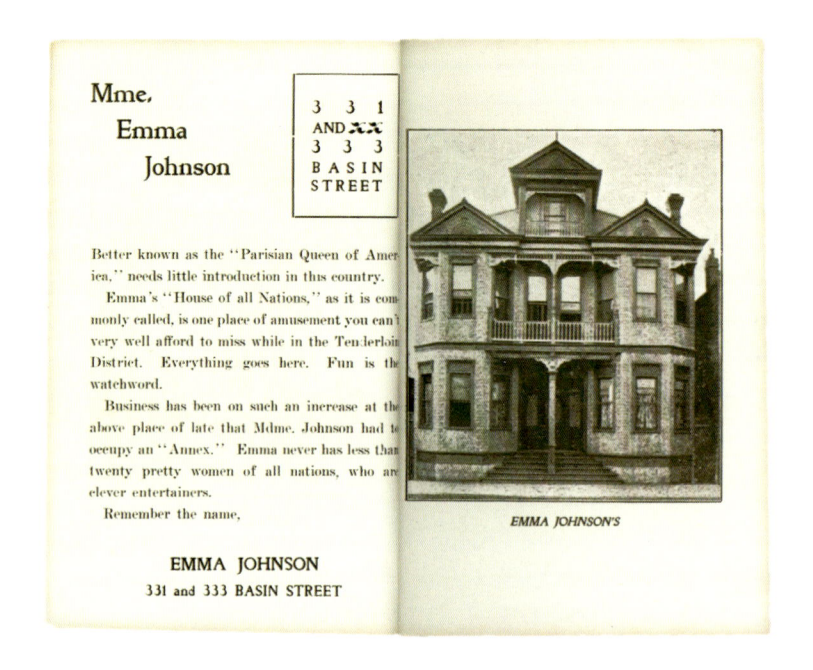

BIBLIOGRAPHY | 80

The advertisement for Irenee Amardeil, "Dealer in Choice Beef, Veal, Mutton, Pork," with stalls 69–76 at the French Market, is the only promotion for a French Market vendor I have found in all of the blue books. The ad includes a residential address at Orleans and Dauphine Streets, along with the telephone number, 2874-F.

Heartman's bibliography includes a photograph identified as a spread from this book (his VI). However, his caption is incorrect; the photograph actually shows pages found in his XII and XIII (No. 10).

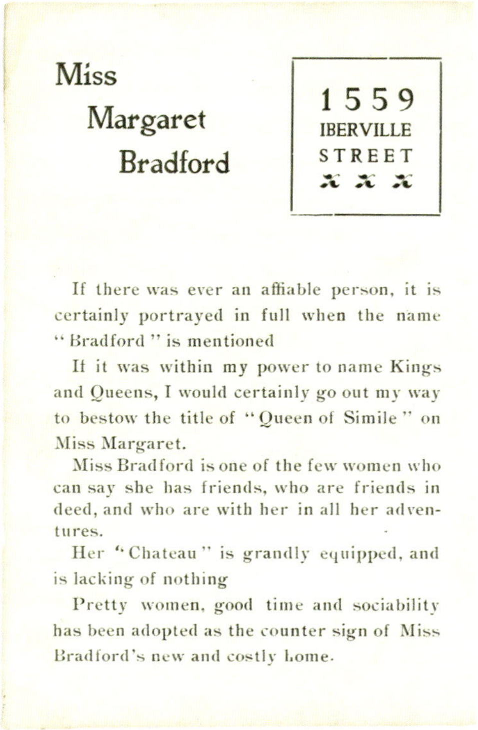

## EDITIONS OF *BLUE BOOK*

# No. 5

### Blue Book | 1906

Cover printed in dark blue ink on lavender-blue paper; interior printed in black and red ink on calendered paper. Seventh edition, 1906. 100 unnumbered pages.

*14.3 cm × 10.5 cm, THNOC, 1969.19.7 (Heartman VII)*

*"Honi Soit Qui Mal y Pense"*

The French balls ("Fun Fun Fun") are advertised again on this *Blue Book*'s first page, taking place on "February 24th and Mardi-Gras Night." By the Carnival season of 1906, *Blue Book* had much more elaborate and sophisticated production values and included far more names and advertisements than the edition produced for the 1900 Carnival season (No. 1). This edition contains the first appearance in *Blue Book* of "Honi Soit Qui Mal y Pense" (shame on him who thinks evil of it), the Middle French phrase associated with Great Britain's Most Noble Order of the Garter. The phrase appears in every subsequent edition, though in different locations. Here it is paired with the image of a female jester previously seen in No. 4. In later editions it accompanies a jovial image of Pierrot and Pierrette bursting through a large red heart, appears on

BIBLIOGRAPHY | 82

the page bearing the preface, and even shows up in an ad for the French balls. The introductory material presented here by Billy News is almost the same as in No. 4.

Listings in the "Names Storyville '400'" directory section are organized geographically by street, then by address, as in Nos. 3 and 4. The madams' names are again in full capitals, but those featured in full-page advertisements are not highlighted with red ink, as in the previous edition. The abbreviations "W," "C," and "Oct." precede women's names. Marks distinguishing Jewish women and those offering fellatio, missing from the last few editions, again appear: a "J" and an asterisk, respectively. Two hundred seventy-one madams or women occupying single addresses are listed, with 182 designated as white, 83 colored, and 6 octoroon. Thirty-four women are identified as "W. J.," although there are none noted as "C. J.," and 34 names are highlighted with an asterisk. Overall, 693 women are listed—501 white, 141 colored, and 51 octoroon.

This edition contains twenty-two full-page brothel ads. Nine familiar photographs of interiors at Josie Arlington's are reproduced here (less the image of her boudoir), as is the photograph of Emma Johnson's Studio. Under the same photographic view of the Star Mansion at 1517 Iberville Street that has appeared in an earlier edition of *Blue Book* is a paragraph that introduces its new madam, Hilma Burt from St. Louis. Great attention is given to the fact that she has taken over "one of the most select houses in the district" and hosts "a coterie of most charming and witty young ladies." This description is notable because it heralds the arrival of an already successful madam from outside New Orleans taking over the management of an established house in Storyville.

Among the usual advertisements for cigars, liquor, and mineral water are some more unusual ones, for Smith's Private Detective Agency and Coburn and Carroll High Class Decorators, both with offices at 309 St.

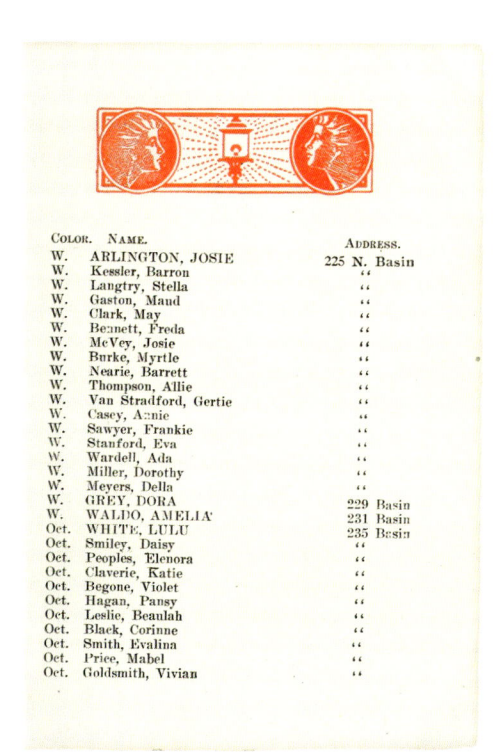

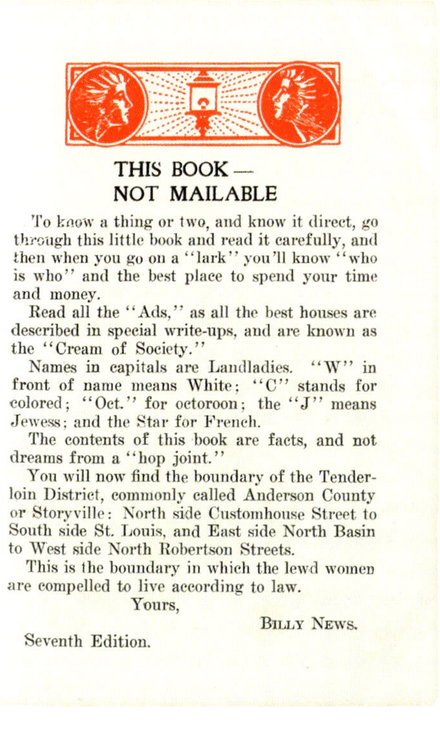

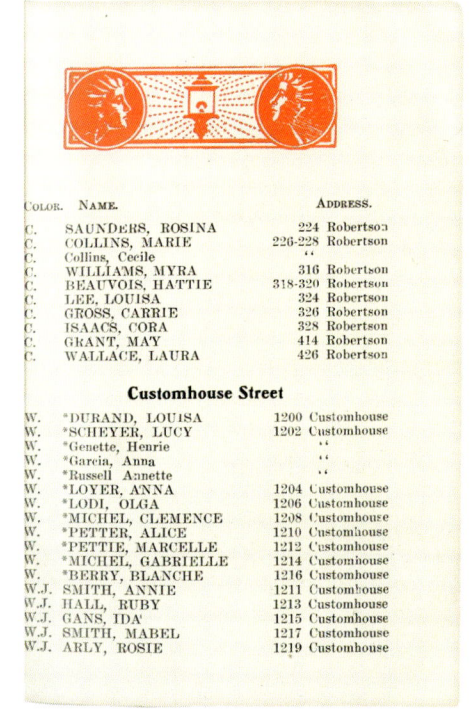

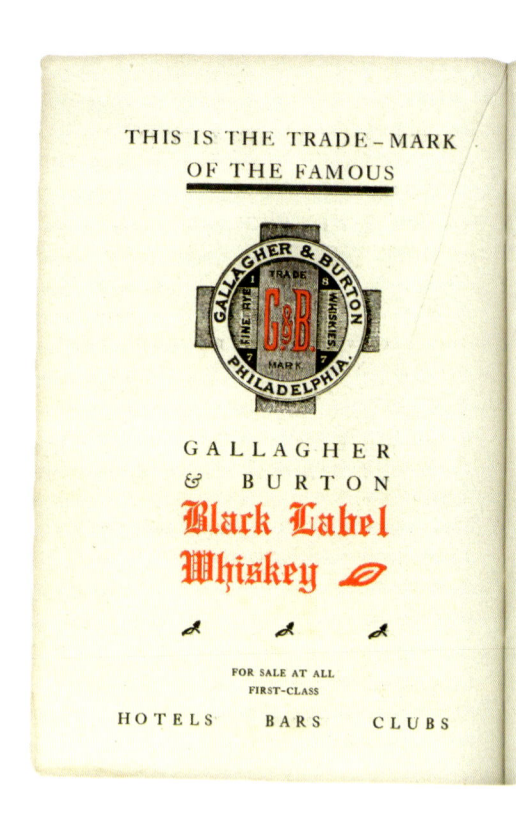

Charles Street, and Central Glass Co., at 518–22 Bienville Street, specializing in decorative mirror, plate, art, and beveled glass. These are the only advertisements for a detective agency or an interior decorator in the Storyville guides, and they demonstrate that advertisers took the local audience for these publications into consideration. Forbidden Fruit, "a new and exquisite cordial . . . a marvellous blending of the juice of the finest selected Grapefruit and the best Old Cognac Fine Champagne," is advertised for sale at Anderson's saloons.

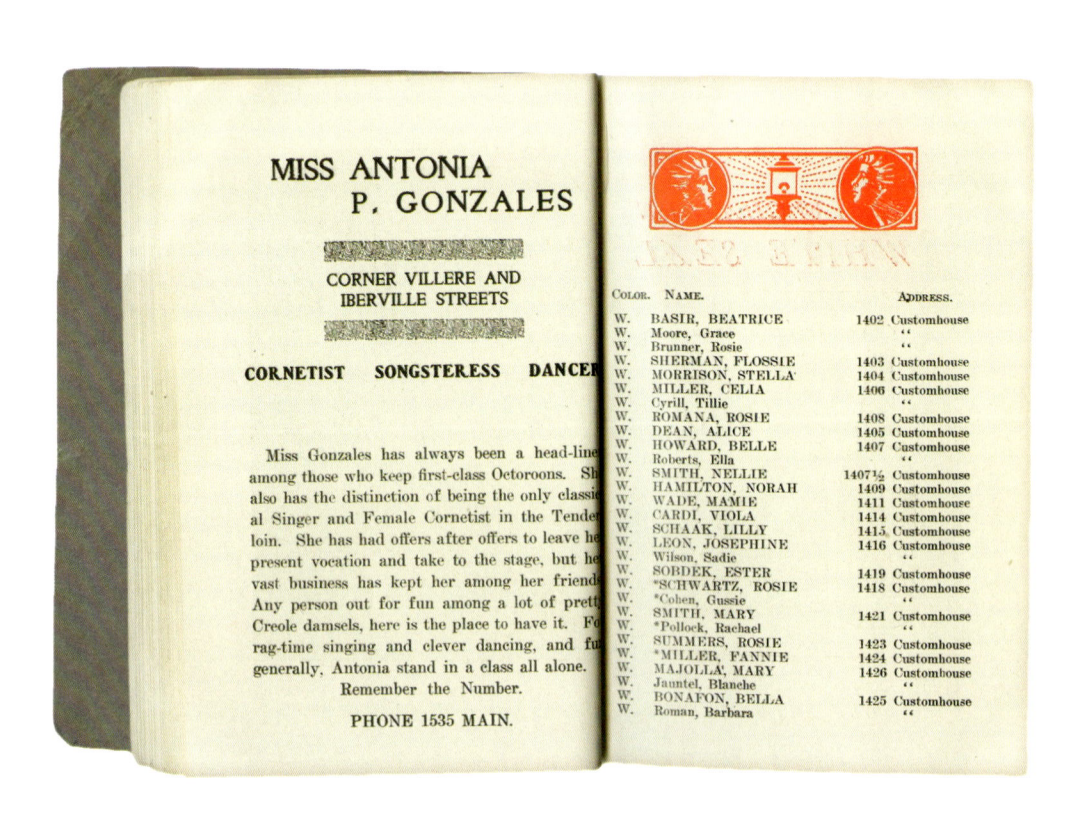

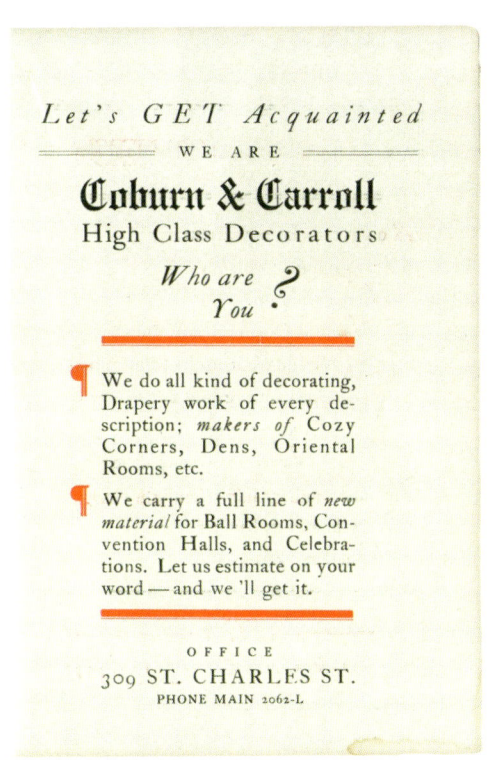

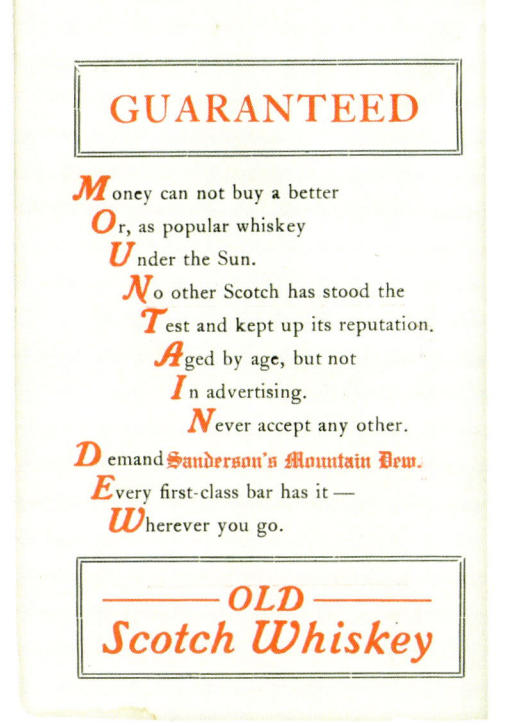

Heartman includes a photograph of the cover of this *Blue Book* on page 57 of his bibliography, and a photograph of a two-page spread on page 59. This is one of only two editions of *Blue Book* among THNOC's holdings printed with both a stated edition number and a year. The other one is No. 6.

EDITIONS OF *BLUE BOOK*

# No. 6

## Blue Book | 1907

Cover printed in dark blue ink on blue-green paper; interior printed in black and red ink on calendered paper. Eighth edition, 1907. 104 unnumbered pages.

14.1 cm × 10.6 cm, *THNOC*, 1969.19.8 (Heartman VIII)

13.7 cm × 10.6 cm, *THNOC*, 86-165-RL

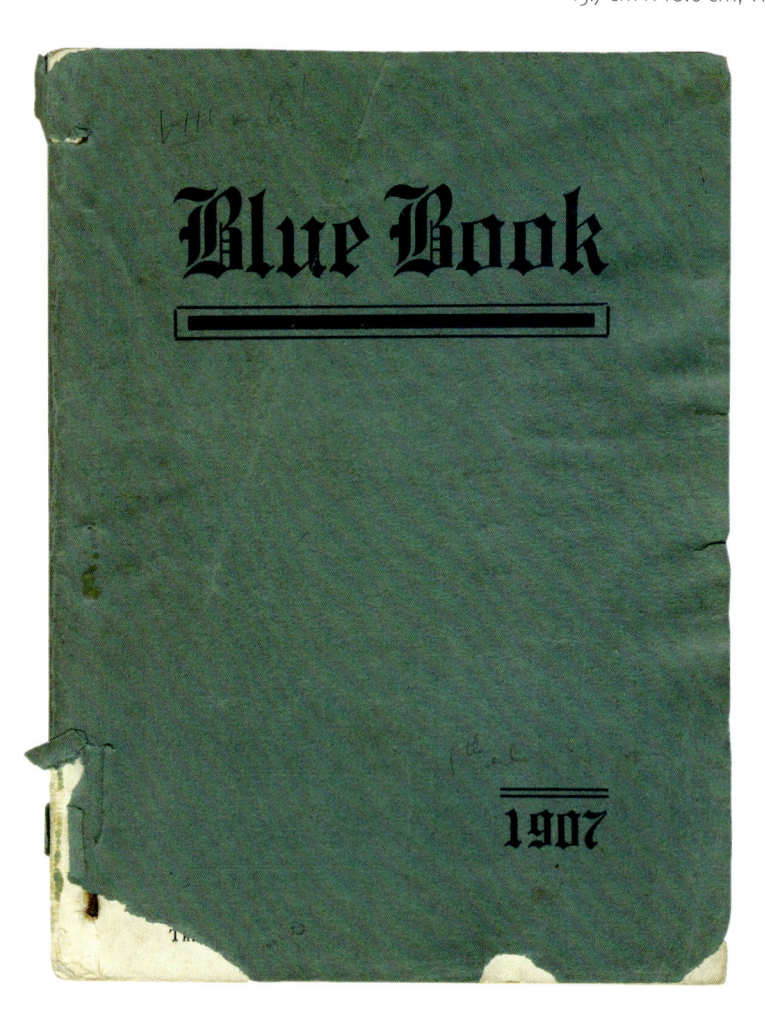

This edition and No. 5 are the only editions of *Blue Book* in THNOC's holdings with both a stated edition and publication year. The advertisement for the French balls features a charming image of a young woman flirting with the viewer over her lowered red mask, and the dates—Saturday, February 9, and Mardi Gras night, which fell on February 12 in 1907—confirm the printed year. Billy News addresses his readers in typical fashion, again boasting, "Everybody who knows to-day from yesterday will say that my Blue Book is the goods right from the spring."

As before, names set in full capital letters are those of landladies as well as of independent operators working solo, and the abbreviations "W" and "C" describe the races of the women listed. Though the preface

BIBLIOGRAPHY | 86

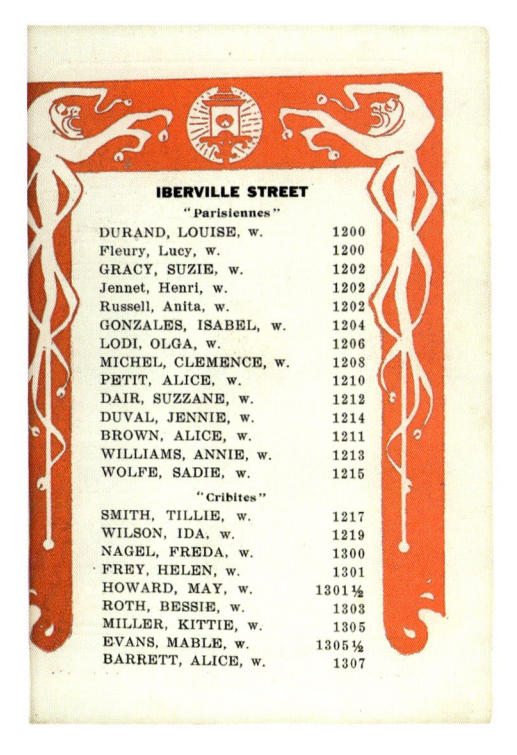

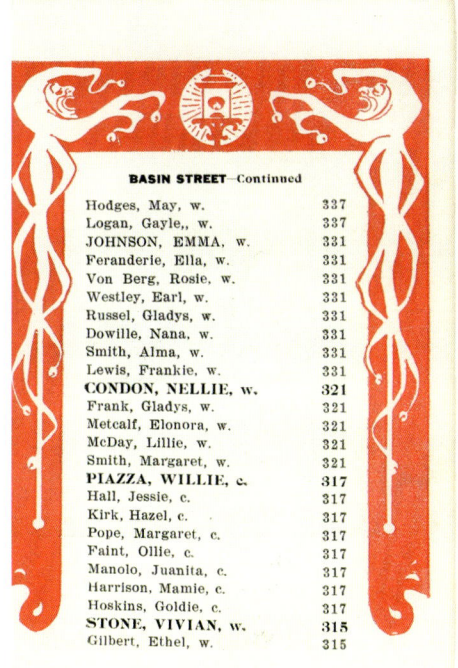

includes the abbreviation "Oct." in its explanation of how to use the book, no octoroon women are actually identified in the directory. Lulu White and Willie Piazza, landladies known for keeping octoroon houses, and identified as such in *Blue Book* until this edition, are for the first time both designated with a "C" here.

The names of the nineteen madams who have full-page ads are further set off in the directory section with boldface capitals. The directory is organized geographically by street and by more or less ascending numeric order, this time starting with Iberville, Bienville, Conti, and St. Louis; then following with N. Franklin (now Crozat), N. Liberty (now Treme), Marais, Villere, Robertson, and N. Basin Streets. Fourteen "Parisiennes," another reference to those specializing in fellatio, are listed at the start of the Iberville Street section, followed by a small section of "Cribites." This designation is unusual because women who worked out of cribs aren't typically included in these publications, and an examination of the associated addresses on a 1908 Sanborn map indicates that many of these structures were large, not the narrow, single-story buildings popularly called cribs. However, rooms in larger houses in the area were often partitioned into smaller, crib-like spaces and rented to individual prostitutes.[3] The term "cribites" doesn't appear in any other Storyville guides. The directory's only other subcategory, "Speakeasies," lists twelve women, all colored, at addresses on Robertson Street. Overall, there are 654 women—445 white, of whom 194 are madams; and 209 colored, of whom 95 are madams.

This edition has a design element not found in any other *Blue Book*. A striking red frame showing two laughing jesters on sticks, facing each other across a glowing lamp, appears on each of the directory pages. As in No. 5, nine photographs of the interiors of the Arlington are reprinted; Heartman stated that there were ten, but he seems to have miscounted. There is the same photograph of Emma Johnson's seen in Nos. 4 and 5.

EDITIONS OF *BLUE BOOK*

# No. 7

Blue | Book

Cover printed in black ink on red paper; interior pages printed in black and red ink on calendered paper.
Ninth edition, undated [1908]. 94 unnumbered pages.

14.6 cm × 10.5 cm, *THNOC*, 1969.19.9 (Heartman IX)

Based on the stated edition number and year printed in its predecessor (No. 6), it is likely that this *Blue Book*, identified in its introduction as the ninth edition, was published in 1908. Further making the case for 1908 is the date given for one of the French balls in the advertisement on the first page—February 29. It happens that 1908 was a leap year, with February 29 falling on a Saturday and Mardi Gras on March 3.

Billy News repeats previous introductions in this *Blue Book*, advising, "To know a thing or two, and know it direct, go through this little book and read it carefully, and then when you go on a 'lark' you'll know 'who is who' and the best place to spend your time and money." For the first time the phrase "Honi Soit Qui Mal y Pense" accompanies an image of Pierrot and Pierrette bursting through a large red heart, rather than

BIBLIOGRAPHY | 90

"Honi Soit Qui Mal y Pense"

the female jester with the white cat on her shoulder. The directory is organized geographically, with the streets of the District appearing in alphabetical order and women listed by their addresses, but St. Louis and Robertson Streets are not included. The reason for this exclusion is unknown; it may be simple neglect. The introduction gives the familiar abbreviations denoting the races of the listed women, although no octoroon women are actually identified in the directory.

There are seventeen full-page ads for brothels, although Margaret Bradford at 1559 Iberville has two distinctly different ads. Bradford's

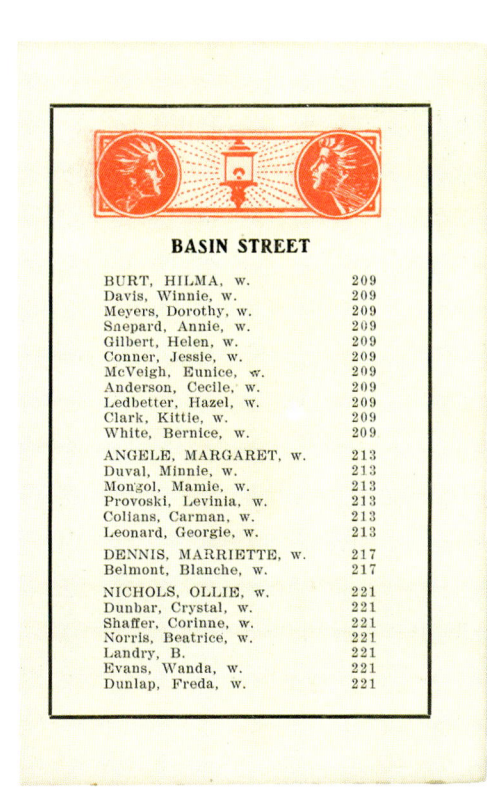

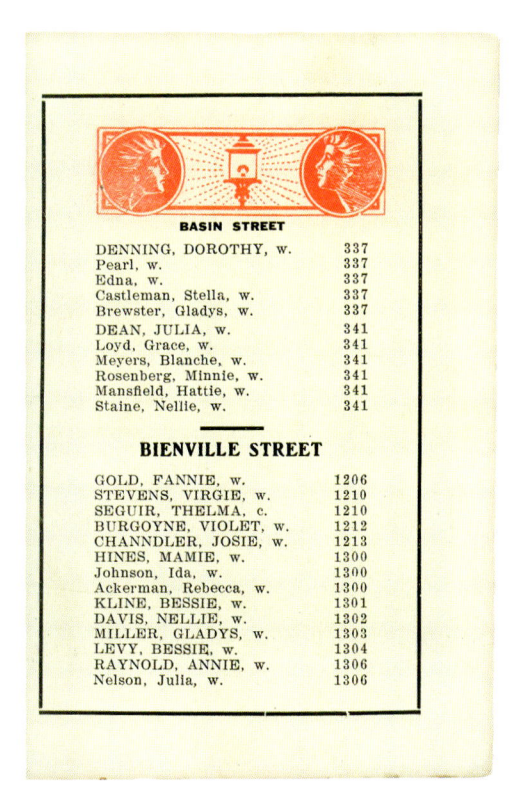

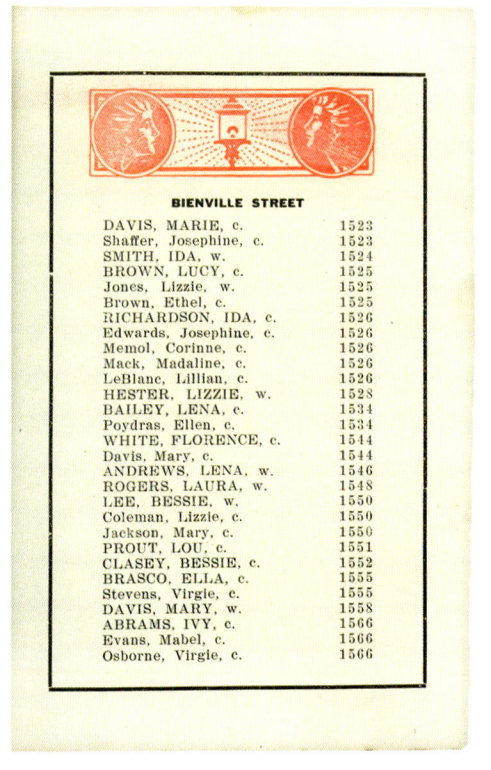

**BASIN STREET**

| | |
|---|---|
| BURT, HILMA, w. | 209 |
| Davis, Winnie, w. | 209 |
| Meyers, Dorothy, w. | 209 |
| Snepard, Annie, w. | 209 |
| Gilbert, Helen, w. | 209 |
| Conner, Jessie, w. | 209 |
| McVeigh, Eunice, w. | 209 |
| Anderson, Cecile, w. | 209 |
| Ledbetter, Hazel, w. | 209 |
| Clark, Kittie, w. | 209 |
| White, Bernice, w. | 209 |
| ANGELE, MARGARET, w. | 213 |
| Duval, Minnie, w. | 213 |
| Mongol, Mamie, w. | 213 |
| Provoski, Levinia, w. | 213 |
| Colians, Carman, w. | 213 |
| Leonard, Georgie, w. | 213 |
| DENNIS, MARRIETTE, w. | 217 |
| Belmont, Blanche, w. | 217 |
| NICHOLS, OLLIE, w. | 221 |
| Dunbar, Crystal, w. | 221 |
| Shaffer, Corinne, w. | 221 |
| Norris, Beatrice, w. | 221 |
| Landry, B. | 221 |
| Evans, Wanda, w. | 221 |
| Dunlap, Freda, w. | 221 |

**BASIN STREET**

| | |
|---|---|
| DENNING, DOROTHY, w. | 337 |
| Pearl, w. | 337 |
| Edna, w. | 337 |
| Castleman, Stella, w. | 337 |
| Brewster, Gladys, w. | 337 |
| DEAN, JULIA, w. | 341 |
| Loyd, Grace, w. | 341 |
| Meyers, Blanche, w. | 341 |
| Rosenberg, Minnie, w. | 341 |
| Mansfield, Hattie, w. | 341 |
| Staine, Nellie, w. | 341 |

**BIENVILLE STREET**

| | |
|---|---|
| GOLD, FANNIE, w. | 1206 |
| STEVENS, VIRGIE, w. | 1210 |
| SEGUIR, THELMA, c. | 1210 |
| BURGOYNE, VIOLET, w. | 1212 |
| CHANNDLER, JOSIE, w. | 1213 |
| HINES, MAMIE, w. | 1300 |
| Johnson, Ida, w. | 1300 |
| Ackerman, Rebecca, w. | 1300 |
| KLINE, BESSIE, w. | 1301 |
| DAVIS, NELLIE, w. | 1302 |
| MILLER, GLADYS, w. | 1303 |
| LEVY, BESSIE, w. | 1304 |
| RAYNOLD, ANNIE, w. | 1306 |
| Nelson, Julia, w. | 1306 |

**BIENVILLE STREET**

| | |
|---|---|
| DAVIS, MARIE, c. | 1523 |
| Shaffer, Josephine, c. | 1523 |
| SMITH, IDA, w. | 1524 |
| BROWN, LUCY, c. | 1525 |
| Jones, Lizzie, w. | 1525 |
| Brown, Ethel, c. | 1525 |
| RICHARDSON, IDA, c. | 1526 |
| Edwards, Josephine, c. | 1526 |
| Memol, Corinne, c. | 1526 |
| Mack, Madaline, c. | 1526 |
| LeBlanc, Lillian, c. | 1526 |
| HESTER, LIZZIE, w. | 1528 |
| BAILEY, LENA, c. | 1534 |
| Poydras, Ellen, c. | 1534 |
| WHITE, FLORENCE, c. | 1544 |
| Davis, Mary, c. | 1544 |
| ANDREWS, LENA, w. | 1546 |
| ROGERS, LAURA, w. | 1548 |
| LEE, BESSIE, w. | 1550 |
| Coleman, Lizzie, c. | 1550 |
| Jackson, Mary, c. | 1550 |
| PROUT, LOU, c. | 1551 |
| CLASEY, BESSIE, w. | 1552 |
| BRASCO, ELLA, c. | 1555 |
| Stevens, Virgie, c. | 1555 |
| DAVIS, MARY, w. | 1558 |
| ABRAMS, IVY, c. | 1566 |
| Evans, Mabel, c. | 1566 |
| Osborne, Virgie, c. | 1566 |

NO. 7 | EDITIONS OF BLUE BOOK | 91

first advertisement says little about the madam herself, but succinctly conveys the idea of a cultured mansion, well-equipped to fulfill the desires of the discriminating gentleman: "There is always something new at the 'BRADFORD' as the refined people call her mansion." Her second ad, while also promoting her "chateau," pretty women, good times, and sociability, emphasizes the Queen of Smile's success: "While still young in years, [Bradford] has, nevertheless proven herself a grand woman, and has also made 'good' as a conductor of a first-class establishment." She is advertised as a woman who has excelled in her chosen profession and is more than capable of providing entertainment to clients who are equally successful in theirs.

The directory lists 175 white madams and 109 colored madams, with many of the names in capitals being the only resident listed at a given address. When the list of a landlady's residents continues to the following page, the landlady's name is repeated at the top of the page, a quirk that only appears in this edition. A total of 697 women are listed, 458 white and 239 colored. Directory pages are headed by the image in red ink of two women in profile facing each other across a glowing lamp first seen in No. 4. Nine of the familiar photographs of the Arlington's interior are reprinted, along with the same exterior view of Emma Johnson's. Heartman erroneously claims that this edition contains the first appearance of an advertisement for an attorney; in fact, P. L. Fourchy, who "Practices in all Courts," has had an advertisement in every edition since 1903 (see No. 3).

Later twentieth-century facsimiles of *Blue Book* reprinted some pages from this ninth edition but also added fake, explicit madams' advertisements (see Nos. 18 and 19). Though these fakes borrow their interior pages from this edition, they typically use a later, more commonly known cover design (first seen on No. 9), rather than the decorative-swag design that frames the title on this edition.

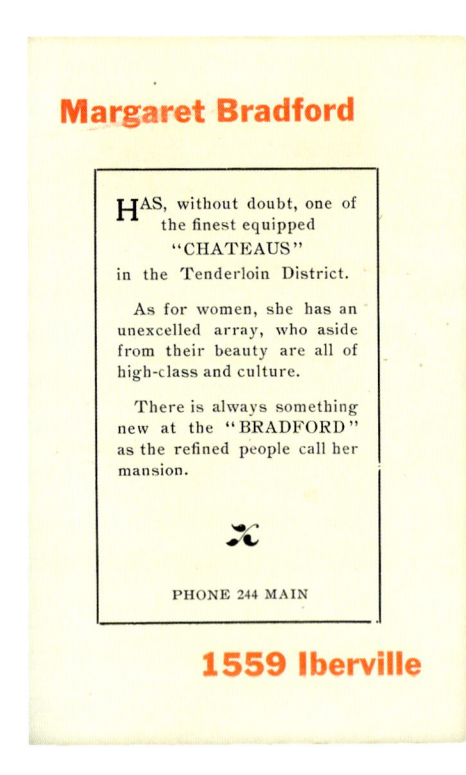

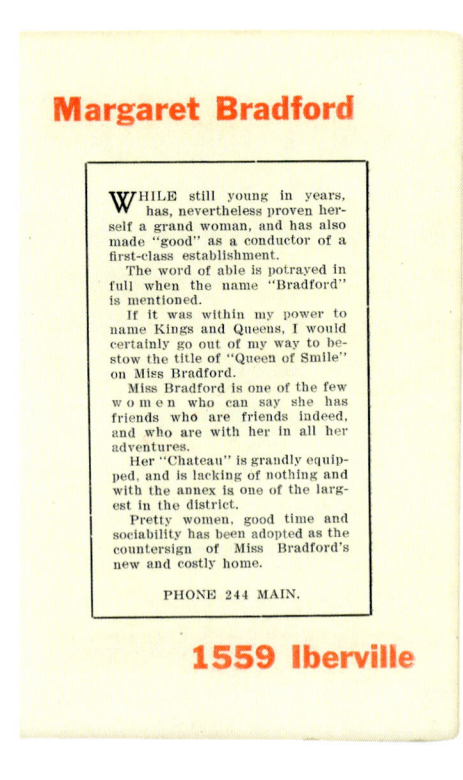

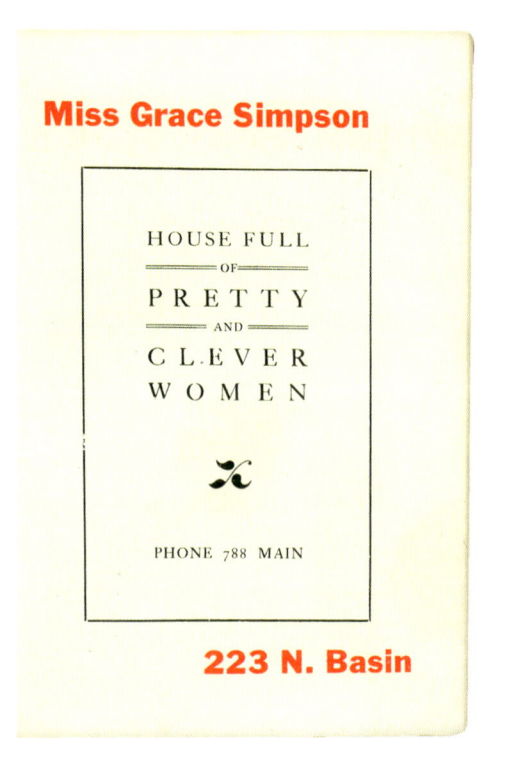

## P. L. Fourchy

Practices in all Courts

Attorney &
Counsellor-at-Law

Residence: 1019 N. Liberty
PHONE 2324-R

Office Hours: 8 to 10 a. m.
PHONE 2493-L    3 to 4 p. m.

Office: 806 Gravier Street
COR CARONDELET

NEW ORLEANS, LA.

---

## JOE TRAVERSE

MANUFACTURING

**JEWELER**

Expert Examination

131 ST. CHARLES STREET
NEAR CANAL    UP-STAIRS

Telephone Main 2027-L    NEW ORLEANS, LA.

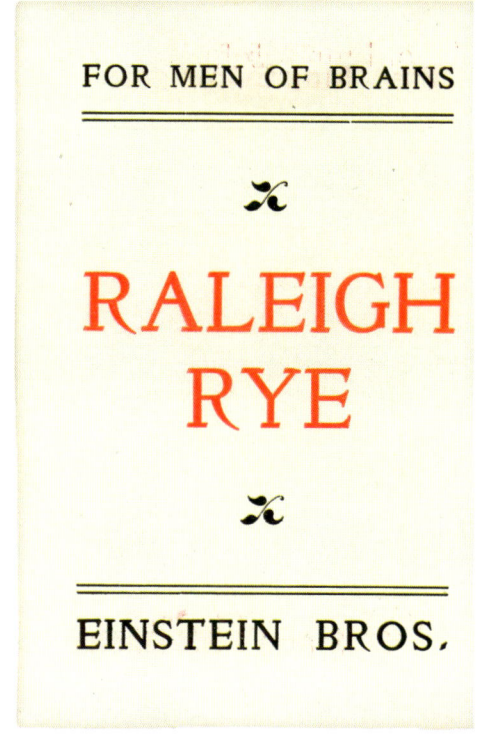

---

FOR MEN OF BRAINS

## RALEIGH RYE

EINSTEIN BROS.

---

## TADEMA CIGAR

THAT MADE

Chas. Meyer & Co.

FAMOUS

Canal and Royal Streets
NEW ORLEANS, LA.

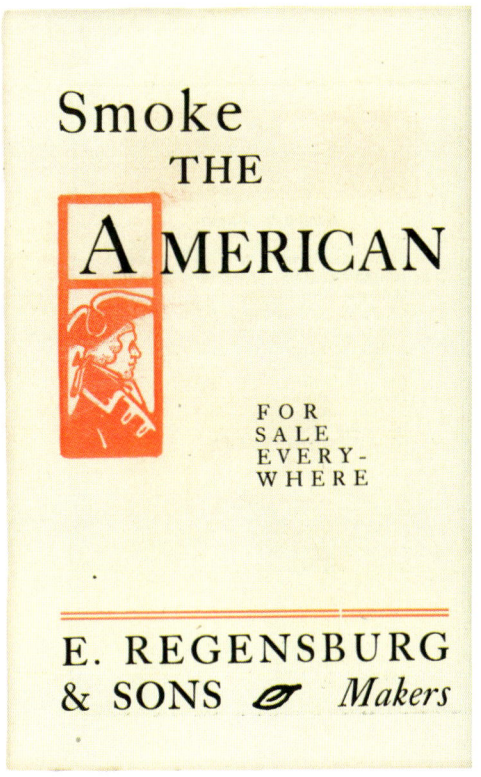

---

Smoke THE AMERICAN

FOR SALE EVERYWHERE

E. REGENSBURG & SONS   Makers

---

## El Principe de Gales

Now King of *Havana Cigars*

FROM
10c to $1.00

LOUISIANA TOBACCO CO.
C. S. FOSTER, PRESIDENT

### EDITIONS OF *BLUE BOOK*

# No. 8
## Blue Book

Cover printed in blue-black ink on gray paper; interior pages printed in black and red ink on calendered paper. Tenth edition, undated [1909]. 96 unnumbered pages.

14.4 cm × 10.9 cm, *THNOC, 1969.19.10* (Heartman X)

Cover printed in blue-black ink on tan paper; interior pages printed in black and red ink on calendered paper. Tenth edition, undated [1909]. 98 unnumbered pages.

14.3 cm × 10.8 cm, *THNOC, gift of Ralph Pons, 77-370-RL*

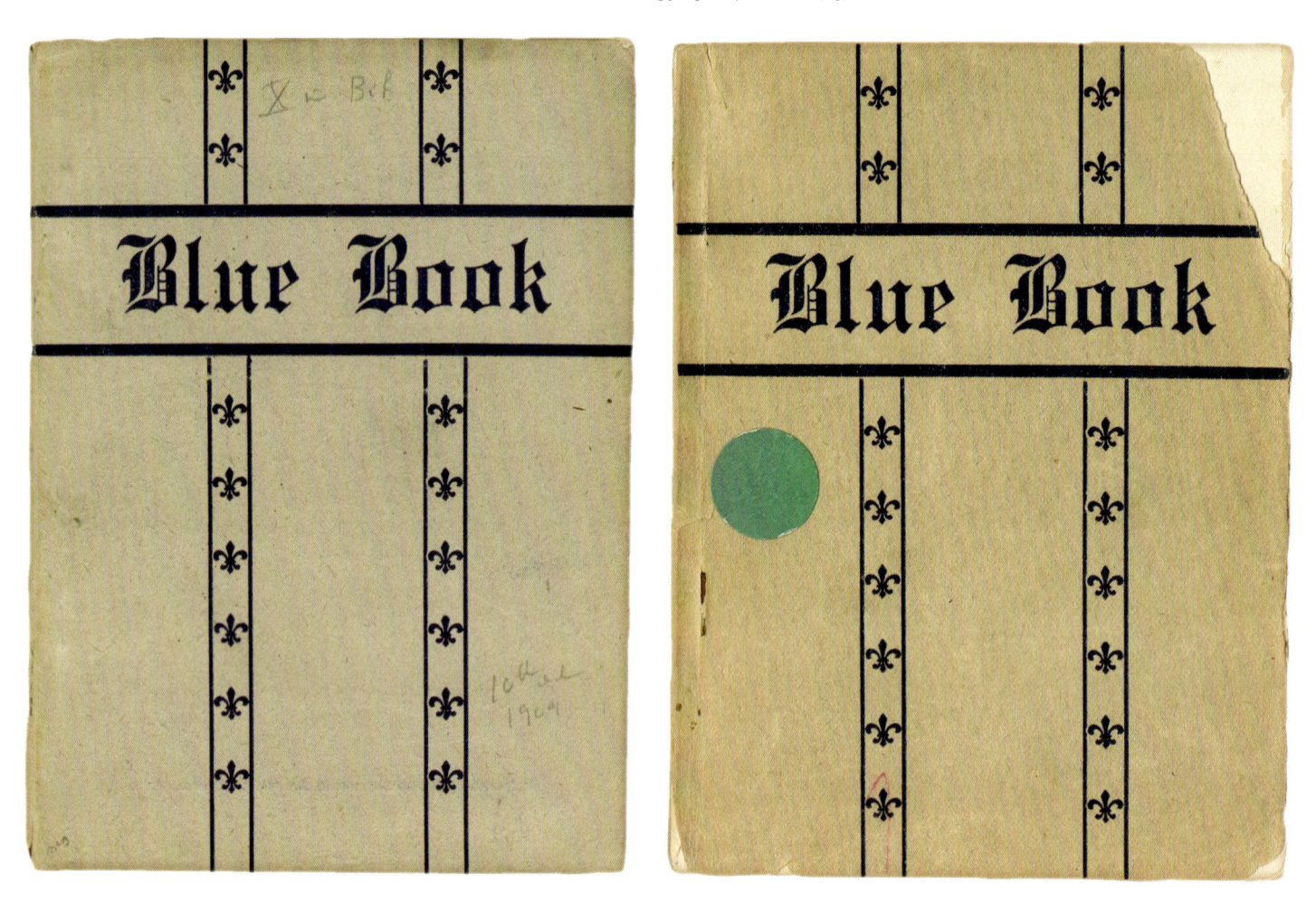

There is a slight difference between the two copies of the tenth edition of *Blue Book* housed at The Historic New Orleans Collection. The copy acquired from the Streeter sale has a gray cover with blue-black printing and ninety-six pages. A copy donated in 1977 has a tan cover with black printing and an added leaf four pages from the back cover. This inserted page—with an ad for Gipsy Shaffer's house on one side and an advertisement for Krug and Co. champagne on the other—has none of the red-ink highlights found throughout both books. Everything else is the same from one book to the other, which may indicate that the copy

> **FUN! FUN!! FUN!!**
> **DON'T MISS THE**
> *French Balls*
> **GIVEN BY THE**
> **C. C. C. Club and**
> **Two Well-Known Gentlemen**
>
> **ODD FELLOWS' HALL**
> **SATURDAY NIGHT BEFORE MADRI GRAS AND MADRI GRAS NIGHT**
>
> ¶ The Balls have been famous for years, so if you are out for a good time don't miss them. Tickets for sale at TOM ANDERSON'S SALOONS, and LAMOTHE'S RESTAURANT, 716 Gravier St.

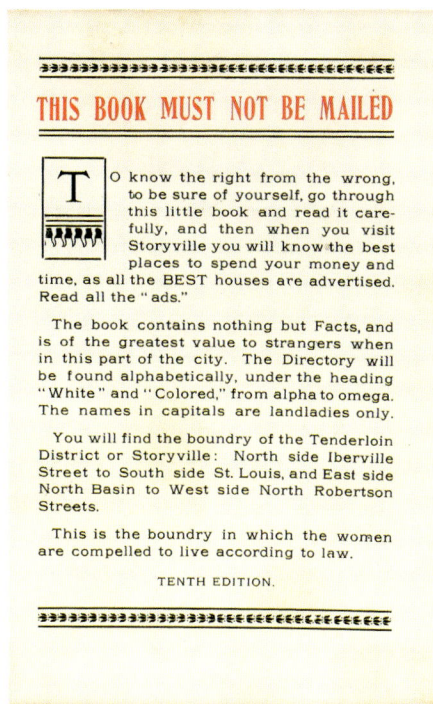

---

## THIS BOOK MUST NOT BE MAILED

To know the right from the wrong, to be sure of yourself, go through this little book and read it carefully, and then when you visit Storyville you will know the best places to spend your money and time, as all the BEST houses are advertised. Read all the "ads."

The book contains nothing but Facts, and is of the greatest value to strangers when in this part of the city. The Directory will be found alphabetically, under the heading "White" and "Colored," from alpha to omega. The names in capitals are landladies only.

You will find the boundry of the Tenderloin District or Storyville: North side Iberville Street to South side St. Louis, and East side North Basin to West side North Robertson Streets.

This is the boundry in which the women are compelled to live according to law.

**TENTH EDITION.**

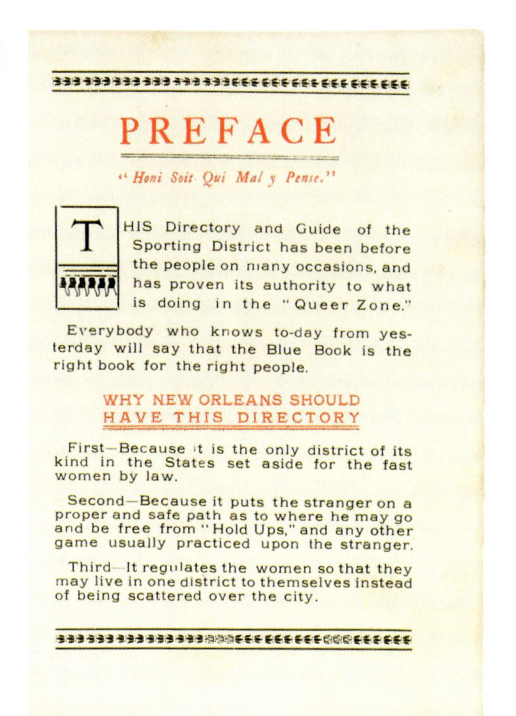

---

## PREFACE
*"Honi Soit Qui Mal y Pense."*

THIS Directory and Guide of the Sporting District has been before the people on many occasions, and has proven its authority to what is doing in the "Queer Zone."

Everybody who knows to-day from yesterday will say that the Blue Book is the right book for the right people.

### WHY NEW ORLEANS SHOULD HAVE THIS DIRECTORY

First—Because it is the only district of its kind in the States set aside for the fast women by law.

Second—Because it puts the stranger on a proper and safe path as to where he may go and be free from "Hold Ups," and any other game usually practiced upon the stranger.

Third—It regulates the women so that they may live in one district to themselves instead of being scattered over the city.

---

with the added page was from a second printing, perhaps even released the following year, considering the fact that no *Blue Book* has been definitively dated to 1910.

The same advertisement from No. 7 for the French balls appears on the first page, with a notable change. This version states that these balls were held on "Saturday night before Madri [*sic*] Gras and Madri [*sic*] Gras night," but for the first time, no actual dates are printed, making it more difficult to date this edition with certainty. This book is identified in its introduction as the tenth edition, and because the ninth edition

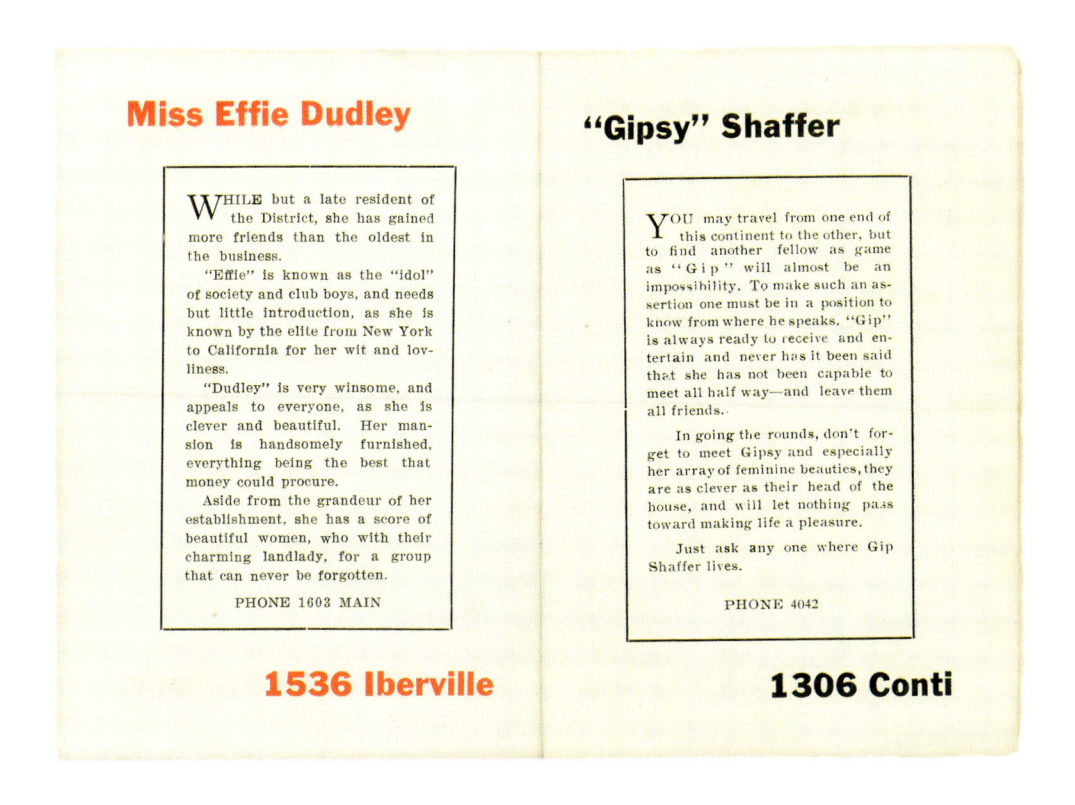

---

### Miss Effie Dudley

WHILE but a late resident of the District, she has gained more friends than the oldest in the business.

"Effie" is known as the "idol" of society and club boys, and needs but little introduction, as she is known by the elite from New York to California for her wit and loveliness.

"Dudley" is very winsome, and appeals to everyone, as she is clever and beautiful. Her mansion is handsomely furnished, everything being the best that money could procure.

Aside from the grandeur of her establishment, she has a score of beautiful women, who with their charming landlady, for a group that can never be forgotten.

PHONE 1603 MAIN

**1536 Iberville**

### "Gipsy" Shaffer

YOU may travel from one end of this continent to the other, but to find another fellow as game as "Gip" will almost be an impossibility. To make such an assertion one must be in a position to know from where he speaks. "Gip" is always ready to receive and entertain and never has it been said that she has not been capable to meet all half way—and leave them all friends.

In going the rounds, don't forget to meet Gipsy and especially her array of feminine beauties, they are as clever as their head of the house, and will let nothing pass toward making life a pleasure.

Just ask any one where Gip Shaffer lives.

PHONE 4042

**1306 Conti**

EDITIONS OF *BLUE BOOK*

# No. 9

## Blue Book

Cover printed in blue-black ink on gray paper; interior printed in red and black ink on calendered paper. No edition number, undated [1912]. 96 unnumbered pages.

14.8 cm × 11 cm, *THNOC, 2012.0141.1*

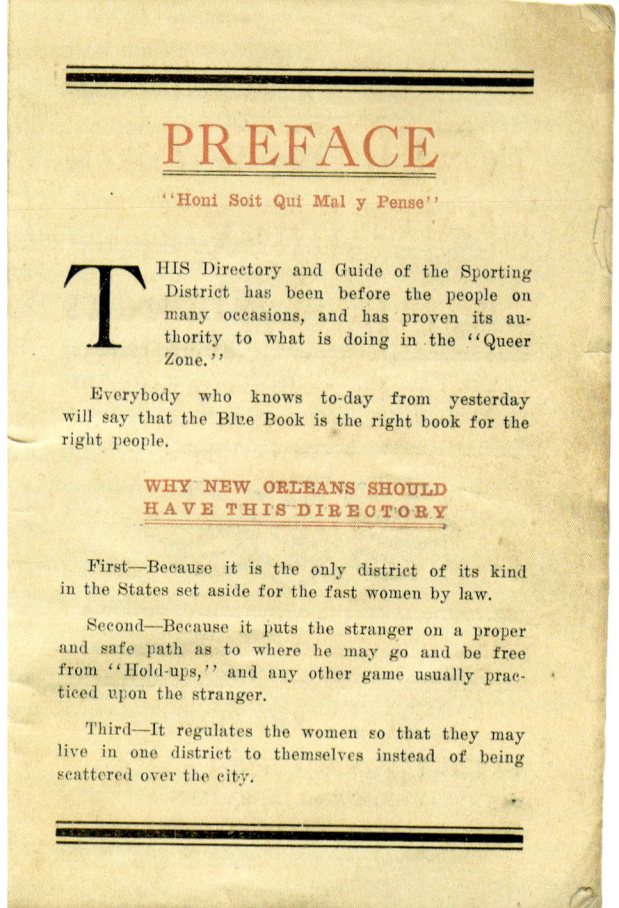

The cover of this edition features a printer's ornament showing a lyre surrounded by lilies and ribbons. This motif appears on later editions (No. 10, for example), but this edition is noteworthy because the ornament is printed upside down. Rose noted this printer's error.[4] Heartman does not make note of the anomaly, but he does describe a *Blue Book*, XI in his bibliography, with a harp motif printed in dark-blue ink on gray cover stock.[5] Heartman's XI was not sold in the Streeter sale, and its current location is unknown (THNOC's copy of this edition was acquired in 2012). The inverted design later appears on the covers of some fake editions (Nos. 19, 21, 22, 23, and 24).

Heartman assigned a date of 1910–11 to this edition. Unfortunately, the advertisement for the French balls on the first page provides no dates to definitively determine the year. Other evidence, however, reveals that it was likely produced in 1912. A full-page advertisement for Lamothe's City Park Restaurant, located at the corner of Alexander and Dumaine Streets, opposite City Park, announces "Fine Banquet Hall and Accommodations for Families" and "Handsome Private Dining Rooms for Auto Parties." This restaurant does not appear in a New Orleans city directory until 1912, so it is unlikely that this *Blue Book* was published before that year. The building is still standing and currently houses one of Ralph Brennan's restaurants, Ralph's on the Park.

The motto "Honi Soit Qui Mal y Pense" appears in the ad for the French balls for the first time and also at the beginning of the preface.

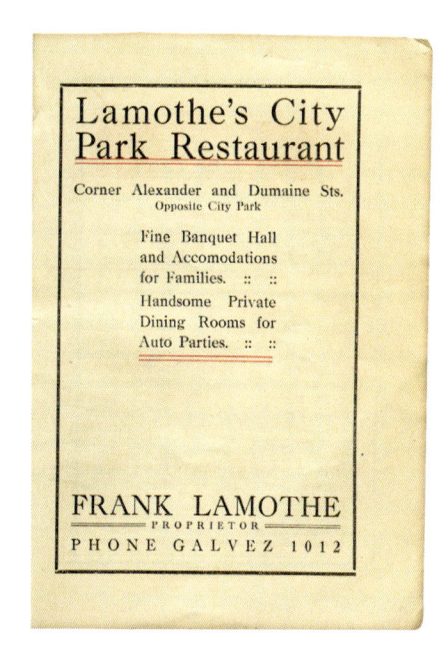

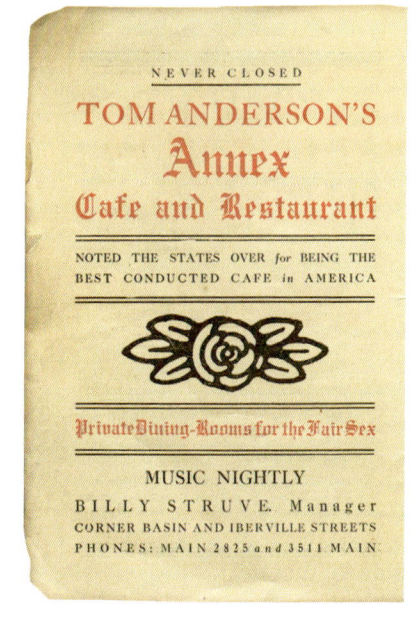

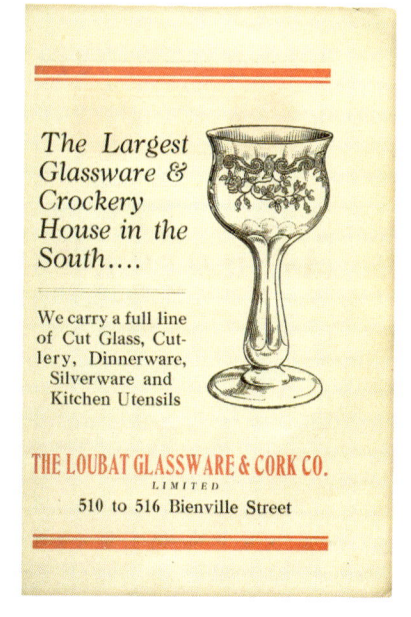

### LETTER "A" (WHITE)

| | |
|---|---|
| Alice, Martha | 1200 Customhouse |
| Arsene, Jeanette | 1202 Customhouse |
| Allen, Ella | 1402 Customhouse |
| Anderson, Patsy | 1526 Customhouse |
| Austin, Annie | 1301 Bienville |
| Alton, Alice | 1320 Conti |
| Alley, Grace | 1414 Conti |
| Arnolds, Grace | 1504 Conti |
| Ashby, Midget | 318 Marais |
| Adams, May | 315 N. Franklin |
| Arnold, Percy | 223 N. Basin |
| Adams, Nellie | 325 N. Basin |
| Alexandria, Violet | 225 N. Basin |
| Arnett, Doroghty | 225 N. Basin |
| Allen, Mamie | 209 N. Basin |
| ARLINGTON, JOSIE | 225 N. Basin |
| Allen, Cecil | 225 N. Basin |
| Andrews, Canell | 209 N. Basin |

### LETTER "B" (WHITE)

| | |
|---|---|
| Brown, Annie | 1308 Customhouse |
| Blach, Ida | 1318 Customhouse |
| Bloom, Rosie | 1320 Customhouse |
| Brown, Josephine | 1208 Customhouse |

### LETTER "P" (COLORED)

| | |
|---|---|
| Perry, Alice | 1527 Customhouse |
| Page, Stella | 1426 Bienville |
| Pratts, Alice | 1527 Bienville |
| Perry, Nettie | 1544 Bienville |
| Porter, Florence | 1564 Conti |
| Pagean, Rosie | 224 N. Robertson |
| PIZZIA, WILLIE, Oct. | 317 N. Basin |
| Pope, Margarette, Oct. | 235 N. Basin |

### LETTER "R" (COLORED)

| | |
|---|---|
| Richardson, Lizzie | 1423 Bienville |
| Robbins, Mabel | 1404 Bienville |
| Rochell, Fannie | 1523 Bienville |
| Ross, Laura | 1429 Conti |
| Riley, Olivia | 1564 Conti |
| Richardson, Lilie | 230 N. Robertson |
| Raymond, Rachel | 225 N. Villere |
| Robert, Emma | 326 N. Marais |
| Reagan, Annetta | 405 N. Marais |
| Roberts, Lucile | 216 N. Liberty |
| Raephel, Bertha, Oct. | 317 N. Basin |
| Richardson, Ollie, Oct. | 317 N. Basin |

### LETTER "W" (COLORED)—Continued

| | |
|---|---|
| Wilson, Mary | 1527 Bienville |
| Williams, Louise | 1518 Bienville |
| Ward, Ella | 1548 Bienville |
| Williams, Alertha | 1548 Bienville |
| Williams, Cora | 1543 Bienville |
| Webster, Annie | 1424 Conti |
| Withfield, Lottie | 1509 Conti |
| Williams, Sarah | 1549 Conti |
| Williams, Stella | 1569 Conti |
| Wong, Juanita | 314 N. Robertson |
| Webb, Albertha | 212 N. Liberty |
| Walter, Louisa | 216 N. Basin |

### OCTOROONS

| | |
|---|---|
| WHITE, LULU | 235 N. Basin |
| PIAZZA, WILLIE | 315 N. Basin |

---

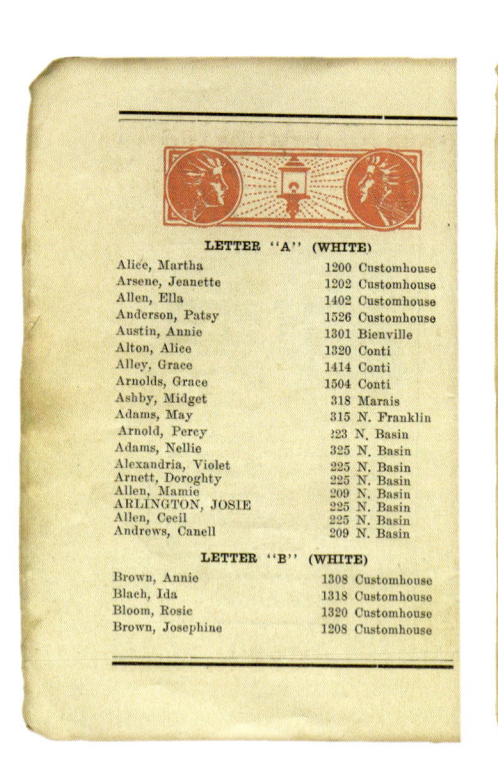

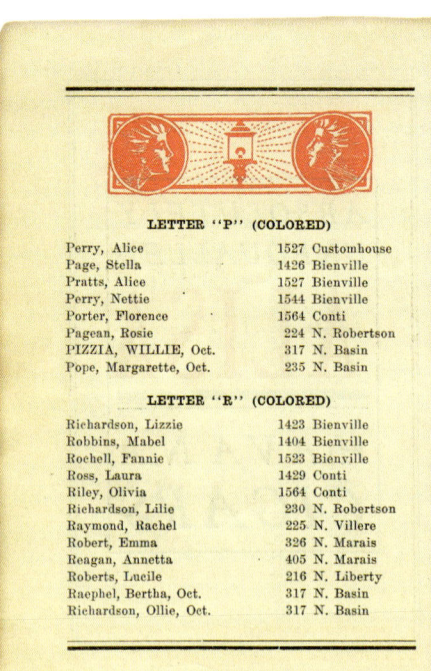

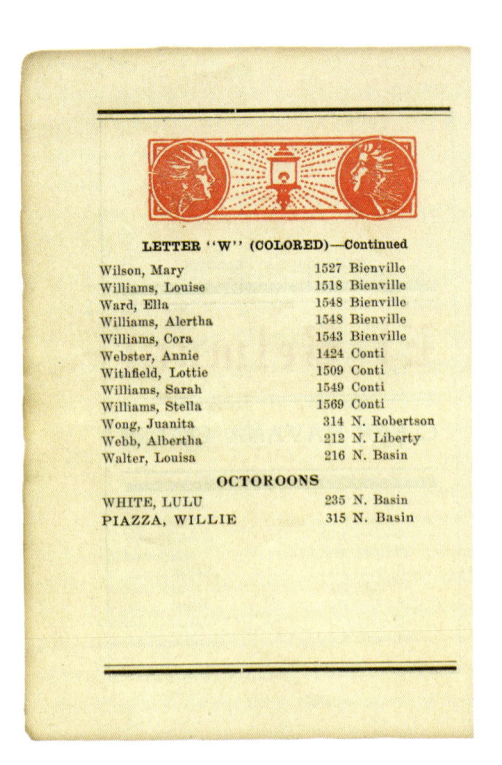

Though the preface and introduction are not credited to an individual, Billy Struve is named as manager in the advertisement for Tom Anderson's Annex, revealing that he was still involved in activities in the District.

As in the directory pages of No. 8, women are divided by race, white prostitutes first and colored prostitutes second, each in a haphazard alphabetical arrangement by first letter of the surname. The landladies' names are again set in full capitals. Of the 602 women listed, there are 382 white prostitutes, including 24 white madams, and 220 prostitutes

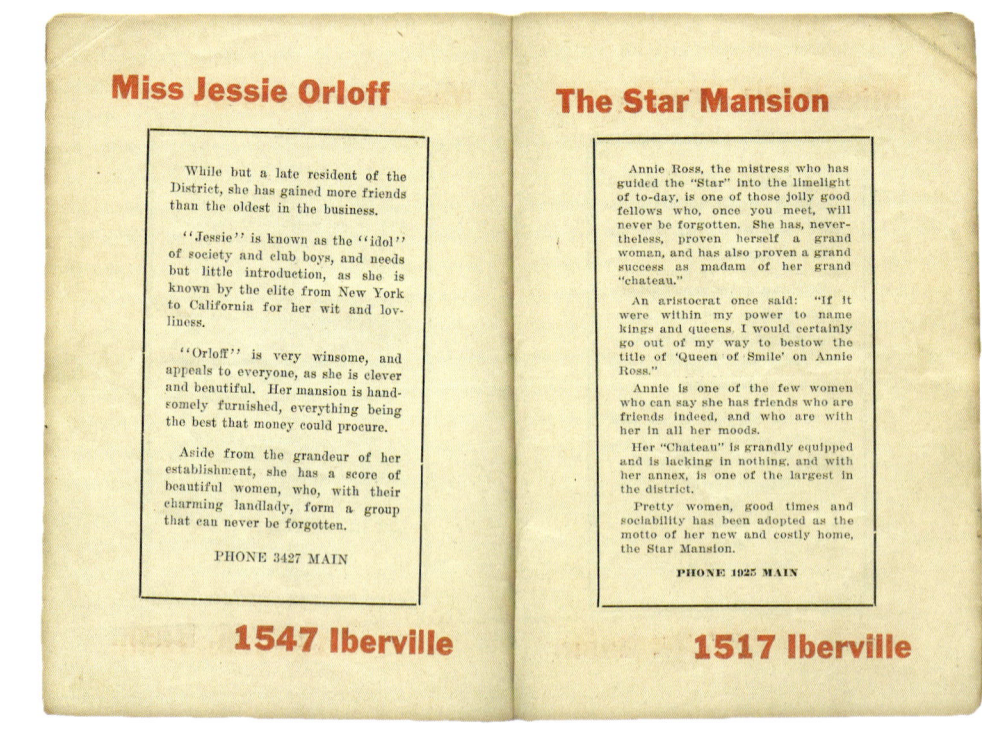

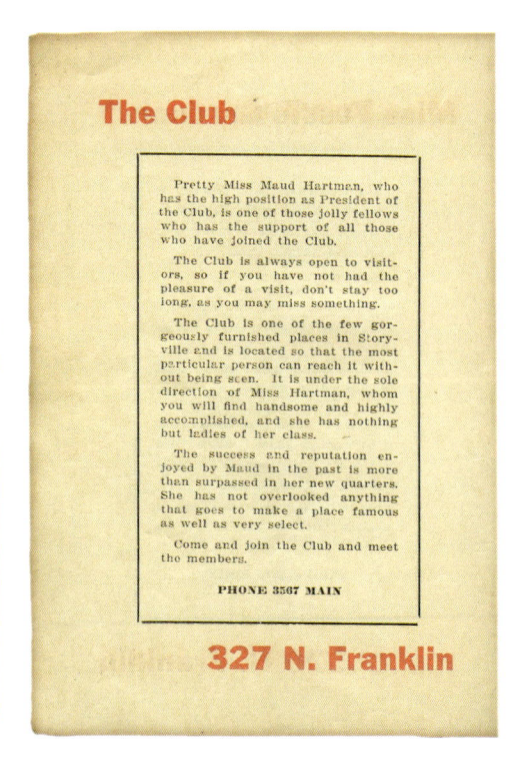

---

## Miss Jessie Orloff

While but a late resident of the District, she has gained more friends than the oldest in the business.

"Jessie" is known as the "idol" of society and club boys, and needs but little introduction, as she is known by the elite from New York to California for her wit and lovliness.

"Orloff" is very winsome, and appeals to everyone, as she is clever and beautiful. Her mansion is handsomely furnished, everything being the best that money could procure.

Aside from the grandeur of her establishment, she has a score of beautiful women, who, with their charming landlady, form a group that can never be forgotten.

PHONE 3427 MAIN

**1547 Iberville**

## The Star Mansion

Annie Ross, the mistress who has guided the "Star" into the limelight of to-day, is one of those jolly good fellows who, once you meet, will never be forgotten. She has, nevertheless, proven herself a grand woman, and has also proven a grand success as madam of her grand "chateau."

An aristocrat once said: "If it were within my power to name kings and queens, I would certainly go out of my way to bestow the title of 'Queen of Smile' on Annie Ross."

Annie is one of the few women who can say she has friends who are friends indeed, and who are with her in all her moods.

Her "Chateau" is grandly equipped and is lacking in nothing, and with her annex, is one of the largest in the district.

Pretty women, good times and sociability has been adopted as the motto of her new and costly home, the Star Mansion.

PHONE 1925 MAIN

**1517 Iberville**

## The Club

Pretty Miss Maud Hartman, who has the high position as President of the Club, is one of those jolly good fellows who has the support of all those who have joined the Club.

The Club is always open to visitors, so if you have not had the pleasure of a visit, don't stay too long, as you may miss something.

The Club is one of the few gorgeously furnished places in Storyville and is located so that the most particular person can reach it without being seen. It is under the sole direction of Miss Hartman, whom you will find handsome and highly accomplished, and she has nothing but ladies of her class.

The success and reputation enjoyed by Maud in the past is more than surpassed in her new quarters. She has not overlooked anything that goes to make a place famous as well as very select.

Come and join the Club and meet the members.

PHONE 3567 MAIN

**327 N. Franklin**

of color. Fourteen of the latter have the designation "Oct." following their names. Only one name in this section is in full capitals (and it is misspelled)—"Willie Pizzia." An unusual feature follows the directory listings for colored prostitutes: a separate category titled "Octoroons." There are only two names printed in this separate category, both in full capitals—Lulu White and Willie Piazza.

There are seventeen full-page advertisements for landladies, starting with Josie Arlington's. In the directory section both Josie Arlington's name and that of her longtime associate, Annie Casey, are in full capitals at the 225 N. Basin address. Eight of the familiar photographs of the Arlington interior are reproduced, with three—the Vienna Parlor, a corner of Arlington's apartment, and the Japanese Parlor—repeated later in the book for good measure. Two photographs of the interior of Hilma Burt's mansion are included, a view of her mirrored ballroom and a parlor. Annie Ross is now identified as the landlady of the Star Mansion at 1517 Iberville Street, once the realm of Ray Owens and Hilma Burt. The photograph of the exterior of Emma Johnson's Studio appears on the penultimate page.

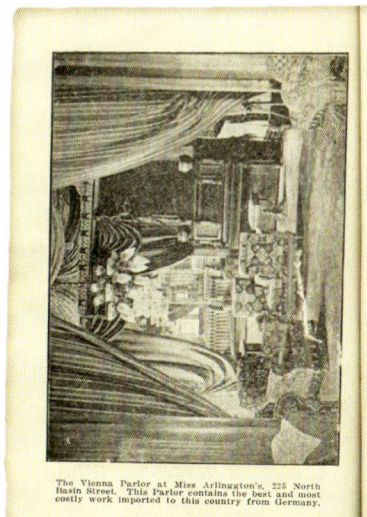

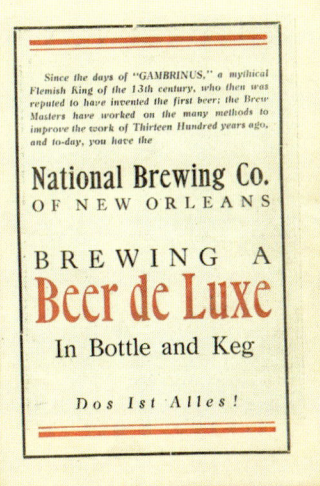

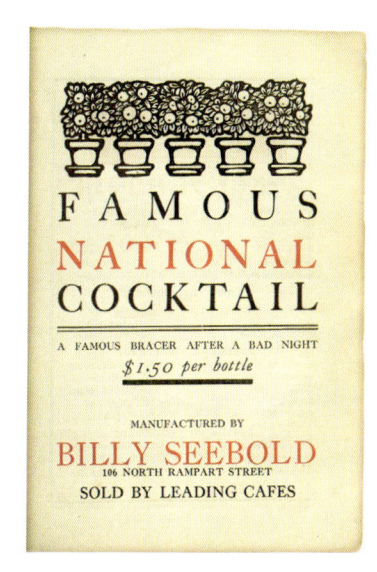

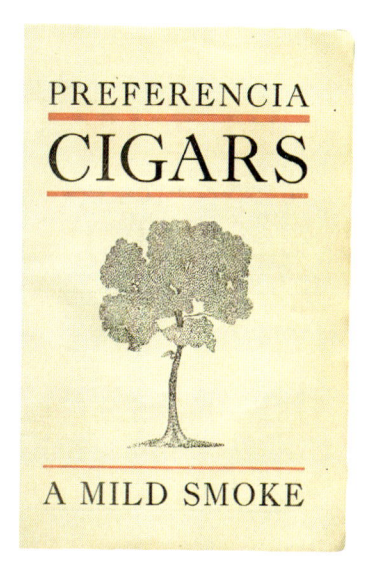

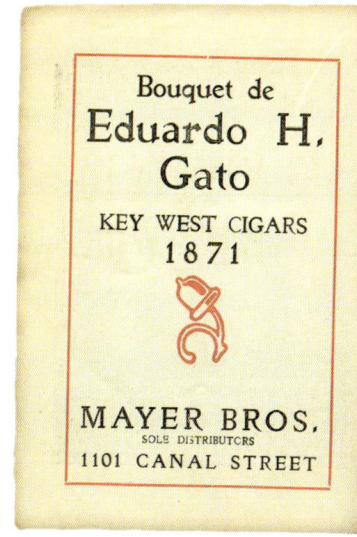

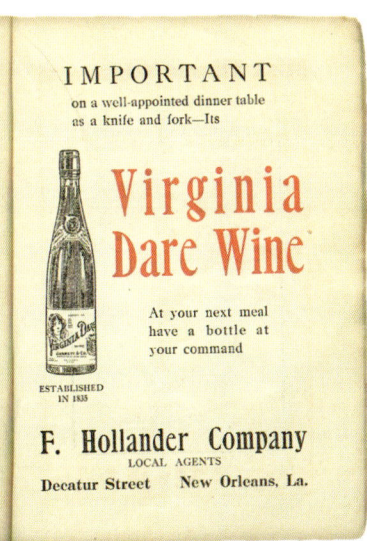

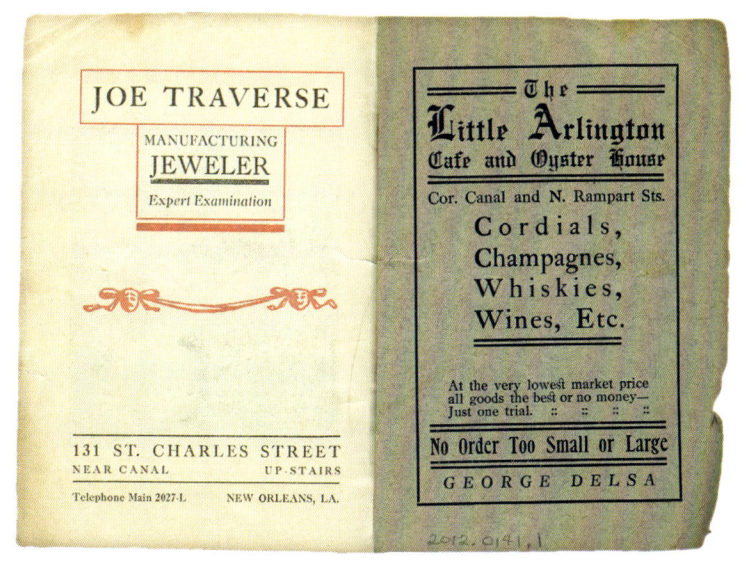

## EDITIONS OF *BLUE BOOK*

# No. 10

## Blue Book

Cover printed in red ink on pale blue-gray paper; interior printed in black and red ink on calendered paper. No edition number, undated [1913–15]. 96 unnumbered pages.

15.1 cm × 11.3 cm, *THNOC, 85-517-RL*

15 cm × 11.2 cm, *THNOC, 1969.19.11* (Heartman XII)

15 cm × 11.5 cm, *THNOC, 1969.19.12* (Heartman XIII)

15 cm × 11.5 cm, *THNOC, 77-2346-RL*

15 cm × 11.3 cm, *THNOC, William Russell Jazz Collection, MSS 536, 92-48-L.62.485*

15.1 cm × 11.5 cm, *THNOC, gift of Mr. and Mrs. E. B. Ludwig III, 2011.0129.2*

15 cm × 11.1 cm, *THNOC, gift of Hélène de la Houssaye Tebo, 2012.0065.1*

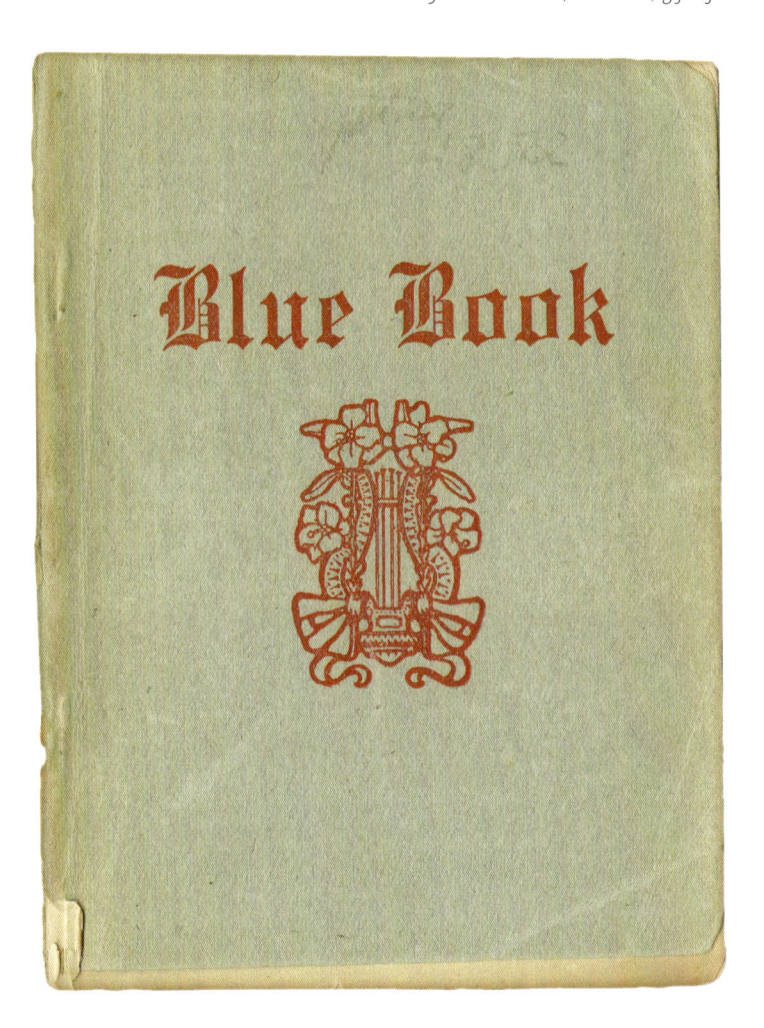

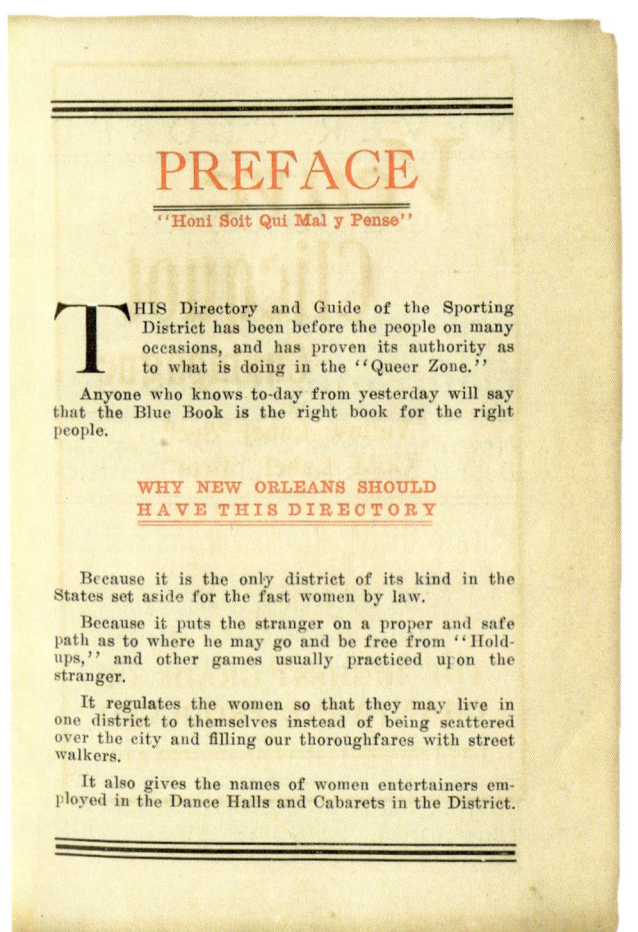

This edition—featuring a correctly oriented printer's ornament showing a lyre surrounded by lilies and ribbons—appears to be the last edition of *Blue Book*. Though it is popularly identified with a publication date of 1915, I believe this edition may have been issued as early as 1913. Because No. 9 was probably produced in 1912, it seems likely that this one may have been released the following year. This guide contains no advertisement for the French balls, which are typically helpful in dating *Blue Book*. By 1911, the powers of moral reform, in the shape of the Law Enforcement League of Louisiana, brought enough pressure to bear upon the district attorney and police headquarters to severely restrict the licentious revelry of these events.[6] Although a French ball ad appears in No. 9, this aspect of Carnival for and by the demimonde had faded away by the time No. 10 was printed. Lacking the usual methods for dating this publication, I combed city directories for overlap with this edition. Bertha Weinthal, who had not appeared in any previous *Blue Book*, became my key. Her full-page advertisement in this edition places her as the madam of a prestigious address, 311 N. Basin, which previously had been under Ella Schwartz's administration since 1905. The New Orleans city directories connect Weinthal with the 311 N. Basin address during the years 1913, 1914, and 1915, which supports my instinct that this edition could have been printed as early as 1913. The directories reveal that before and after this time Weinthal was letting furnished rooms at locations in the French Quarter. Another clue may further narrow the date. The full-page advertisement for the brothel at 225 N. Basin simply identifies it as "The Arlington," with no mention of its famous madam, Josie Arlington (all previous versions of this ad name her), and Anna Casey is listed in the directory section as the house's madam. Arlington died on February 14, 1914, just ten days before Mardi Gras, following a lengthy illness.

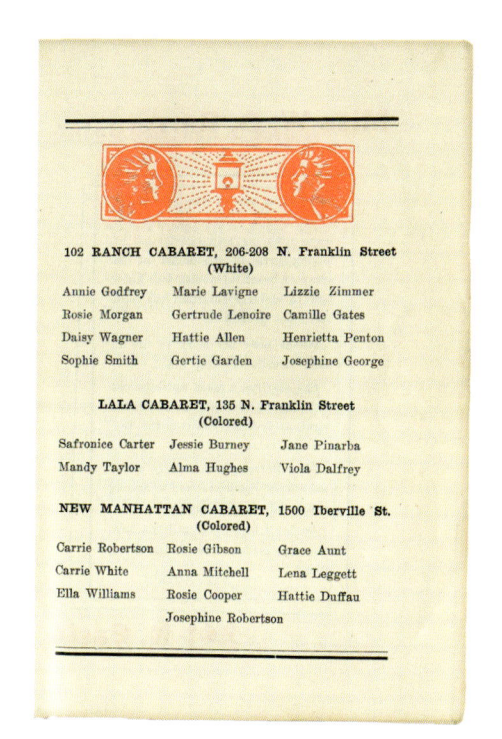

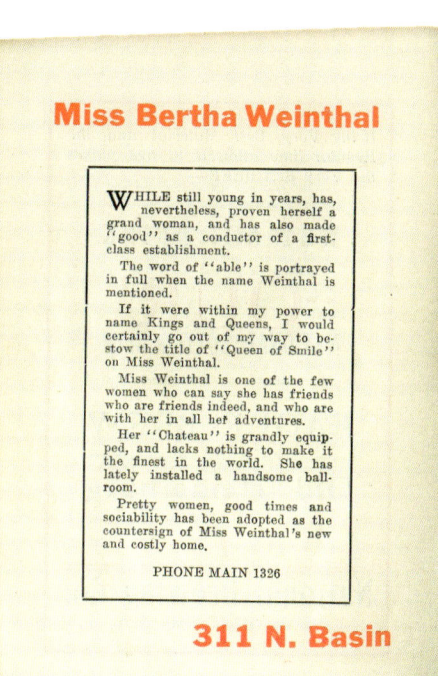

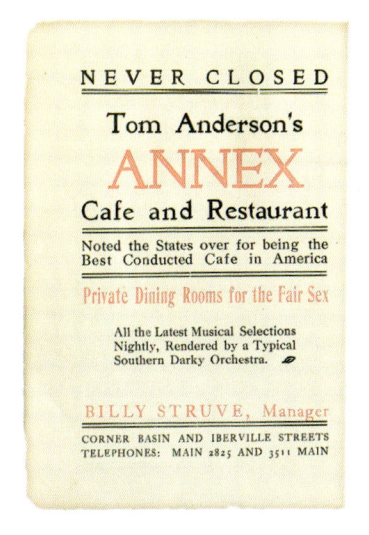

The introductory material is not signed, but Billy Struve is identified as manager in the advertisement for Tom Anderson's Annex Cafe and Restaurant on the second page. A fourth and final reason has been added to suggest "Why New Orleans Should Have This Directory": "It also gives the names of women entertainers employed in the Dance Halls and Cabarets in the District." In this edition, for the first time, the directory has a section featuring cabarets and the women who worked in them. Though commercial sex was certainly on offer at these venues, the primary selling point appears to have been musical entertainment and dancing.

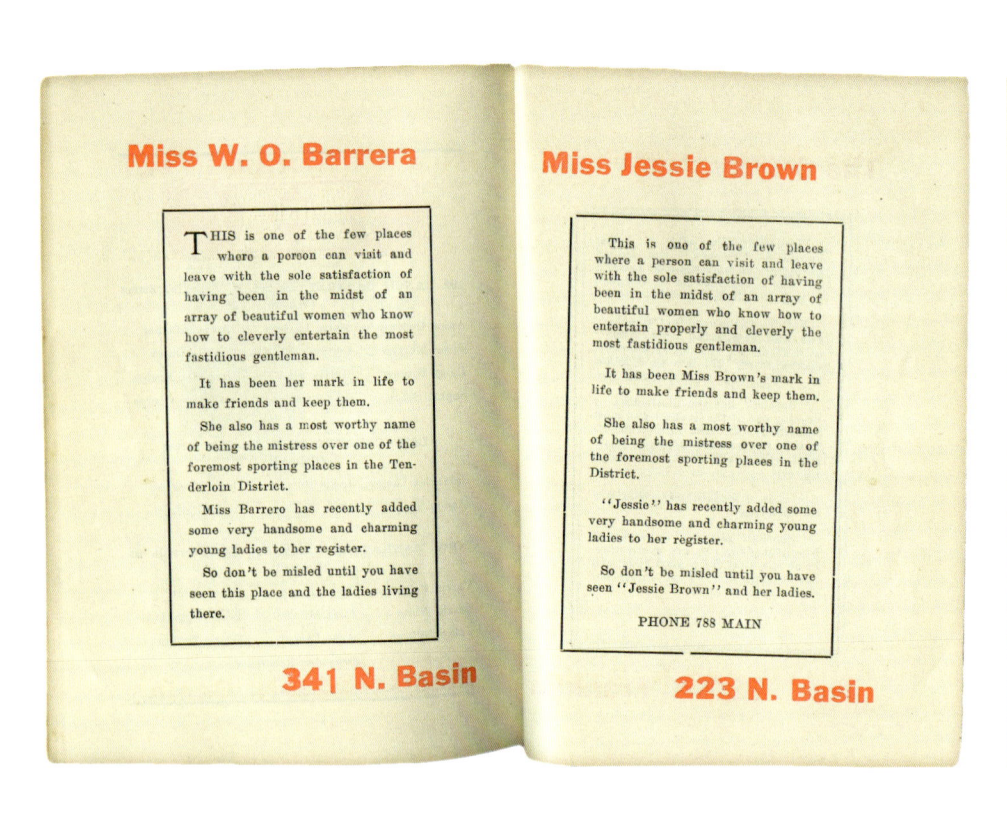

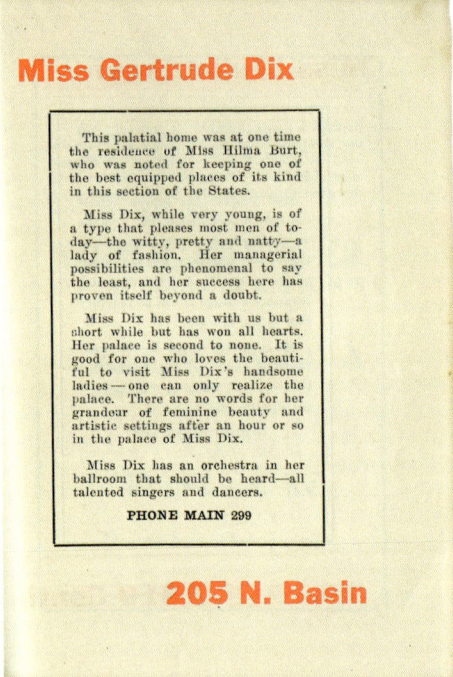

The directory section contains entries for 332 white prostitutes; 20 white landladies, their names set in full capitals; 7 octoroon prostitutes; 2 octoroon landladies, their names also set in full capitals; and 234 colored women, though none are designated as landladies. Two pages of "Late Arrivals," women recently arrived in the District, list 45 women, only four designated as colored. There are seven white cabarets with names of 71 women and two colored cabarets with names of 16 women.

This edition contains twenty-three full-page brothel advertisements, including the first appearance of Gertrude Dix, madam of 209 N. Basin, formerly managed by Hilma Burt. Dix and Thomas C. Anderson married in 1928, long after the closing of Storyville.[7] There is again the photograph of Emma Johnson's at 331–33 N. Basin, and the familiar drawing of the facade of the Arlington at 225 N. Basin accompanying its full-page advertisement. Notably absent are any photographs of brothel interiors. Facing Bertha Weinthal's full-page ad is a theatrical photograph of the "Oriental Danseuse" Rita Walker, a "guest" at Weinthal's establishment described as "one of the first women in America to dance in her bare feet." She is artfully posing on a leopard skin, scantily dressed in exotic selections from her "$5000 wardrobe which she uses for her dances."

Heartman was in possession of two copies of this edition—his XII and XIII. He considered them different editions, but examination of the two copies reveals that they are identical. The content presented in XII is exactly the same as that in XIII—page by page, name by name, advertisement by advertisement, and misprint by misprint; even the "Late Arrivals" sections contain the same names. Heartman assigned a date of

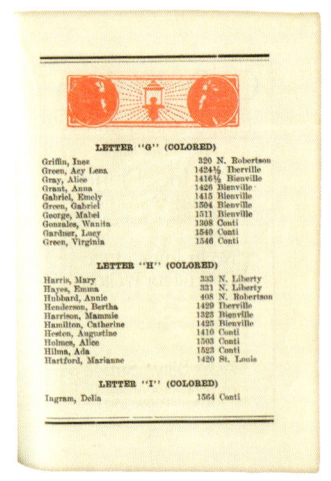

1911–12 to his XII and believed that XIII, which he dated to 1915, was the "Last Blue Book Issued." He described the color of XII's cover stock as "greenish gray,"[8] although the inside of the cover is the same shade of pale blue-gray as many other copies of this edition in our holdings. The covers of XII and another copy in THNOC's holdings (2011.0129.2), however, do appear very slightly more green than blue, and some color fading over time should be taken into account. The intensity and tone of the red printing throughout the pages of all these copies varies widely. As there is nothing in their contents to indicate that these are separate editions, I consider them copies of the same. Among the various mistakes Heartman made in his bibliography, he reproduces a spread from this edition on page 55 showing the cabaret listings, erroneously identified there as pages from the 1905 *Blue Book* (No. 4). Cabarets are not included in *Blue Book* until this edition.

This edition is the one that is most often seen today at sales and auctions; whether it had a higher print run or simply a better survival rate is unknown. A facsimile reprint of it was published in 2013 (No. 25).

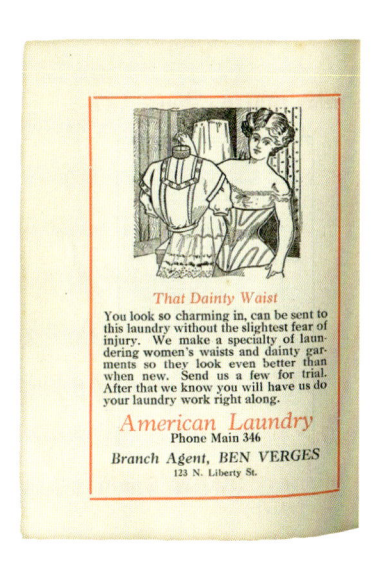

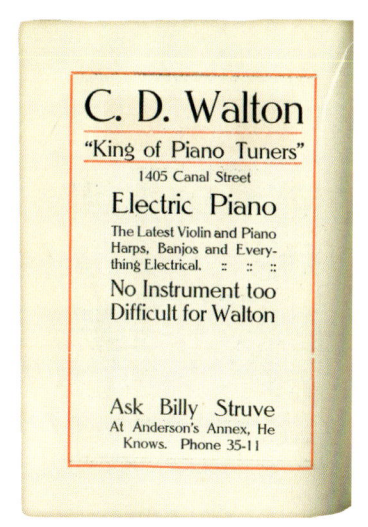

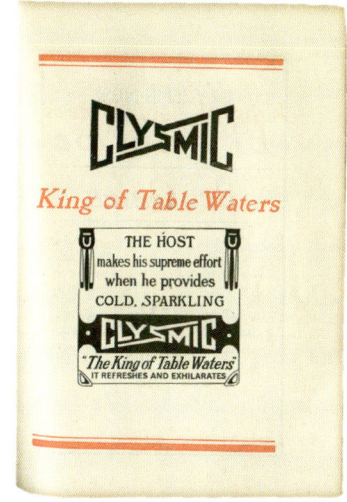

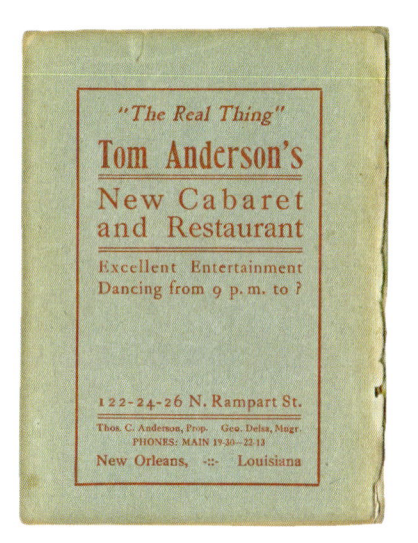

There appears to have been a printing of this edition in which all of the text and design elements of the interior pages are printed only in black ink, with none of the rubrication seen in THNOC's seven identical copies. I have examined a copy of this item that is in private hands, and its size, the cover printing, and the quality of the paper are exactly the same as THNOC's seven. There is one other exception—three staples are used to bind the text block rather than the usual two seen in most issues. The printing on the interior pages, the overall wear, and the accumulation of rust around the staples leads me to believe that, even lacking the red-ink highlights of the others, this one is also of the Storyville period.

## ALTERNATIVE STORYVILLE-ERA GUIDES

# No. 11
## NEW MAHOGANY HALL

Cover printed in black ink on tan paper; interior pages printed in black ink on calendered paper.
No edition number, undated [1898–99]. 24 unnumbered pages.

12 cm × 7.5 cm, *THNOC*, 56-15

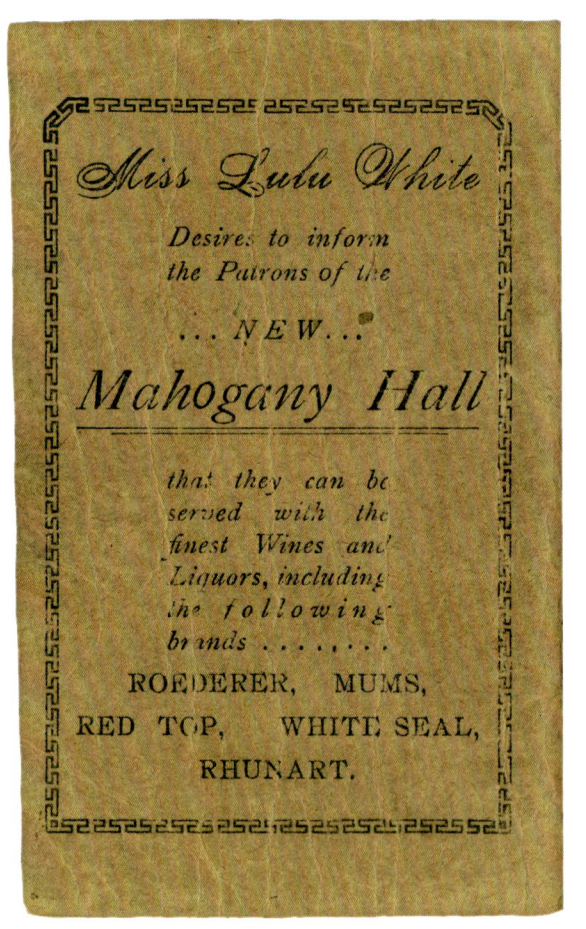

Lulu White, one of Storyville's most notorious madams, presided over one of its most famous brothels, Mahogany Hall, which offered only octoroon women. She was unexcelled in self-promotion. This is the second of two known Mahogany Hall booklets produced by White (THNOC does not own a copy of the first). This guide was issued shortly after she moved into her palatial new house at 235 N. Basin Street in 1898; hence, *New Mahogany Hall*. This booklet contains small, grainy black-and-white portrait photographs of twenty-one of her prostitutes—the same twelve as in her previous souvenir booklet, plus nine new women. Two of the women in *New Mahogany Hall*, Annie Stone and Margaret Levy, are listed in the 1900 *Blue Book* (No. 1) working for other madams, Pearl Knight at 229 N. Basin and Willie Piazza at 319 N. Basin. This helps set the date as between 1898 and 1899.

BIBLIOGRAPHY | 106

### Victoria Hall.

A member of Miss White's Club, as accomplished as she is beautiful, a form equal to Venus, a voice not unlike Patti. How could a more accurate description be printed, and what more could be said.

### MISS LULA WHITE.

This famous West Indian octoroon first saw the light of day thirty-one years ago. Arriving in this country at a rather tender age, and having been fortunately gifted with a good education it did not take long for her to find out what the other sex were in search of.

In describing Miss Lulu, as she is most familiarly called, it would not be amiss to say that besides possessing an elegant form she has beautiful black hair and blue eyes, which have justly gained for her the title of the "Queen of the Demi-monde."

Her establishment, which is situated in the central part of the city, is unquestionably the most elaborately furnished house in the city of New Orleans, and without a doubt one of the most elegant places in this or any other country.

She has made a feature of boarding none but the fairest of girls—those gifted with nature's best charms, and would, under no circumstances have any but that class in her house.

As an entertainer Miss Lulu stands foremost, having made a life-long study of music and literature. She is well read and one that can interest anybody and make a visit to her place a continued round of pleasure.

And when adding that she would be pleased to see all her old friends and make new ones. What more could be added?

Your old friend

### Georgie Wilson,

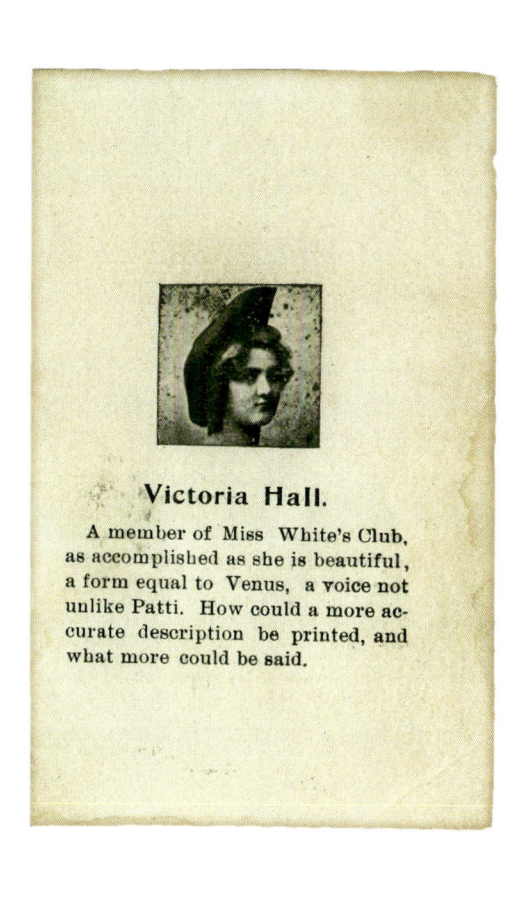

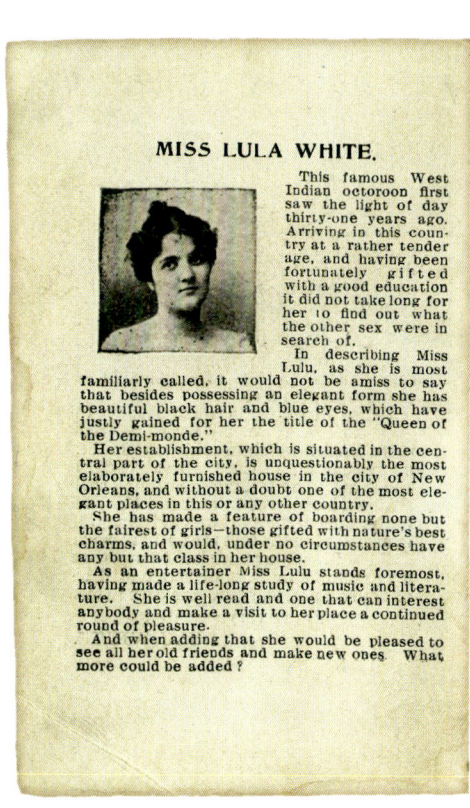

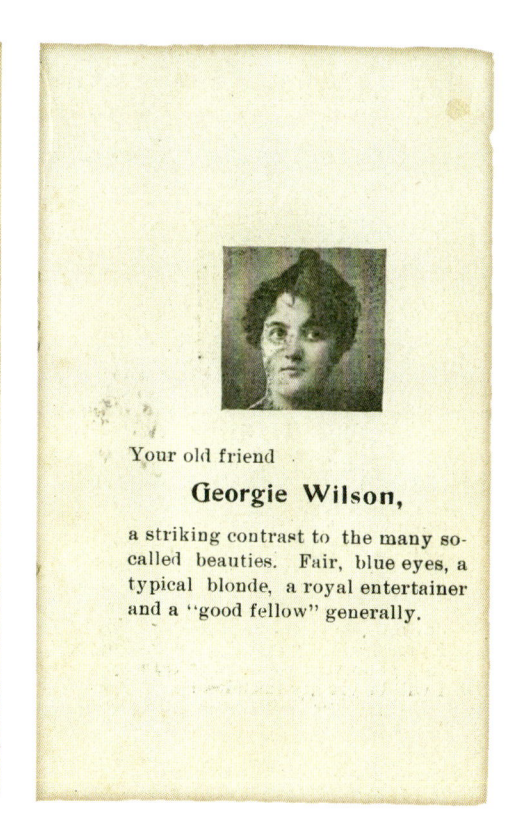

a striking contrast to the many so-called beauties. Fair, blue eyes, a typical blonde, a royal entertainer and a "good fellow" generally.

The book also purports to show a portrait of "Miss Lula White" herself (even in her own publication, a madam could not be sure her name would be spelled correctly). Al Rose claims that the photograph of White is actually of another of her prostitutes, Victoria Hall.[9] Upon close examination, however, it is apparent that yet another woman in *New Mahogany Hall*, "Your old friend Georgie Wilson," bears an even more striking resemblance to "Lula," right down to her topknot and spit

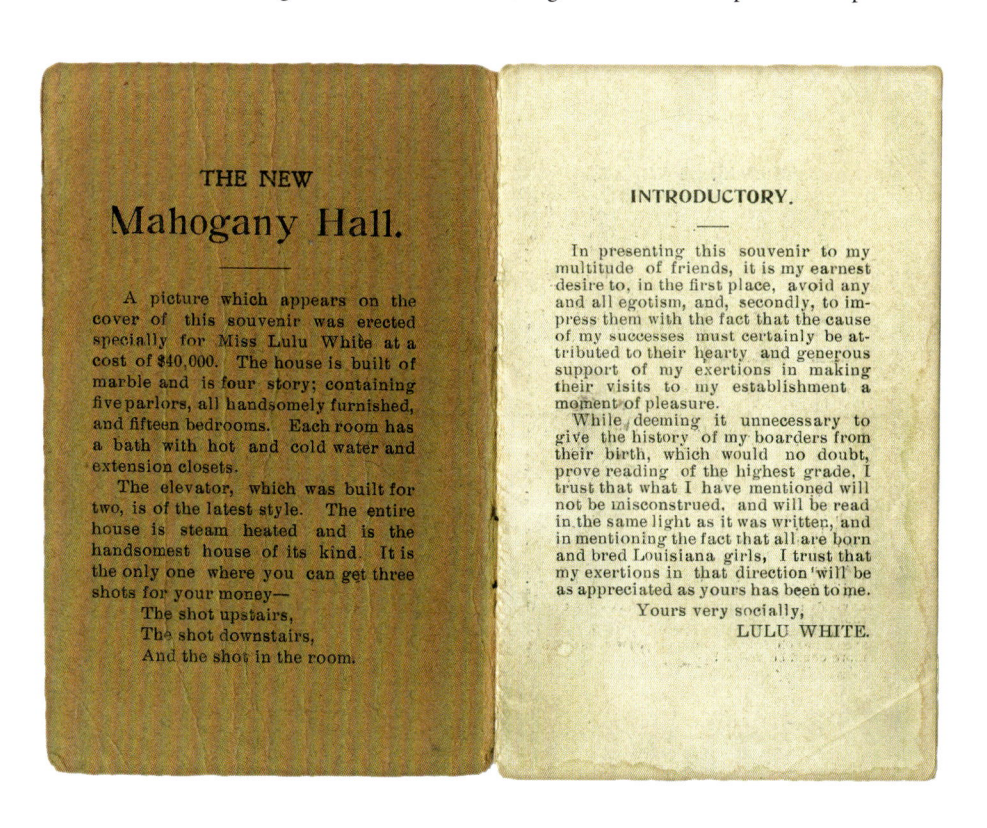

### THE NEW Mahogany Hall.

A picture which appears on the cover of this souvenir was erected specially for Miss Lulu White at a cost of $40,000. The house is built of marble and is four story; containing five parlors, all handsomely furnished, and fifteen bedrooms. Each room has a bath with hot and cold water and extension closets.

The elevator, which was built for two, is of the latest style. The entire house is steam heated and is the handsomest house of its kind. It is the only one where you can get three shots for your money—

The shot upstairs,
The shot downstairs,
And the shot in the room.

### INTRODUCTORY.

In presenting this souvenir to my multitude of friends, it is my earnest desire to, in the first place, avoid any and all egotism, and, secondly, to impress them with the fact that the cause of my successes must certainly be attributed to their hearty and generous support of my exertions in making their visits to my establishment a moment of pleasure.

While deeming it unnecessary to give the history of my boarders from their birth, which would no doubt, prove reading of the highest grade, I trust that what I have mentioned will not be misconstrued, and will be read in the same light as it was written, and in mentioning the fact that all are born and bred Louisiana girls, I trust that my exertions in that direction will be as appreciated as yours has been to me.

Yours very socially,

LULU WHITE.

NO. 11 | ALTERNATIVE STORYVILLE-ERA GUIDES | 107

curl. It is obvious that a different head shot pose of the woman identified as Wilson taken at the same session was chosen to portray White.

The inside cover contains a brief description of New Mahogany Hall, a four-story marble structure containing five parlors; a two-person elevator; steam heat; and fifteen bedrooms, each having its own bath with hot and cold water, a luxury at a time when many houses in New Orleans and elsewhere did not have indoor plumbing. *New Mahogany Hall* claims that this house is the only one "where you can get three shots for your money—The shot upstairs, The shot downstairs, And the shot in the room," a reference to oral, anal, and vaginal sex.[10] The introduction is signed in print, "Yours very socially, Lulu White," followed by a short biography of the madam in which she is described as a "famous West Indian octoroon," and "Queen of the Demi-monde" with "black hair and blue eyes."

Heartman does not mention this souvenir specifically but states that "there were many more issues including some very tiny ones which were gotten out by individual establishments,"[11] although he does not identify any madams who issued their own promotional booklets. White's are the only single-madam blue books I have seen; if other women produced their own guides, such souvenirs have not turned up in collections with which I am familiar.

❧ ❧ ❧

I have also examined a copy of the first known Lulu White souvenir booklet, now in a private collection. In October 2007, Neal Auction Company of New Orleans offered a small lot of Storyville and cabaret memorabilia from the estate of New Orleans author and collector Al Rose, among which was the earlier booklet, titled *In Remembrance of a Visit to Lulu White's*.[12] The cover features elaborate printer's ornaments, incorporating several fleurs-de-lis, and gives the address as 166 Customhouse Street (now 930 Iberville Street, in the French Quarter, although the building was demolished years ago), the address where White operated her brothel from 1890 until 1898.[13]

This earlier souvenir booklet was probably produced between 1890 and 1894 and mentions twelve women, all of whom are featured in her later brochure, but does not contain portrait photographs. It is 13.2 cm by 7.3 cm and contains eight numbered pages, one of the few instances in all of these directories where pagination is employed. The top of every verso page reads "Lulu White's Octoroon Club," and the header of every recto page repeats the street address. At the foot of each page are statements regarding the quality and availability of beer and wines "always on hand." The introduction and short history of White are identical to those in her later souvenir booklet, except here she is described as having "blonde hair and blue eyes."

### Middie Cook.

Miss White's house would be incomplete without Middy Cook. She is everything that one desires—charming, pretty, sweet. There are lots of pebbles on the beach, but there is only one Middy Cook. She is a native of Alabama, and a girl to be proud of. Call and see her.

### "Chippie" McKee.

The name often tells the tale. Miss Chippie is a young lady whom any man would call to see the second time. Why? Because she can make your visit one never to be forgotten. You may have heard Paderewski play the piano, but hear Miss Chippie. While we do not claim that she is a superior player, we do say, with emphasis, that she can interest you equally as well—demure, petite. "Nuff sed."

### Annie Stone.

Who has not heard of this beauty of Louisiana? Not any who has lived in New Orleans. Miss Stone is one of the best entertainers in New Orleans; and if she can not show you a royal time no one can. Make up a club, and go in a crowd to see Miss White and don't forget to ask for Miss Stone. You will have a great time.

### Petite Irene Mantley.

There are others, lots of others, but there is only one Irene Mantley, who has accomplished that which others have failed to do—to win your esteem at once. Can sing you a song, can play a violin or mandolin solo, and if you are in search of a good time, desire to come in contact with a good fellow, look no further, but invite yourself to Miss White's Octoroon Club and ask for Miss Mantley.

### Jennie Leverie.

A member of Miss White's Club, is this young lady. Formed after a model of Venus, the Goddess of Love, a voice that is rich for song, of gentle disposition is the gift of Miss Leverie. What more would one desire? Miss Leverie was born in the Empire State and was a resident of Buffalo.

### Corine Meyers.

The poet has said that there are others, lots of others, but there is only one Corine Meyers, and we do not stretch the point when we re-echo and say that this is true. She can sing a song and rob the canary of its sweet voice. She can perform on any musical instrument, and is a bosom friend in a short while.

### Margaret Levy.

This young lady has gained during her brief stay in this city a vast multitude of friends, who unite in saying that there are lots of girls in the city but only one Margaret Levy. This young lady has an aptitude for gaining friends, and what is better, keeping them. As an entertainer she is above the average and she extends to all an invitation to visit her.

### The beautiful Estelle Russell,

now a member of high standing in Miss White's famous Octoroon Club, a few years ago one of the leading stars in Sam T. Jack's Creole Show, which assertion alone should test the capacity of Miss Lulu's commodious quarters every night.

Gentlemen, don't fail, when visiting Miss White's, to ask for Miss Estelle, for you miss a treat if you do not.

### Lulu Morris.

Pretty Lulu Morris is how this young lady's friends speak of her. We can not do the lady justice as words of ours are inadequate to express her beauty and accomplishments. If you would know her, call at Miss White's and be introduced to Miss Morris.

### Birdie White.

The above young lady who has during her brief stay in this city, gained a multitude of friends, who unite in saying that "there's lots of girls, but only one Birdie White." She has solved the mystery of gaining friends and keeping them, which is in itself a wonderful accomplishment. As an entertainer she is above par, and cordially extends an invitation to her gentlemen friends to visit her during the Carnival, or any other time.

### Ida McClelland.

This young lady, who needs but little introduction from the fact that she is universally known as the famous dancer who created such furore at the New York clubs a short time ago.

Many will, no doubt, recognize in this clever Creole the petite figure which caused men to go into raptures at the World's Fair, while visiting the Midway, and when we say that you must see her to properly appreciate her many charms we hope that you will take this hint.

### Florence Mandley.

This young lady scarcely needs any introduction for she has already made for herself a national reputation, for she is the famous dancer who created such a sensation by her grace at the New York clubs a short time back.

Many will be able to recognize in this clever Creole the petite figure which caused the men to go into raptures, while taking in the sights of Miss White's Club, and when we say that you must be personally acquainted with her before you can appreciate her many charms we hope that you will take the hint.

ALTERNATIVE STORYVILLE-ERA GUIDES

# No. 12

THE RED BOOK | A Complete Directory of the Tenderloin

Cover printed in black ink on red paper; interior pages printed in black ink on plain paper;
No edition number, undated [1901]. 24 numbered pages.

14.4 cm × 9.5 cm, *THNOC, 1969.19.5* (Heartman V)

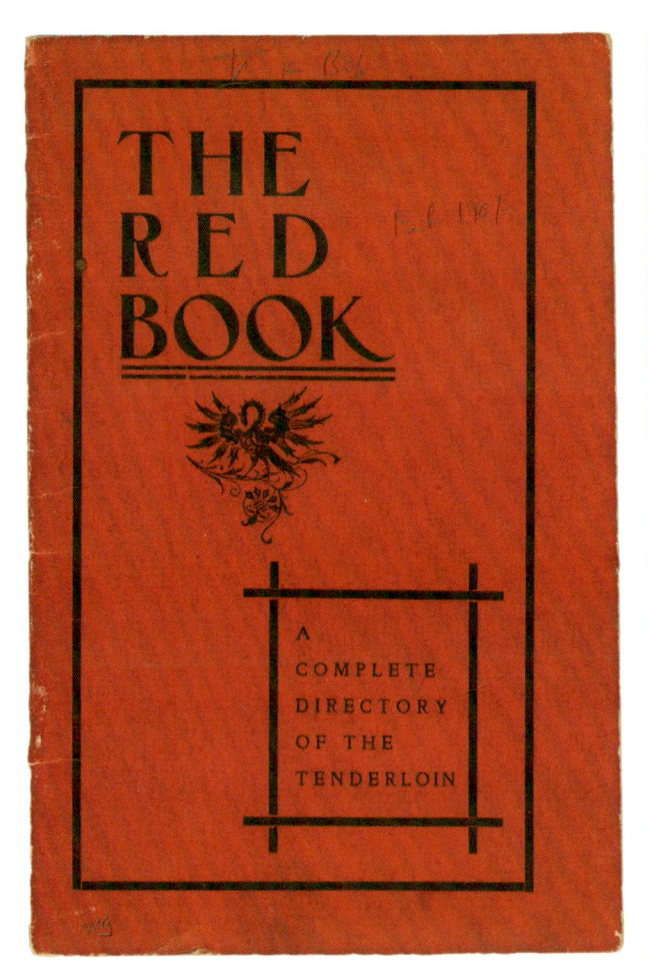

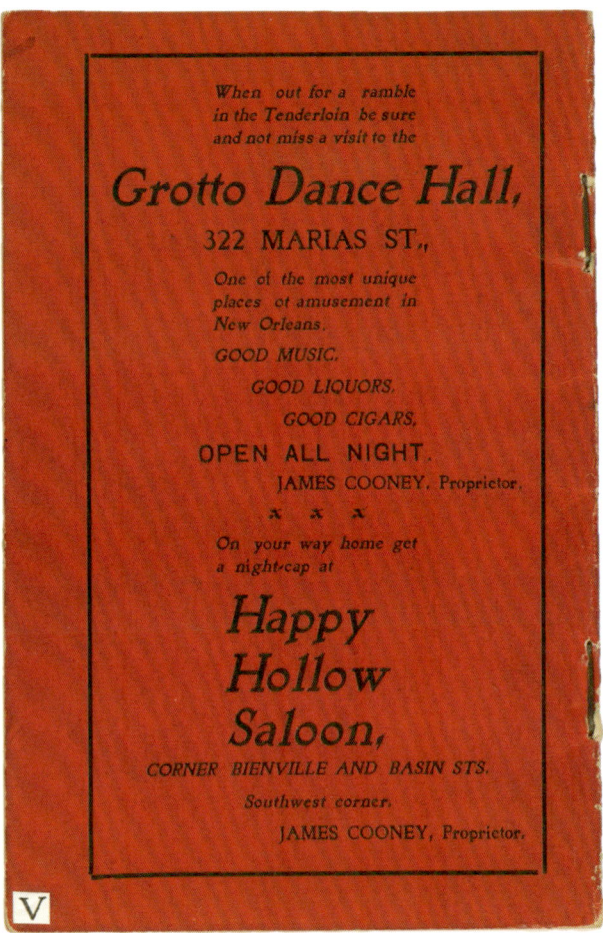

*The Red Book* seems to be the only example of a rival guide to *Blue Book*. It is of a better production quality than that more famous publication, with more intricate printers' embellishments, more artistic page layouts, and fewer grammatical horrors. There is no pithy introduction, nor coy attribution of authorship, and no advertisements for any of Tom Anderson's establishments, all consistent elements in *Blue Book*. Despite its selling points, this guide appears to have been published only once.

The first page of *The Red Book* states, "A Directory of the Tenderloin: Being a comprehensive and accurate record of the addresses of the sporting ladies in that portion of town commonly known as Storyville" and encourages the reader to "give them a call, boys, You'll get treated right." "The Red Book" appears at the top of each page, and the book, unlike most Storyville guides, employs pagination. "The Limits of the Tenderloin as Prescribed by Law" are given on page 3, accompanied by a map. Only three full-page advertisements for specific mansions—Josie Arlington's, Lulu White's, and Mae Burton's—appear in the guide. A brief, three-line ad at the bottom of page 24 encourages those looking for a "light lunch" to go to Fred Wagner's, and two advertisements on the outside back cover promote the Grotto Dance Hall and the Happy Hollow Saloon, both managed by James Cooney. Page 12 features an advertisement for a journal "devoted to sporting, amusements and the humorous side of life," called the *Sporting Life*, published by Wm. C. Moulton and Co., which was released "every Saturday, at 629 Poydras Street."

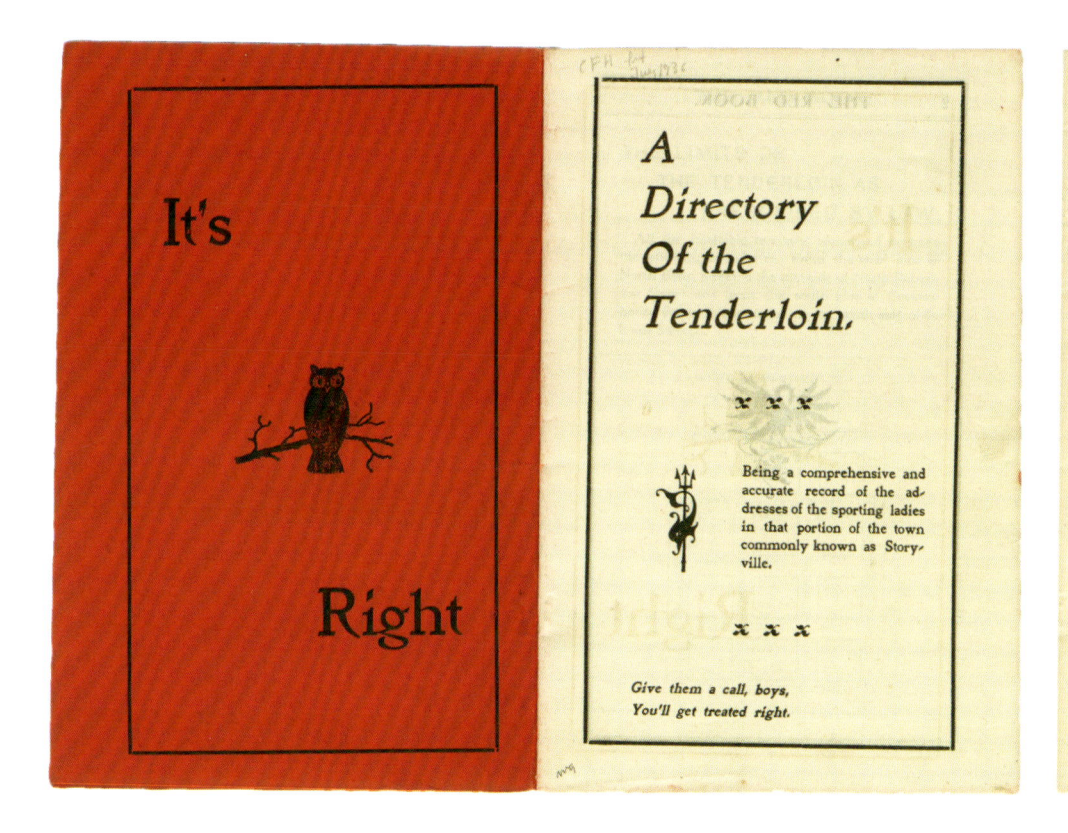

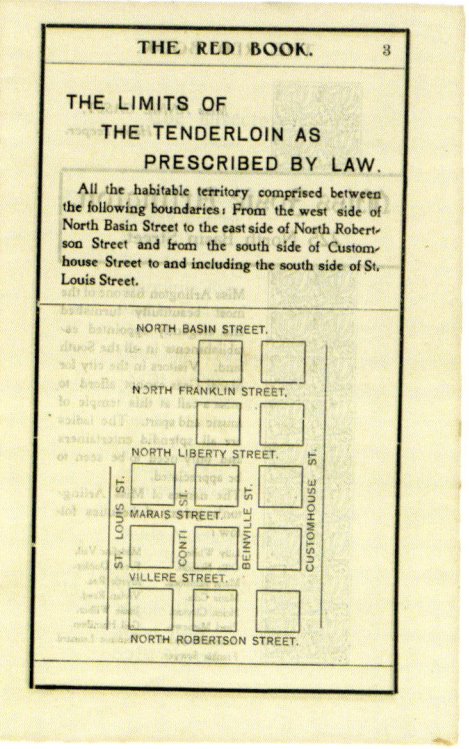

A full-page advertisement announces the dates for the C. C. C. Ball (Saturday, February 16) and the Two Well-Known Gentlemen Ball (Tuesday, February 19). Mardi Gras was on February 19 in 1901. It seems that there were two distinct guides to Storyville produced in 1901, this one and No. 2. Heartman includes photographs of the first page (which he erroneously identifies as the cover) and additional pages in his bibliography, on pages 51 and 53. He incorrectly dates this book to "about 1903."[14] In determining the date of this guide, Rose concluded that it had to have been published prior to 1904 based on his belief that Customhouse became Iberville in that year.[15] However, the New Orleans city directory reveals that 1901 was the year that most of Customhouse Street was renamed Iberville. Idiosyncratically, the portion that crossed Storyville, from N. Rampart to N. Claiborne, retained its old name until 1906, when the entire street, from the river to the lake, officially became Iberville.

The directory is organized by street address, and there is no indication of the prostitutes' races. One hundred thirteen landladies are indicated by capital letters, and 218 other women are listed. Only one photograph appears in this guide: a full-page, full-length image of "The Famous Lulu White. Queen of the Octoroons." Whether this photograph actually depicts White is unclear, since an image of a different woman portrays White in her own souvenir booklet (No. 11).

As *The Red Book* is so different from others of its genre, it is probable that it was produced by another publisher, perhaps the printer whose ads appear in it on pages 6 and 12. Both advertisements for Alltmont, printer, give the address 727 Common; the second ad, which lists prices for printing jobs, drops one "l" from the name and gives an additional address—139 Carondelet. Both addresses (and a seemingly fluid approach to spelling this surname) can be verified in the New Orleans city directory for 1901. There, Samuel Alltmont, bookseller, appears at 139 Carondelet, and under "printers" in the directory's business section is a listing for Samuel Altmont at 727 Common. The second Alltmont ad in *The Red Book* includes the date February 1901, further confirming this guide's year of publication.

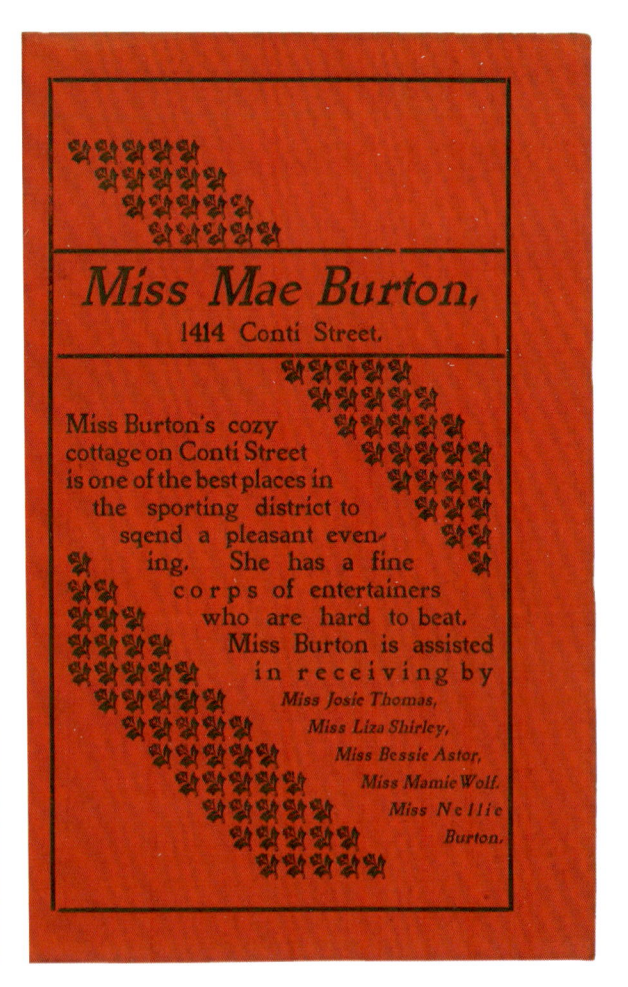

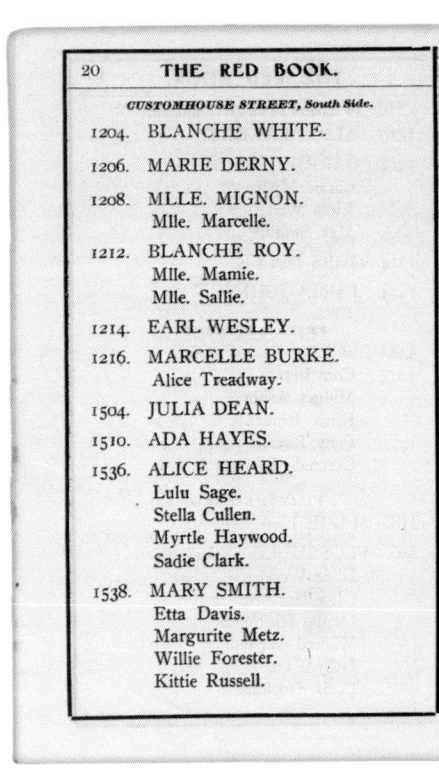

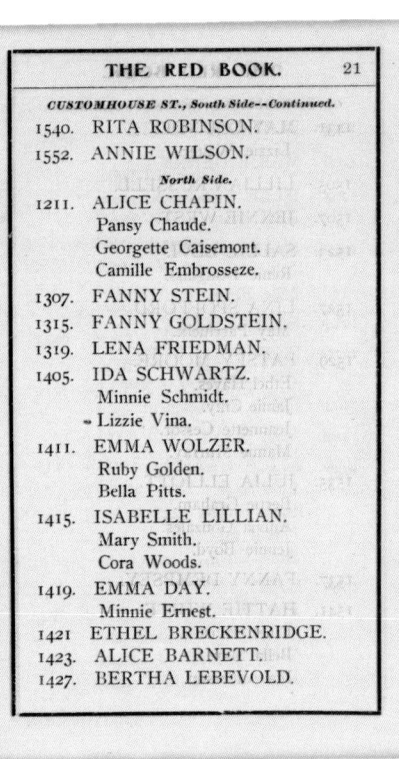

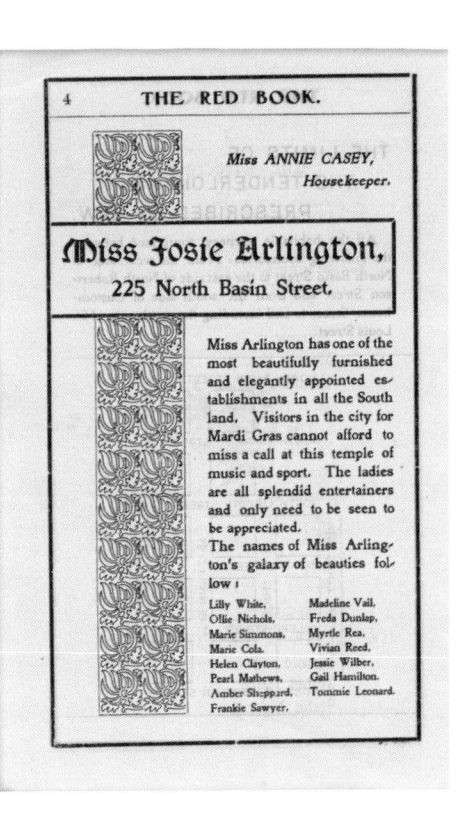

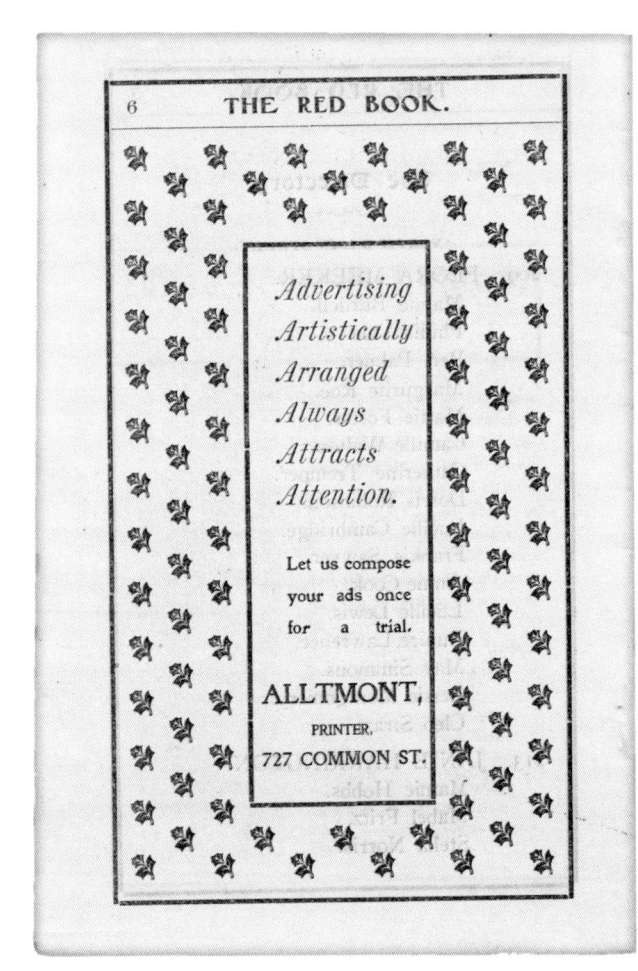

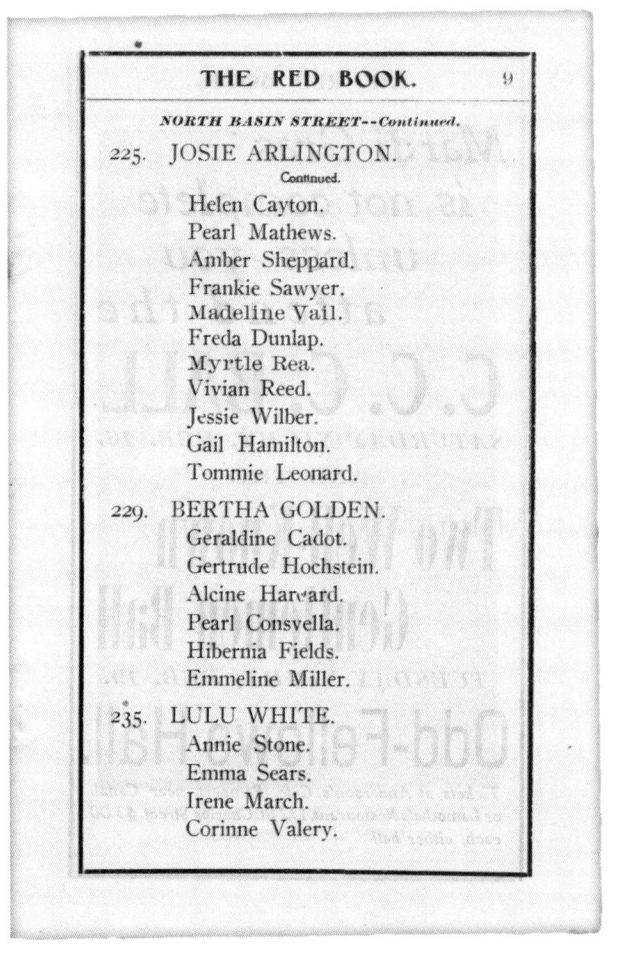

## THE RED BOOK. — 20

**CUSTOMHOUSE STREET, South Side.**

- 1204. BLANCHE WHITE.
- 1206. MARIE DERNY.
- 1208. MLLE. MIGNON.
  Mlle. Marcelle.
- 1212. BLANCHE ROY.
  Mlle. Mamie.
  Mlle. Sallie.
- 1214. EARL WESLEY.
- 1216. MARCELLE BURKE.
  Alice Treadway.
- 1504. JULIA DEAN.
- 1510. ADA HAYES.
- 1536. ALICE HEARD.
  Lulu Sage.
  Stella Cullen.
  Myrtle Haywood.
  Sadie Clark.
- 1538. MARY SMITH.
  Etta Davis.
  Margurite Metz.
  Willie Forester.
  Kittie Russell.

## THE RED BOOK. — 21

**CUSTOMHOUSE ST., South Side—Continued.**

- 1540. RITA ROBINSON.
- 1552. ANNIE WILSON.

**North Side.**

- 1211. ALICE CHAPIN.
  Pansy Chaude.
  Georgette Caisemont.
  Camille Embrosseze.
- 1307. FANNY STEIN.
- 1315. FANNY GOLDSTEIN.
- 1319. LENA FRIEDMAN.
- 1405. IDA SCHWARTZ.
  Minnie Schmidt.
  Lizzie Vina.
- 1411. EMMA WOLZER.
  Ruby Golden.
  Bella Pitts.
- 1415. ISABELLE LILLIAN.
  Mary Smith.
  Cora Woods.
- 1419. EMMA DAY.
  Minnie Ernest.
- 1421. ETHEL BRECKENRIDGE.
- 1423. ALICE BARNETT.
- 1427. BERTHA LEBEVOLD.

## THE RED BOOK. — 4

Miss ANNIE CASEY,
Housekeeper.

**Miss Josie Arlington,**
225 North Basin Street.

Miss Arlington has one of the most beautifully furnished and elegantly appointed establishments in all the South land. Visitors in the city for Mardi Gras cannot afford to miss a call at this temple of music and sport. The ladies are all splendid entertainers and only need to be seen to be appreciated.

The names of Miss Arlington's galaxy of beauties follow:

| | |
|---|---|
| Lilly White. | Madeline Vail. |
| Ollie Nichols. | Freda Dunlap. |
| Marie Simmons. | Myrtle Rea. |
| Marie Cola. | Vivian Reed. |
| Helen Clayton. | Jessie Wilber. |
| Pearl Mathews. | Gail Hamilton. |
| Amber Sheppard. | Tommie Leonard. |
| Frankie Sawyer. | |

## THE RED BOOK. — 6

*Advertising*
*Artistically*
*Arranged*
*Always*
*Attracts*
*Attention.*

Let us compose your ads once for a trial.

**ALLTMONT,**
PRINTER,
727 COMMON ST.

## THE RED BOOK. — 9

**NORTH BASIN STREET—Continued.**

- 225. JOSIE ARLINGTON.
  *Continued.*
  Helen Cayton.
  Pearl Mathews.
  Amber Sheppard.
  Frankie Sawyer.
  Madeline Vail.
  Freda Dunlap.
  Myrtle Rea.
  Vivian Reed.
  Jessie Wilber.
  Gail Hamilton.
  Tommie Leonard.
- 229. BERTHA GOLDEN.
  Geraldine Cadot.
  Gertrude Hochstein.
  Alcine Harvard.
  Pearl Consvella.
  Hibernia Fields.
  Emmeline Miller.
- 235. LULU WHITE.
  Annie Stone.
  Emma Sears.
  Irene March.
  Corinne Valery.

ALTERNATIVE STORYVILLE-ERA GUIDES

# No. 13

Sporting Guide, | OF THE | TENDERLOIN DISTRCT | OF NEW ORLEANS, LA. | WHERE THE FOUR-HUNDRED CAN BE FOUND

Cover printed in black ink on orange-red paper; interior printed in black ink on plain paper.
No edition number, undated [1902]. 24 unnumbered pages.

11.5 cm × 8 cm, *THNOC*, 1969.19.3 (Heartman III)

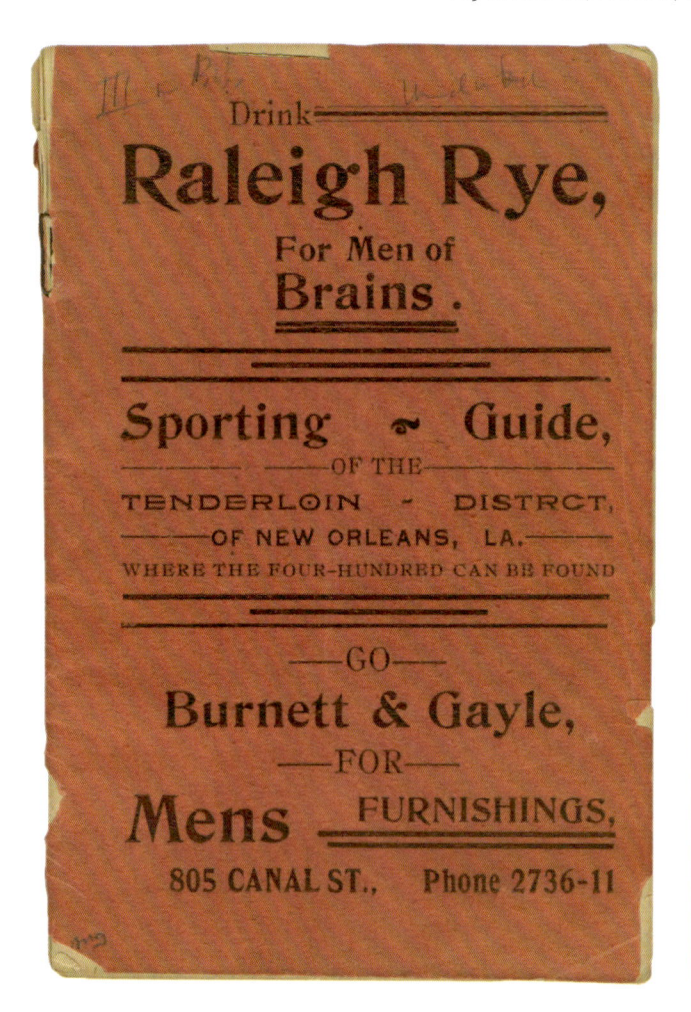

The uncredited "Introductory" that opens this guide is probably the most straightforward in any of the blue books in projecting an illusion of the elite: "This volumn [sic] is published for the benefit of the upper 'Four Hundred' who desire to visit the Tenderloin District with safety and obtain the desired pleasure accruing from beauty and pleasure, which can be accomplished by following this guide." This book lacks a directory section, and is composed largely of advertisements. The first and last four pages are ruled and have the word "Memorandum" at the top of each.

This guide was likely published in 1902. Burnett and Gayle, a men's clothing store that advertised on the cover of this guide, appears in the

BIBLIOGRAPHY | 114

### FRENCH PALLACE STUDIO.

Miss Emma Johnson is the proprietor of the French Pallace Studio, No. 331 North Basin Street, and it has the name of being the only Frst-Class house of this kind in the city and the boys who are acquainted with Emma's Palace, will say the same. Here are some of the handsome all round young entertainers who are always willing and ready:

Miss Ella Smith,
" Andry Duyon,
" Earl Wesley,
" Flossey Nickless,
" Allice Shermann,
" Lucial Davies,
" Margarette DeFerandy,
" Violet DeMagmette,
" Josephine Joe,
" Emily Erwin,
" Marrie Jacobs,

### MISS ANTONIA P. GONZALES.

### 217 N. Basin Street.

Miss Antouia P. Gonzales is the only Cornetist Songsertress Dancer and Violinest in the Tenderloin District. Miss Antonia herself plays the Cornet and Violin and in fact she is an all round entertainer; also has some beautiful girls. Here are some of her bells:

Miss Lilian McLean,
" Josephine Madison,
" Daisy Allan,
" Marie DeSantos,
" Irma Meyers.

---

New Orleans city directories only between 1902 and 1904. Antonia P. Gonzales, who is identified as the landlady of 217 N. Basin in this issue, is listed at that address in the 1902 and 1903 New Orleans city directories. By the time the 1903 *Blue Book* (No. 3) was printed, Gonzales had moved her operation to Villere Street, at the corner of Customhouse, supporting the idea that *Sporting Guide* was issued before 1903.

Full-page madams' advertisements similar to those found in *Blue Book* follow the introduction in no particular order, each with extravagant descriptions of cultivated landladies and costly furnishings, as well as

---

### MISS JESSIE BROWN,

### 1542 Customhonse Street.

Miss Jessie Brown who is running the Mansion at 1542 Customhouse Street, has one of the cossiest and finest furnished appartments and she is without doubt one of the best fellow you ever met. She has a good word for every body. Miss Brown has only been keeping house a short while as she comes direct from Chicago and she did not fail to bring some of the finest girls there was to be found and for entertaining they can't be beat. Here are their names.

Mess Camille Reims,
Ruth Jordan,
Mary Howard,
Nellie Jerome,
Lula Walker.

### MISS BERTHA GOLDEN,

The Egyptian Princess,
from Alexandria, Egypt.

NOW AT
### 213 N. Basin street.

Miss Bertha Golden who was formerly with the Sam T. Jacks Tenderloin Company who was at the old St. Charles Theatre three years ago and created such an excitement with her muscle dance and living pictures, and who has traveled all over the world with the above and several other companies, and holds the world record, is now at 213 Basin street. To convince yourself, give her a call and we will assure you that she can't be beat. She also has some of the most beautiful entertainers. Here are some of the names:

Miss Josie Freeman, housekeeper,
Clara Fass, Ollie Burk Wilson,
Mamie Alexander, Geraldine Cadot,
Minnie McLain, Annie Stevenson,
Audrey Andrews, Vivian Garrett,
Louise Marks.

a casual disregard for correct spelling and punctuation. Most of these advertisements conclude with listings of the "beautiful entertainers" and "young, charming, and well cultivated ladies" housed therein. Ten madams and sixty-four women are named in these ads. Illustrating the appeal of new women from outside the District is a half-page ad for "Misses Isabell & Mabell," which announces that they "have just arrived from New York." Bertha Golden is hailed as "The Egyptian Princess, from Alexandria, Egypt," emphasizing the exotic. A particularly cavalier approach to spelling is presented in ads for Nettie Green, the "propprietress of one of the finest asignation house in the city," and Emma Johnson, sometimes identified as "French Emma," who was in charge of the French Pallace Studio. Only a single photograph appears in the book: a small portrait of Willie V. Piazza (called "the most charming young Landlady of Basin street" in her ad on a previous page) wearing a high-collared, printed dress with her hair upswept under a stylish hat.

In addition to the advertisements for rye and men's clothing on the front cover and for florist J. W. Davis on the back cover, this guide contains half-page advertisements for three saloons, including Anderson's Annex. On a page near the end of this guide is a brief list of phone numbers for a few of the larger brothels and saloons. The bottom of this page features the warning, "This book not mailable." Heartman states that this is the first such reference to postal restrictions determined by the Comstock Law to appear in the Storyville guides[16]; however, this warning appears in an early edition of *Blue Book*, likely published in 1901 (No. 2). Heartman also includes a photograph of a two-page spread from this book on page 45 of his bibliography.

THE

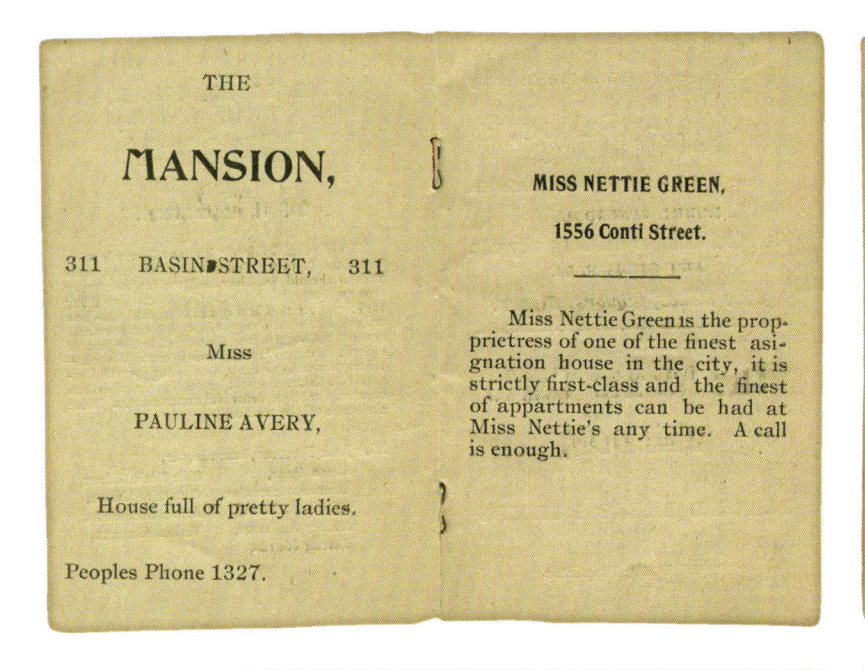

MANSION,

311   BASIN STREET,   311

Miss

PAULINE AVERY,

House full of pretty ladies.

Peoples Phone 1327.

---

**MISS NETTIE GREEN,**

1556 Conti Street.

Miss Nettie Green is the proprietress of one of the finest asignation house in the city, it is strictly first-class and the finest of appartments can be had at Miss Nettie's any time. A call is enough.

---

Don't forget to drop in and see the **Pretty Pictures** in the

**Viking Saloon,**

H. L. SPURGEON, Prop.

in your Rounds to or from the Tenderloin.

LADIES WINE ROOM.

Cor. Customhouse and Burgundy Sts.
NEW ORLEANS, LA.

**Fine Wines, Liquors, Cigars.**

**The Monte Carlo SALOON,**

BASIN AND BIENVILLE STREETS

FRANK TURO, Proprietor.

---

**MISS OLLIE NICHLES,**

221 N. Basin stret.

Phone 1663.

Speaking of the many landladies on Basin street, Miss Ollie Nichles is one of the youngest and most handsome landladies in the business. Miss Nichles has appeared before the better class of sporting gentlemen of this community, and never has her reputation been other than a highly cultivated lady. As an entertainer and for keeping the best entertainers that can be got, and for conversational acquirements she has no aqual. So, when you go out for a good hot time don't overlook her house. The beautiful women therein are,—

Misses Nellie Levand, of Atlanta,
    Sadie McLain, New York,
    Ethel Gilmore, Beaumont, Texas,
    Gladys Morton, Minneapolis,
    Hilda McLain, St. Louis,
    Mabel Shaw, Chicago,
    Alma Ellis, Atlanta,
    Gertrude VonClare, Canada.

---

**MISS DOROTHY DENNING,**

313 N. Basin street.

Miss Dorothy Denning is now located at 313 N. Basin, her new mansion, which is without doubt one of the most exquisitely furnished apartments on Basin street, everything being of new make. Her paintings and cut glass, is certainly a grand selection. Miss Denning is the most beautiful, young, handsome and charming Landlady in the Tenderloin, and all her girls are of the same type. She keeps nothing but young, charming and well cultivated ladies, and one visit means remembrance always. Here are her stars:

Miss Lillian Erwin,
  " Alice Knott,
  " Daisy Harris,
  " Marie Best,
  " Lela Roadery,
  " Carrie Stevens,
  " Vivian Stewart,
  " Virgil Opal.

---

Everybody Knows

**Anderson's Annex . . . .**

CUSTOMHOUSE AND BASIN STS.

**MISSES ISABELL & MABELL,**
1417 Customhouse St.

**ANNOUNCEMENT!**

That there are two of the swellest girls to be found in the Tenderloin, at present, running the House 1417 Customhouse St. Boys if you are looking for fine treatment and good lookers, call on these two girls, their names are

**ISABELL & MABELL.**

These two girls have just arrived from New York.

---

**A FEW PHONES.**

| | |
|---|---|
| OLLIE NICHOLS | 1663 |
| DOROTHY DENNING | 3554 |
| JESSIE BROWN | 3235 |
| BERTHA GOLDEN | 1892 |
| JOSIE ARLINGTON | 1888 |
| THE MANSION | 1327 |
| FLO MEEKER | 14-24 |
| PAULINE AVERY | 169 |
| FRANK TORO | 2575 |
| ANDERSON'S | 28-28-12 |
| ANDERSON'S ANNEX | 31-0-9 |

—x—

(This book not mailable.)

---

MEMORANDUM.

---

**Notice.**

Want everybody to know that J. W. DAVIS, The Florist, will be open by the first of December for business, with the best cut flowers the Chicago Market affords, such as Carnations, Ferns, Brides and Bridesmaids Violets, Etc.

The cheapest cut flowers in the city.

805 Canal St., Cor. Burbon.

Phone............

ALTERNATIVE STORYVILLE-ERA GUIDES

# No. 14
## *HELL-O*

Printed in black ink on cherry-red paper.
No edition number, undated [1903]. 8 unnumbered pages.

7.3 cm × 5.8 cm, *THNOC*, 1969.19.2 (Heartman II)

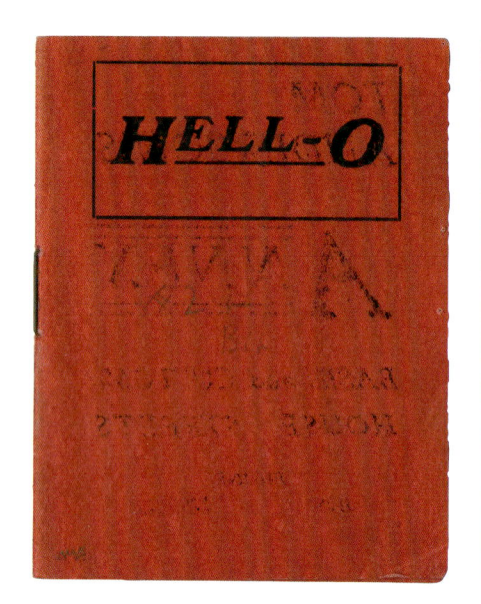

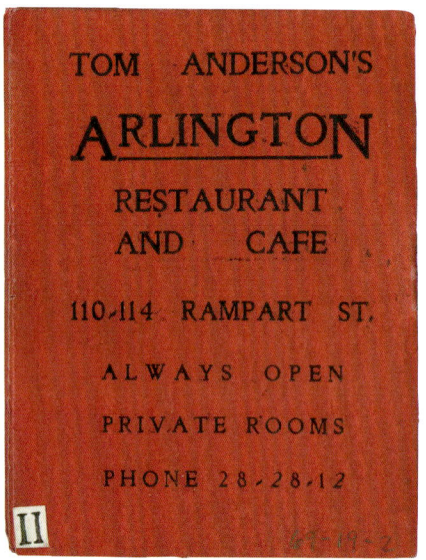

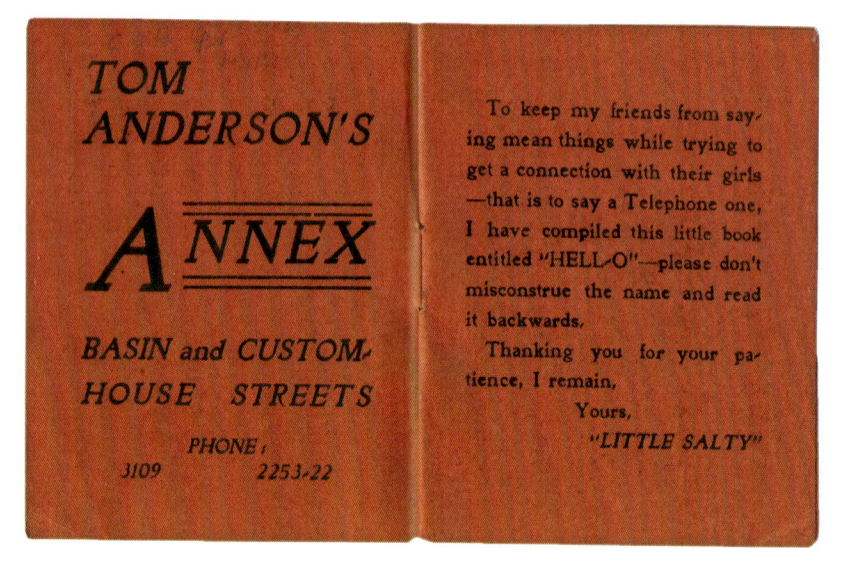

There are no elaborate, descriptive advertisements for madams in this tiny guidebook, printed entirely on cherry-red paper. The three advertisements in *Hell-O* are all for businesses owned by Tom Anderson—Anderson's Annex, corner Basin and Customhouse Streets; Anderson's Stag at Gravier Street, opposite the St. Charles Hotel; and Anderson's Arlington Restaurant and Cafe, at 110–14 Rampart. Anderson opened the Annex in 1901, so this guide couldn't have been produced prior to that year.[17] The addresses of three madams listed in *Hell-O*—Nina Jackson, Ray Owens, and Mai Tuckerman—match their addresses as given in the 1903 *Blue Book* (No. 3). Tuckerman's address is further corroborated by the 1903 city directory (where her first name is spelled May), which suggests that this book was produced in 1903. An argument for an earlier date might be Antonia Gonzales's listing at 217 N. Basin, her address in 1902; by the time the 1903 *Blue Book* was published, she had moved her operations to Villere, at the corner of Customhouse.

*Hell-O*'s brief introduction is signed "Little Salty." He states that he has compiled the guide in order to aid "friends" "trying to get a connection with their girls—that is to say a Telephone one." Regarding the title of his publication, he begs his readers "please don't misconstrue the name and read it backwards." Whether "Little Salty" was responsible for two later issues in this format, "*The Lid*" and "*The Scout*," may never be known, but Struve and Anderson are the likely men behind the pseudonym. After all, the only advertisements are for Anderson's establishments, and Struve was his right-hand man. These no-frills guidebooks, having only basic information, were small enough to be concealed, perhaps in a memorandum book, and were certainly less bulky than the full-size *Blue Book* that Struve was producing simultaneously.

Thirty-one women from Basin, Conti, Villere, Bienville, and Customhouse (now Iberville) Streets are listed, some with phone numbers. Six of these women appear on a separate page under the heading "Octoroons." Probably all are madams; many of the women listed have been previously identified as madams in other Storyville-era blue books, and this small guide seems to have been complied as a quick reference to the District. One establishment, the Firm, appears only by name, at 223 Villere Street, and one woman, Lizzie Curtis, is listed well outside of the confines of Storyville, at 420 Howard Street.

Heartman includes a photograph of a two-page spread from this small guide on page 43 of his bibliography. A fake version of *Hell-O* appeared in the mid-1960s (see No. 17).

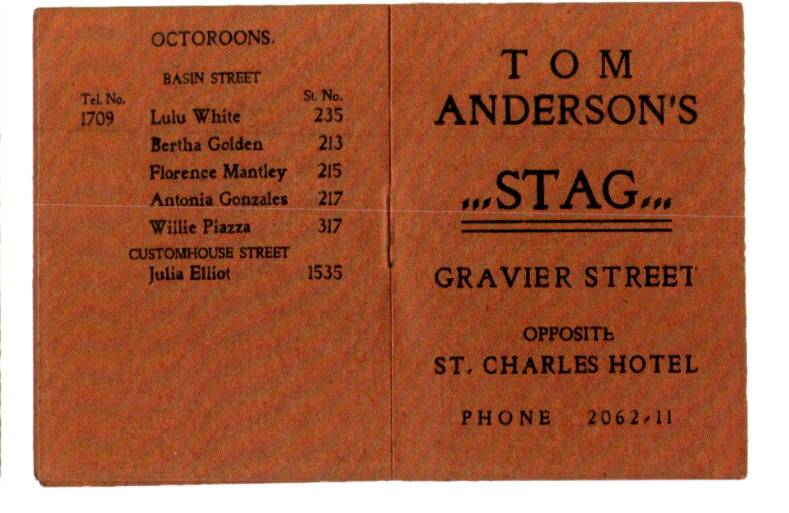

FAKES AND FACSIMILES

# No. 16

FROM THE SCARLET PAST | of fabulous NEW ORLEANS | SOUVENIR EDITION | OF THE WORLD FAMOUS TENDERLOIN DIRECTORY | 'THE BLUEBOOK' | with a brief | STORY OF STORYVILLE

Cover printed in black ink on tan, textured paper; interior pages printed in black ink on plain paper.
New Orleans: Thurman W. Reeves, 1951. 20 unnumbered pages.

15.9 cm × 9.5 cm, *THNOC, 77-1371-RL*

15.9 cm × 9.5 cm, *THNOC, 1969.19.14*

15.9 cm × 9.5 cm, *THNOC, 77-2347-RL*

15.9 cm × 9.5 cm, *THNOC, 85-224-RL*

15.9 cm × 9.5 cm, *THNOC, William Russell Jazz Collection, MSS 536, 92-48-L.62.484*

15.9 cm × 9.5 cm, *THNOC, T130701.1513.10*

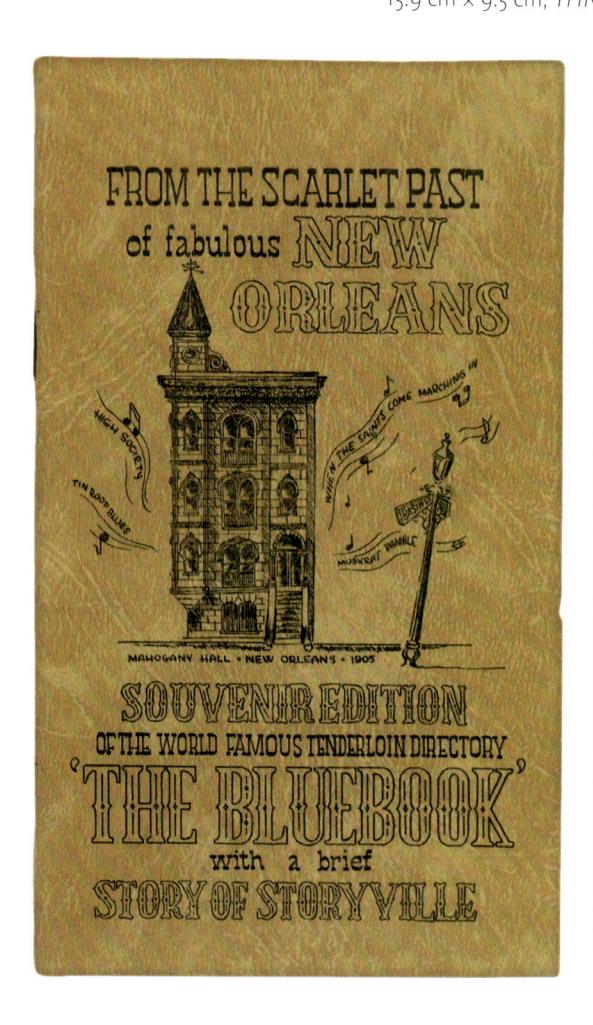

Thurman W. Reeves (1906–1966) published this hodgepodge souvenir booklet in 1951. *From the Scarlet Past* contains a brief history of Storyville and short essays on the blue books, with emphasis on Lulu White and her brothel. It reproduces many pages from White's souvenir booklet *New Mahogany Hall* (No. 11), featuring photographs and

BIBLIOGRAPHY | 122

descriptions of her prostitutes. Photographs of the covers of two *Blue Book* editions (Nos. 2 and 5) are also included. Most of Reeves's casual observations are unencumbered by historical research, but he does make a point about the continuing appeal of these little directories: "Blue Books today are considered rare Americana, and are consequently choice collectors' items. Demand for them is far greater than the supply, and incredible though it may sound, originals command prices exceeding some of our great classics of literature. Believe it or not."

Reeves was born September 16, 1906, in Laurel, Mississippi, to Thomas W. and Viola Reeves. He married Jessie Price, had three daughters, and resided for much of his life in Hattiesburg, where he was a machinist and operated Reeves Auto Shop. He died in New Orleans on June 23, 1966, and was buried in Laurel, Mississippi.[19] He appears in a 1949 New Orleans city directory as a machinist for American Bakeries. No New Orleans city directories were published for the years 1950 and 1951, around the time of this pamphlet's publication. Hattiesburg city directories place him in that city between 1953 and 1963. In 1956, his entry notes that he is a mechanic at Higgins Industries in New Orleans, and from 1959 through 1963, entries list him as an employee at Ingalls Shipbuilding firm in Pascagoula, although he still resided in Hattiesburg. After 1964, he is not listed in either Hattiesburg or New Orleans city directories.[20] A brief 1951 article in the *Times-Picayune* reports that Reeves "recently did much research on the original 'Blue Books' of New Orleans," but says nothing of his publication or anything further about him.[21] This little booklet about the blue books apparently is the only item Reeves published. To produce it, he must have owned or had access to authentic Storyville guides, especially Lulu White's *New Mahogany Hall*, since that work is reproduced so extensively.

The Historic New Orleans Collection owns several copies of *From the Scarlet Past*. One copy (1969.19.14) belonged to collector Thomas W. Streeter and was part of lot 4290 in Streeter's posthumous auction, purchased in 1969 by L. Kemper Williams, which formed the foundation of THNOC's holdings on prostitution. Another (92-48-L.62.484) in the extensive William Russell Jazz Collection, composed of items relating to early New Orleans jazz music and musicians, is inscribed "To Bill Russell Best Regards Thurman W. Reeves."

**FAKES AND FACSIMILES**

# No. 17
## HELL-O

Cover and interior printed in black ink on dark red-orange paper.
No edition number, undated [mid-1960s]. 8 unnumbered pages.

*7.5 cm × 5.6 cm, THNOC, William Russell Jazz Collection, MSS 536, 92-48-L.62.488*

At first glance, this seems to be a copy of the Storyville-era *Hell-O* (No. 14). However, aspects of its production suggest that it is a fake printed in the mid-1960s. It is significantly different from the copy of *Hell-O* noted in Heartman's bibliography and acquired for THNOC by General Williams from the Thomas W. Streeter sale in 1969. The red paper it is printed on is of a slightly different hue and texture from the original, and it uses a different typeface. The title, specific lettering of the first ad, and the name "Little Salty" are not italicized, as they are in the genuine *Hell-O*, and the letterspacing causes the text to wrap differently. These differences cause me to believe that this is a fake.

According to local printer and publisher Justin D. Winston, who also published in the 1970s under the pseudonym Faruk von Turk, this book was produced as part of an elaborate ruse played upon Al Rose in 1965.[22] Apparently it worked, because this fake is photographically represented in full as a genuine Storyville-era blue book on page 134 of Rose's *Storyville, New Orleans*, and two copies are included in his papers at the Hogan Jazz Archive at Tulane University. In the late 1990s, a private collector found more than fifty copies of this publication in a small box at a garage sale in Metairie, a suburb of New Orleans.

BIBLIOGRAPHY | 124

## TOM ANDERSON'S ANNEX

BASIN and CUSTOMHOUSE STREETS

PHONE:
3109    2253-22

---

To keep my friends from saying mean things while trying to get a connection with their girls—that is to say a Telephone one, I have compiled this little book entitled "HELL-O" — please don't misconstrue the name and read it backwards.

Thanking you for your patience, I remain,

Yours,

"LITTLE SALTY"

---

### BASIN STREET

| Tel. No. | | St. No. |
|---|---|---|
| 211 | Flo Meeker | 1424 |
| 1663 | Ollie Nicholls | 221 |
| 788 | Grace Simpson | 223 |
| 1888 | Josie Arlington | 227 |
| 167 | Pauline Avery | 311 |
| 3554 | Dorothy Denning | 313 |

### CONTI STREET

| Tel. No. | | St. No. |
|---|---|---|
| 1793 | Ray Owens | 1306 |
| 1114 | Mrs. Barron | 1320 |
| | Nina Jackson & Co. | 1418 |
| | Gypsy Shaeffer | 1414 |
| 1406 | Maud Livingston | 1550 |
| 1786 | Alice Thompson | 1558 |
| 1810 | Garnet Runiart | 1548 |

### VILLERE STREET

| Tel. No. | | St. No. |
|---|---|---|
| | The Firm | 223 |

### BIENVILLE STREET

| Tel. No. | | St. No. |
|---|---|---|
| 766 | Lou Prout | 1551 |
| 1558 | Maud David | 1632 |

### N. ROBERTSON STREET

| Tel. No. | | St. No. |
|---|---|---|
| 2913-22 | Cora Isaacs | 328 |

### CUSTOMHOUSE STREET

| Tel. No. | | St. No. |
|---|---|---|
| 1024 | Camille Lewis | 1559 |
| 3235 | Jessie Brown | 1542 |
| 1973 | Jennie Hope | 1540 |
| | May Smith | 1538 |
| 3427 | Fanny Lambert | 1547 |
| 1715 | May O'Brien | 1549 |
| | Alice Heard | 1535 |

### ST. LOUIS STREET

| Tel. No. | | St. No. |
|---|---|---|
| 1944 | Mai Tuckerman | 1424 |

### HOWARD STREET

| Tel. No. | | St. No. |
|---|---|---|
| 1670 | Lizzie Curtis | 420 |

---

## OCTOROONS

### BASIN STREET

| Tel. No. | | St. No. |
|---|---|---|
| 1709 | Lulu White | 235 |
| | Bertha Golden | 213 |
| | Florence Mantley | 215 |
| | Antonia Gonzales | 217 |
| | Willie Piazza | 317 |

### CUSTOMHOUSE STREET

| | Julia Elliot | 1535 |
|---|---|---|

---

## TOM ANDERSON'S ...STAG...

GRAVIER STREET

OPPOSITE
ST. CHARLES HOTEL

PHONE 2062-11

FAKES AND FACSIMILES

# No. 18

### The | Blue | Book | GUIDE TO PLEASURE | For Visitors to the Gay City | Directory to the Red-Light District | of New Orleans in the Gay Nineties

Cover printed in black ink on medium blue paper; interior printed in black ink on heavy paper.
1963. 80 unnumbered pages.

16.2 cm × 10 cm, *THNOC, William Russell Jazz Collection, MSS 536, 92-48-L.62.483*

Cover printed in black ink on pale blue paper; interior printed in black ink on heavy paper.
Undated [1963?]. 80 unnumbered pages.

15.9 cm × 10.2 cm, *THNOC, gift of Linda Kaplan, 2006.0423*

The two copies of this fake—based on a genuine ninth-edition *Blue Book* (No. 7)—in THNOC's holdings are slightly different. A copy in the William Russell Jazz Collection has "© 1963" printed on its cover. The second copy has no printed date, and several of the pages toward the middle of the book appear in a different order. Both have fewer pages than the original (the genuine No. 7 has 94 pages) and present these

BIBLIOGRAPHY | 126

### Miss Lulu White

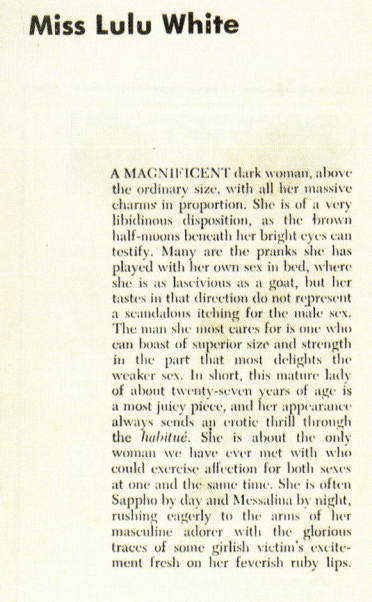

A MAGNIFICENT dark woman, above the ordinary size, with all her massive charms in proportion. She is of a very libidinous disposition, as the brown half-moons beneath her bright eyes can testify. Many are the pranks she has played with her own sex in bed, where she is as lascivious as a goat, but her tastes in that direction do not represent a scandalous itching for the male sex. The man she most cares for is one who can boast of superior size and strength in the part that most delights the weaker sex. In short, this mature lady of about twenty-seven years of age is a most juicy piece, and her appearance always sends an erotic thrill through the *habitué*. She is about the only woman we have ever met with who could exercise affection for both sexes at one and the same time. She is often Sappho by day and Messalina by night, rushing eagerly to the arms of her masculine adorer with the glorious traces of some girlish victim's excitement fresh on her feverish ruby lips.

**235 N. Basin**

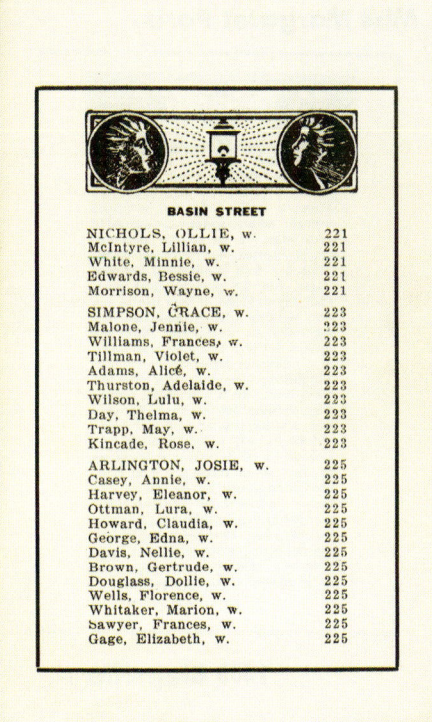

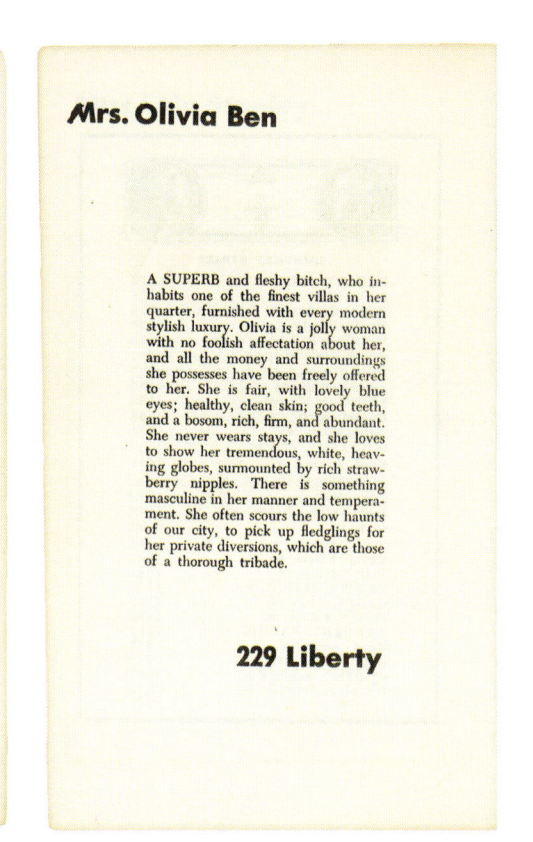

---

**BASIN STREET**

| | |
|---|---|
| NICHOLS, OLLIE, w. | 221 |
| McIntyre, Lillian, w. | 221 |
| White, Minnie, w. | 221 |
| Edwards, Bessie, w. | 221 |
| Morrison, Wayne, w. | 221 |
| SIMPSON, GRACE, w. | 223 |
| Malone, Jennie, w. | 223 |
| Williams, Frances, w. | 223 |
| Tillman, Violet, w. | 223 |
| Adams, Alice, w. | 223 |
| Thurston, Adelaide, w. | 223 |
| Wilson, Lulu, w. | 223 |
| Day, Thelma, w. | 223 |
| Trapp, May, w. | 223 |
| Kincade, Rose, w. | 223 |
| ARLINGTON, JOSIE, w. | 225 |
| Casey, Annie, w. | 225 |
| Harvey, Eleanor, w. | 225 |
| Ottman, Lura, w. | 225 |
| Howard, Claudia, w. | 225 |
| George, Edna, w. | 225 |
| Davis, Nellie, w. | 225 |
| Brown, Gertrude, w. | 225 |
| Douglass, Dollie, w. | 225 |
| Wells, Florence, w. | 225 |
| Whitaker, Marion, w. | 225 |
| Sawyer, Frances, w. | 225 |
| Gage, Elizabeth, w. | 225 |

---

### Mrs. Olivia Ben

A SUPERB and fleshy bitch, who inhabits one of the finest villas in her quarter, furnished with every modern stylish luxury. Olivia is a jolly woman with no foolish affectation about her, and all the money and surroundings she possesses have been freely offered to her. She is fair, with lovely blue eyes; healthy, clean skin; good teeth, and a bosom, rich, firm, and abundant. She never wears stays, and she loves to show her tremendous, white, heaving globes, surmounted by rich strawberry nipples. There is something masculine in her manner and temperament. She often scours the low haunts of our city, to pick up fledglings for her private diversions, which are those of a thorough tribade.

**229 Liberty**

---

pages out of order. None of the photographs of brothel interiors in the original are reproduced here. The introductory page that identifies the original as the ninth edition can be seen in both copies.

The most striking difference between this publication and No. 7 becomes apparent when several of the full-page madams' ads are examined. Fifteen decidedly fake ads—most replacing the photographs of brothel interiors that appear in the original—are interspersed with reproductions of thirteen genuine ads. How can the fake ones be identified? For one, the typography and overall design of the fake ads are different: the genuine ads may include phone numbers, frames, or decorative fleurons, but the fake ones do not employ any of these elements. For another, phrases in these ads such as "lascivious as a goat," "a most juicy piece," "insignificant actress whores," "plump, firm bottom," "take her in the rear," "fleshy bitch," and "tantalizing nipples" are not seen in any genuine Storyville guides that I have examined. Perhaps the producer of this cut-and-paste book felt that the all-too-tame ninth edition needed some spice to further titillate a mid-twentieth-century purchaser of such a souvenir.

In Storyville-era blue books, there are almost no detailed physical descriptions of madams in their advertisements, and no specific descriptions of any special sexual talents. Interestingly, this facsimile contains two ads—one genuine and one fake—for the same madam, Cora DeWitt. The genuine ninth-edition ad describes DeWitt as "the mistress of a first-class establishment" and a "whole-soled [sic] member of the fair sex who is sterling and a jolly good fellow." A few pages earlier, the fake ad calls her "a frank and genial whore, who carries on her trade without disguise, and glories in her shame" and emphasizes "her small, hard, pointed breasts," concluding, "The warm place at her side in bed is never without a wealthy occupier." Though the genuine ad describes the women who worked for her as "jolly good girls," the fake ad makes no mention of these women, only fabricates sexual attributes for DeWitt. Margaret Bradford also has two ads in this fake, and both are genuine (a quirk of the ninth edition *Blue Book*, No. 7).

The directory section of this book is unaltered and matches that found in No. 7. In creating the fake ads, the compiler sometimes took the names of actual madams and wrote new, more scandalous copy for them. Other fake ads feature the names of women listed in the directory as prostitutes, rather than madams. There is one exception. The very last ad in this booklet written in the more salacious style is for Maria Henry, who "possesses every vice in the harlot's catalogue." Her name does not appear in the directory, and her address, "7, Avenue Victor Hugo," would place her on a notable thoroughfare in Paris's sixteenth arrondissement near the Arc de Triomphe. Victor Hugo has never been the name of a street in New Orleans. This cavalier attitude toward the accuracy of names and addresses is a holdover from the genuine blue books.

## Miss Cora DeWitt

CORA, as all the boys call her, needs but little to tell that she is the mistress of a first-class establishment.

Here is one whole-soled member of the fair sex who is sterling and a jolly good fellow.

No one knows what a good, jovial person Cora is until they have had the pleasure of meeting and forming her acquaintance.

She also has a lot of jolly good girls as guests, who are the "goods," as one would term them. Don't overlook Cora.

PHONE 3884 MAIN

**1537 Iberville**

## Miss Cora Dewit

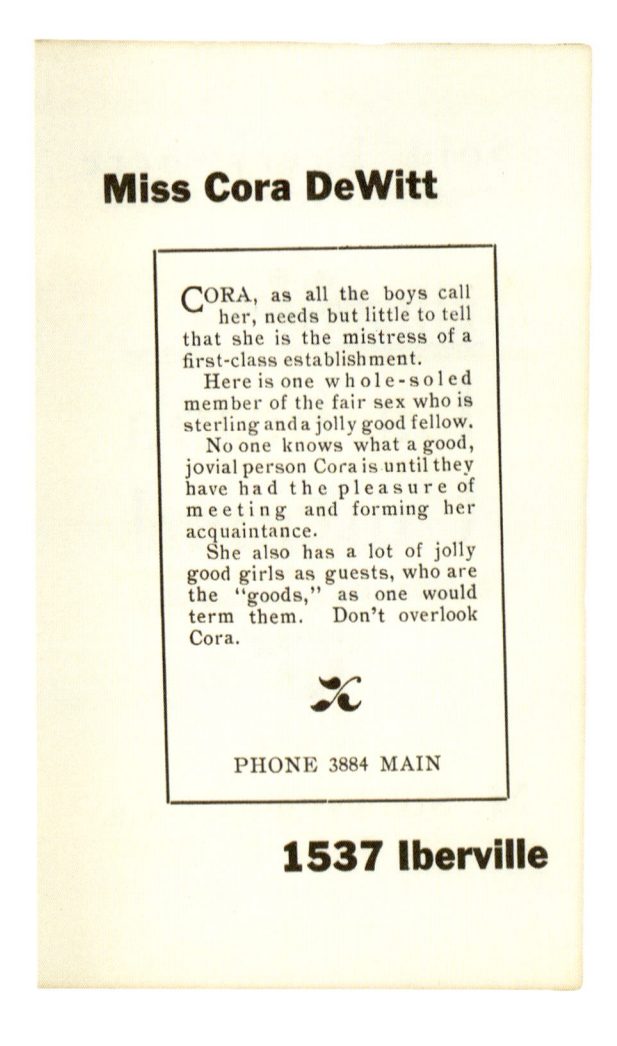

A FRANK and genial whore, who carries on her trade without disguise, and glories in her shame. She is about four-and twenty; short; plump; with nice, dark eyes, and sweeping eyelashes that shine out with renewed luster, as her raven locks are dyed fair. She comes from the south, and is very well made, while her small, hard, pointed breasts must meet with the approval of all *connoisseurs* of a jolly, devil-may-care disposition. The warm place at her side in bed is never without a wealthy occupier.

**1535 Iberville**

### Miss Isabelle Joiner

SHE is one of the most ferocious tribades in N.O. She is as pale as an aristocratic lady of fashion; with chestnut hair, worn in plain bands on her forehead, and her eyes are like those of a cat, being as green and deep as the sea. Her mouth is superb, with full, luscious lips of rosy tint, and teeth of alabaster whiteness. Indeed, such eyes and such teeth are enough to make the fortune of any woman, and Isabelle does a deal of business and earns plenty of money. Her person is slight, well-built, and she is very graceful in her manner. She was born in an obscure country village some twenty-six years ago, and at the age of fifteen was debauched by a yokel, in a field of rising corn. A fervent priestess of Venus, she is capable of offering twenty sacrifices in one night on the altar of love, and all the money she gets from the men, she offers to any woman who takes her fancy, keeping herself foolishly poor.

### 1204 Iberville

### Mrs. Saidie Gold

SHE is of middle height, she looks thin till undressed, but her beautiful bosom, and plump, firm bottom soon draw a cry of astonished delight from the lucky amateur. Her figure is incomparably fine, and her skin is of wonderful texture, causing her robust thighs to feel like satin to the touch. Her hair and eyes are dark brown, the eyebrows are black, and she has a lovely mouth, with a most sensual upper lip. Her age is now about twenty-six, and she is just the piece required for a right down, reckless rake, who wants a mistress who will refuse him absolutely nothing, but cheerfully bow to his every whim, even when he tries to realize, as much as possible, the ardent, but cruel pastimes of a Tiberius or a Caligula.

### 1216 Iberville

### Miss H. Camille

WE do not believe that a more ugly, insignificant little black thing has ever trod the common path. She has made a meteor-like appearance and we can only ascribe the share of worship she receives to the glamor thrown round a woman by the footlights. But no girl need ever despair in this city, as long as she is not squeamish in bed, but will sigh, "I love you!" to every man, whether he be a handsome youth, fresh from a bath of perfume, or a hoary old sniffer, who abhors soap and water. Camille lives with a poor clerk, earning a few dollars weekly, but the indigent scribe carefully keeps in the background, while his mistress is earning the wherewithal to buy her unscrupulous Romeo a winter coat.

### 1527 Iberville

### Miss Lulu Stanley

A YOUNG, dark, slight actress, who is very expert in the numerous ramifications of her art. She shows at her best when the visitor chooses her ruby mouth as the altar on which to pour out his sacrifice to Venus, and is exceedingly smart when the *blasé* amateur implores her to take up a bunch of twigs, adorned with colored ribbons, and gaily whip him along the road to pleasure. The most aristocratic bums have bled with joy beneath her tingling birch, and her lectures to her grown-up pupils are fantastic and eloquent in the extreme.

### 218 Liberty

### Miss Dollie Dollars

THIS is another of the insignificant actress whores, who crowd the stage, and are always ready to receive the spectators after their performance. This lump of lechery is a third-rate opera-bouffe girl; small, dark, and thin; with a pointed nose, and an agreeable bearing. She has been passed from hand to hand for the last five or six years, so that she thoroughly knows her business, and is expert in the art of pleasing a man of slightly salacious tastes.

### 226 Villere

### Miss Maria Henry

A CHARMING, baby face, with lovely eyes, pretty little nose, teeth like a terrier's, and chestnut locks, not disfigured by hair dye. Her charms are in symmetrical proportion, but her breasts and buttocks are soft; now about twenty-eight, has been for some years the toy of the general public. She possesses every vice in the harlot's catalogue, being an inveterate sucker of women's seed, and a facile Ganymede for rich sodomites. She will obey the orders of all who can afford to pay very highly to play with her softened globes, or recline on her flabby belly.

### 7, Avenue Victor Hugo

**FAKES AND FACSIMILES**

# No. 20
### Blue Book | *TENDERLOIN* | "400."

Cover printed in black ink on medium-blue paper; interior pages printed in black ink on calendered paper. Undated [1970s]. 24 unnumbered pages.

*14.1 cm × 11 cm, THNOC, gift of Friends of Jefferson Public Library, 2003.0268*

---

Although the cover design of this book is a reduced version of the early *Blue Book* featuring a lady with a fan (No. 1), the facsimile pages are from the edition with the inverted lyre and lilies motif on the cover (No. 9). The book was printed for the Institute of Louisiana Music and Folklore (ILMF), a nonprofit organization formed in 1974. The center spread states that ILMF, "through film and other media, attempts to preserve and document aspects of our unique Louisiana heritage."[26] With its smeared pages, this poorly executed reprint appears to have been produced quickly, perhaps intended as a souvenir for distribution at ILMF-sponsored events. Interspersed with seven facsimile full-page madams' advertisements are contemporary ads for several local businesses active in the 1970s, including Antoine's Restaurant, WDSU-TV, and Napoleon House. One of these, Loubat, a kitchen equipment supplier, actually advertised in the Storyville-era guides. Loubat's ad in this book reproduces elements of its *Blue Book* ad from 1912 (No. 9).

BIBLIOGRAPHY | 132

### 'ALWAYS GOOD'

**Molly's Irish Pub**

732 TOULOUSE STREET
1107 DECATUR STREET
NEW ORLEANS, LA.

JIM & CAROL MONAGHAN

---

### FIRST IN NEW ORLEANS

**6 WDSU-TV**
NEW ORLEANS

---

### Voodoo Museum

Finest Gris-Gris from Original Recipes

††††††

Expert
Palm ◊ Tarot ◊ Gypsy
Readings

Wholesale ◊ Retail
Open 7 days – 10 a.m. to Midnight
739 Rue Bourbon
Telephone 523-2906     New Orleans, La.

---

The Largest Glassware & Crockery House in the South....

We carry a full line of Cut Glass, Cutlery, Dinnerware, Silverware and Kitchen Utensils

**THE LOUBAT GLASSWARE & CORK CO.**
LIMITED
510 to 516 Bienville Street

---

### Miss May Evans

Miss Evans is one woman among the fair sex who is regarded as an all-round jolly good fellow, and one who is always laughing and making all those around her do likewise.

While nothing is too good for May, she is admired and befriended by all who come in contact with her.

May recently erected a handsome mansion in North Franklin Street, that would be beautiful on Fifth Avenue, New York, or on one of the boulevards about Chicago or Philadelphia. See for yourself.

May has the honor of keeping one of the quietest establishments in the city, where beautiful women, good wine and sweet music reign supreme.

What more can a person expect? Just think of it! "Pretty women, wine and song."

In the palace of a king one could not expect more.

The signal of "May's" mansion is: "Let's all live and enjoy life while we can."

PHONE 1190 MAIN

**315 N. Franklin**

---

### Napoleon House
*Since 1797*

Enjoy your favorite drink while listening to our collection of classical recordings.

**500 CHARTRES ST.
NEW ORLEANS, LA.**

---

A list of supporters for ILMF's events includes the *Vieux Carré Courier*, a French Quarter newspaper that ceased publication in 1978. Another ad gives a clue as to when this book was produced—one for Orleans Medalarts, which states that it made a medal for the 1975 Port of New Orleans Storyville Ball. This fake was likely produced sometime between 1974 and 1978, perhaps by another listed supporter, Von Turk's Offel Offset.

FAKES AND FACSIMILES

# No. 22

## Blue Book

Cover printed in dark blue ink on light gray paper with bluish threads incorporated throughout; interior printed in black ink on plain paper. Undated [1970s]. 96 unnumbered pages.

14.6 cm × 10.6 cm, *THNOC, William Russell Jazz Collection, MSS 536, 92-48-L.62.487*

A slightly different fake based upon the Storyville-era No. 9 features the inverted lyre and lilies design on the cover, done in dark blue ink on light gray paper with bluish threads incorporated throughout the stock. As seems to be typical of these fakes, the pages are not in the same order as they are in the original. Hilma Burt's is the first of the madams' ads in this book (Josie Arlington's ad is first in the source material), but the directory listings are in the correct order, beginning with white prostitutes whose surnames start with "A."

However, the creators of this fake did make an effort to include authentic details. Unlike some other fakes based on No. 9, this copy reproduces the advertisements appearing on the inside front cover (Veuve Clicquot), inside back cover (Little Arlington Cafe and Oyster House), and back cover (Paddock Dry Gin and Tube Rose Rye Whisky) of the original. In addition, most fakes are stapled through the center of the book block; this publication is side stitched through the left edge, with the cover glued over the staples, like copies of the genuine *Blue Book* are.

This fake is one of the approximately 16,000 items in the William Russell Jazz Collection. Russell's extensive collection of documents and memorabilia includes many of his notes about individual pieces. One of his typed notes filed with (but not attached to or inserted in) this copy states, "This Monochrome reproduction of the 1909 Bluebook was produced by The New Orleans Jazz Museum and Mr. George E. Anding from an original in the collection of Mr. Al Rose and printed by Minit Printit, Inc." He seems to have changed his mind about the source date at some point: on the cover of his copy, Russell wrote the year 1909, then scratched it out and wrote "prob 1910–1911." I believe his copy was based on No. 9, which I argue was printed in 1912. The rest of the information in Russell's note helps us date this fake. The New Orleans Jazz Museum opened in 1961 and went bankrupt in 1973. After a period in storage, its collections were donated to the Louisiana State Museum in 1977. Minit Printit filed as a Louisiana business corporation in February 1970. Therefore, it seems clear that this souvenir guide was likely produced sometime during the early 1970s.

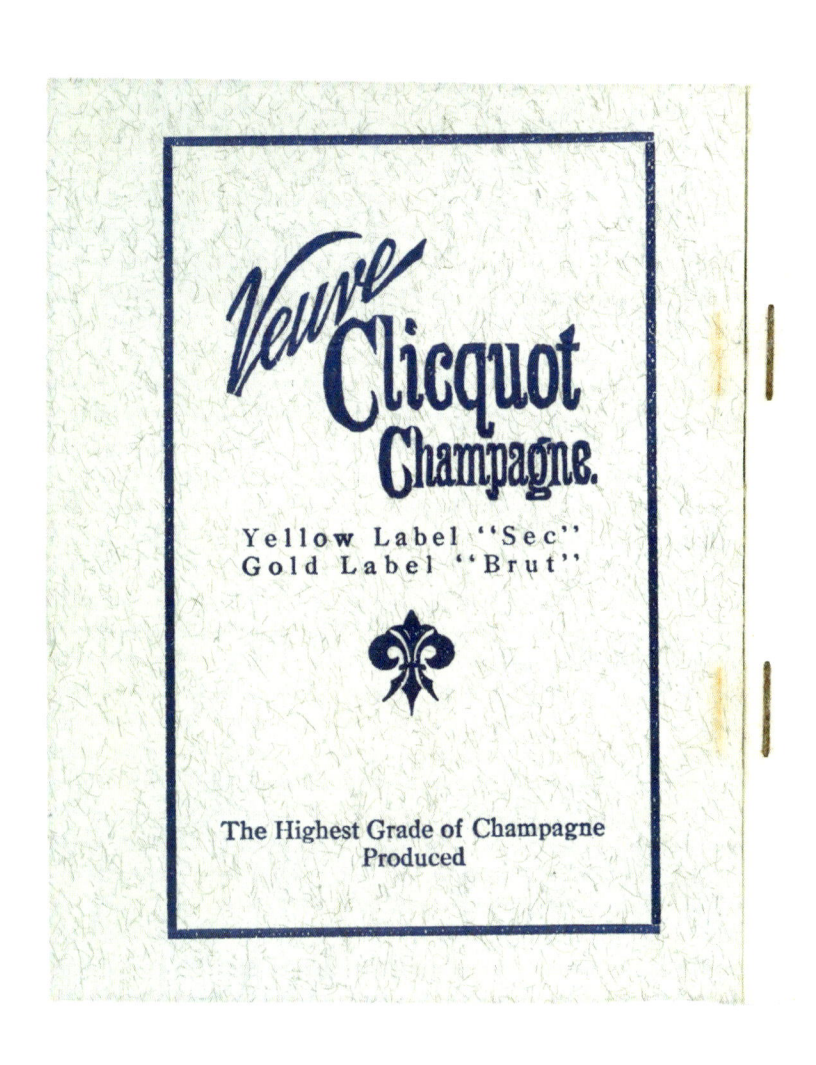

FAKES AND FACSIMILES

## No. 23
### Blue Book

Cover printed in black ink on pale blue paper; interior printed in black and red ink on plain paper. Undated [1980s]. 96 unnumbered pages.

13.7 cm × 10.8 cm, *THNOC, gift of Aubrey Armbruster, 2013.0288*

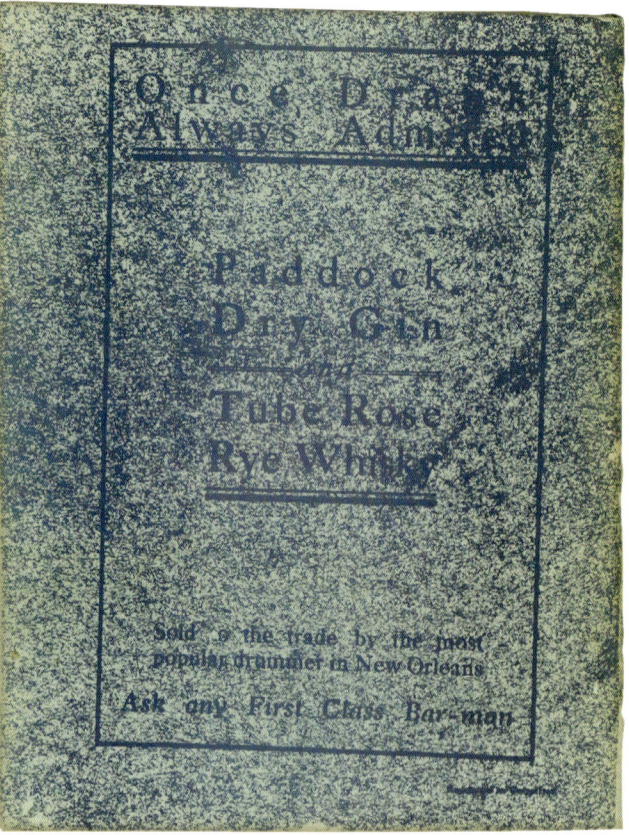

Another fake based on No. 9 replicates the two-color printing of the original—unlike most other post-Storyville reproductions, which are usually printed entirely in black. The cover printing, featuring the inverted lyre and lilies motif, is darkly mottled and could be a poorly executed photoreproduction of the cover of No. 22, which has dark fibers incorporated throughout the paper. A line of type on the lower right corner of the back cover may hold the clue to the identity of the creator of this book. Unfortunately, it is tantalizingly illegible. Like other reproductions based on No. 9, all of the pages are here, but they are out of order. The content aligns poorly on the pages. Some pages are set crookedly; others bleed off the bottom. Photographs and other printed elements throughout are poorly reproduced.

Aspects of this publication's production initially led me to believe that it was a Storyville-era guide. This publication, like No. 22, is side stitched through the left edge, with the cover glued over the staples, like copies of the genuine *Blue Book* are. Additionally, rubrication is typically not found in fakes. Despite these points, the reproduction quality overall, the type of paper stock used, and the illegible line of type on the back cover—seemingly a credit line—have convinced me that this is not a genuine Storyville-era publication, and that it was probably produced after the fakes and facsimiles of *Blue Book* that I date to the 1970s.

NO. 23 | FAKES AND FACSIMILES | 139

FAKES AND FACSIMILES

## No. 24

THE BLUE BOOK | of New Orleans | Edited by Jay Moynahan

Cover and spine debossed in black on dark red buckram cloth; interior printed in black ink on plain paper. Spokane, WA: Chickadee Publishing, 2006. Limited edition of 500 numbered copies (THNOC's, 188/500), plus five author's copies. 127 numbered pages.

16.8 cm × 9.5 cm, *THNOC, 2011.0262*

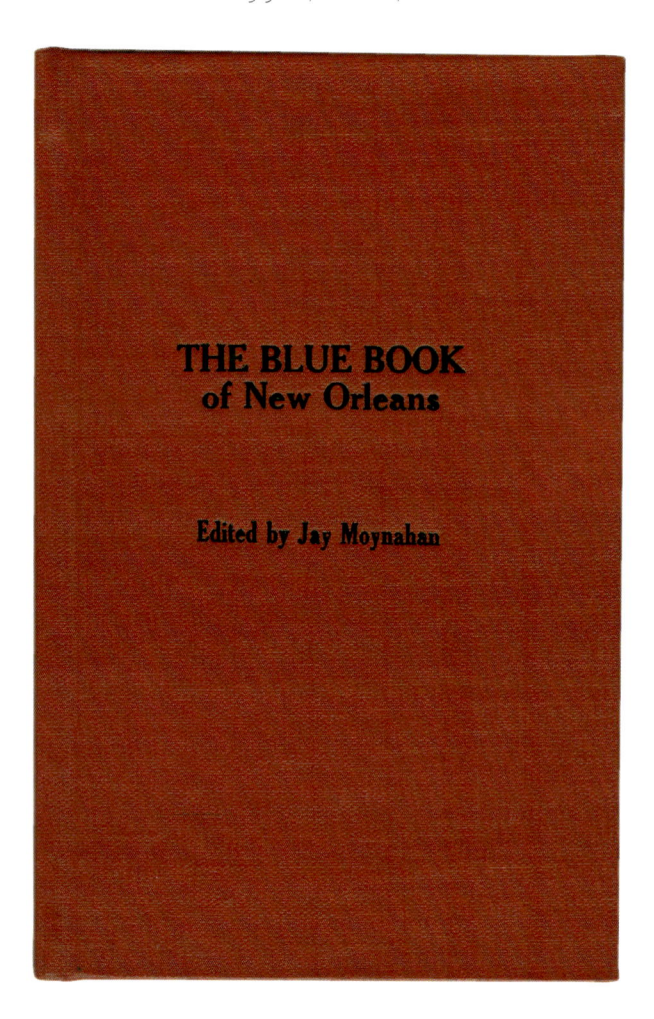

Jay Moynahan's publication includes a brief essay on Storyville and the blue books, reprints the introductory material from Reeves's 1951 souvenir (No. 16), and reproduces an edition of *Blue Book* on pages 19–116, though it's clear that his source material was a 1970s facsimile rather than a genuine Storyville-era guide.[27] Moynahan, referencing research by Shreveport historian Eric Brock, claims to have reproduced "the true 1911–1912 edition." Brock appears to have used Heartman's bibliography as his source (Heartman assigned a date of 1911–12 to his XII, see No. 10).[28] However, this is not a reproduction of No. 10; it is closest to the fakes discussed in Nos. 21 and 22, both of which are based upon No. 9. The Veuve Clicquot ad that appears on the inside front cover of

BIBLIOGRAPHY | 140

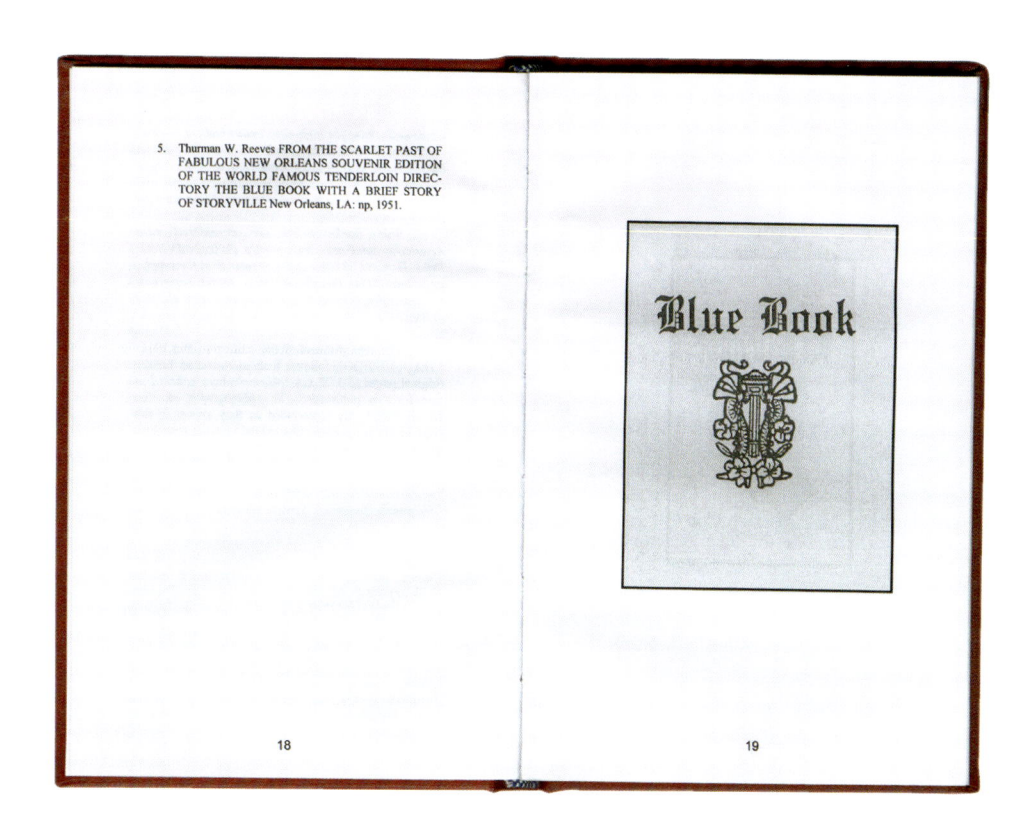

5. Thurman W. Reeves FROM THE SCARLET PAST OF FABULOUS NEW ORLEANS SOUVENIR EDITION OF THE WORLD FAMOUS TENDERLOIN DIRECTORY THE BLUE BOOK WITH A BRIEF STORY OF STORYVILLE New Orleans, LA: np, 1951.

No. 9 is reprinted in Moynahan's version (as it is in Nos. 21 and 22), and the page containing three reasons justifying the District and these guides is repeated, but the order of the advertisements differs from that of the genuine No. 9. Josie Arlington's is the first full-page madam's ad in the original publication; here, Hilma Burt's is the first. The advertisements on the inside and outside back cover of No. 9 are not reproduced; Moynahan presents these as blank pages. The directory pages are presented in the correct order in Moynahan's publication, beginning with "A" for white prostitutes. The pages are reproduced in this publication at a smaller size than *Blue Book* and the fakes he seems to have drawn upon. Moynahan speculates incorrectly that the original cover was probably printed on red paper stock, but this is not true of the genuine and fake *Blue Book* editions whose content he actually reproduces (Nos. 9, 21, and 22), nor the edition he claims to reprint (No. 10).[29]

Moynahan, a retired professor, has been collecting material about prostitution in the American West, Alaska, and western Canada since the early 1990s. Spurred by the discovery that a distant relative was a madam in a Colorado mining town in the 1870s, coupled with a desire to show what life was like for frontier prostitutes, Moynahan has produced at least fifty publications in his Sportin' Women Series for Chickadee Publishing.[30] This book is one of only two hardcover facsimiles (No. 25 is the other); all Storyville-era blue books, as well as most fakes, are paperbacks.

**FAKES AND FACSIMILES**

# No. 25
## Blue Book

Cover and spine debossed in silver on navy blue simulated leather; interior printed in black and dark red ink on plain paper. Carlisle, MA: Applewood Books, 2013. 100 unnumbered pages.

*16 cm × 11.3 cm, THNOC, 2013.0357*

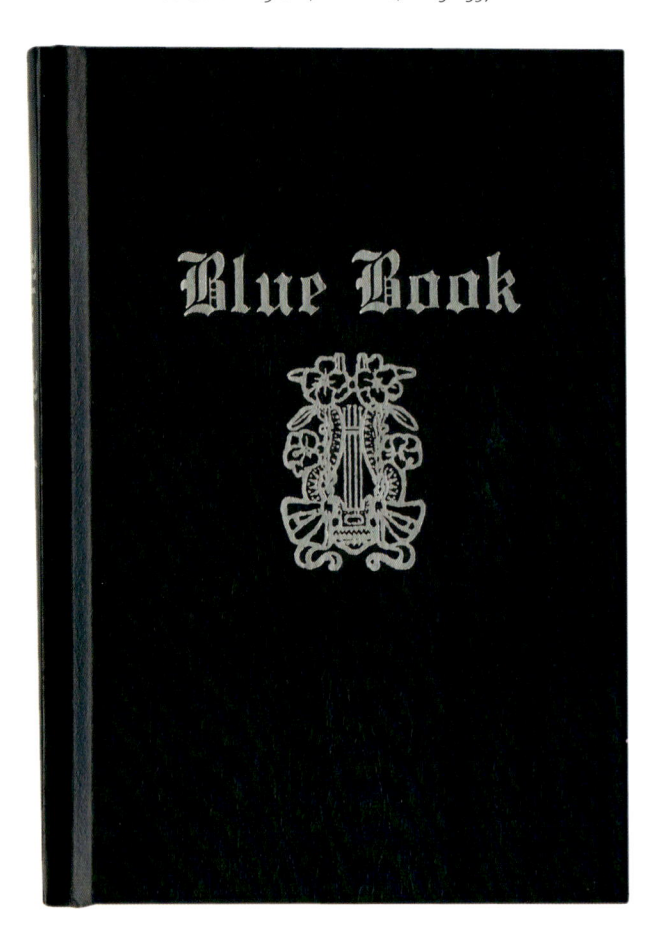

Other than the publisher's title page, copyright information, and a brief introduction, this book in the Applewood after Dark series is a reproduction of the Storyville-era *Blue Book* of 1913–15 (No. 10). According to Phil Zuckerman, president of Applewood Books, the original book was photographed; then parts were refined digitally.[31] This reproduction slightly enlarges text and design elements from the original pages. The directory section and madams' ads have been newly typeset. Some of the design elements, such as the header depicting two women in profile facing a glowing red lamp, have been cleaned up, though others do not show the fine linework of the original illustrations. The final product is a close facsimile that thoughtfully replicates the design and printing of its source material.

Like the Storyville-era guides, this modern reprint contains its own mistakes: the publisher's introduction incorrectly identifies Thomas C.

Anderson and Anderson's Saloon as "Thomas C. Alexander" and "Alexander's Saloon" and erroneously states that *Blue Book* was published "from about 1909 to 1915." The facsimile was reproduced from a copy in the possession of Judith Lafitte, who with her husband, Tom Lowenburg, owns Octavia Books, an independent bookstore in Uptown New Orleans. Applewood was careful to replicate a quirk of this specific copy: the small, penciled check mark a previous owner placed by the name of white prostitute Dolly Wells in the directory section.

This facsimile, one of only two hardcover editions (No. 24 is the other), has stylish rose-colored endpapers that repeat the lyre and lilies motif so strongly associated with *Blue Book*.

# NOTES

1. For an interview with a woman who worked in the District as a child, see Rose, *Storyville*, 148–50.
2. Heartman, "*Blue Book*," 50.
3. "City Will Control Segregated Area Under New System," *Times-Picayune*, January 24, 1917, p. 4, c. 5–6.
4. Rose, *Storyville*, 142.
5. Heartman, "*Blue Book*," 67.
6. Leathem, "'A Carnival,'" 227–28.
7. Rose, *Storyville*, 44.
8. Heartman, "*Blue Book*," 69.
9. Rose, *Storyville*, 126.
10. The meaning of this phrase can be found in Flexner, *Listening to America*, 453.
11. Heartman, "*Blue Book*," 74.
12. Neal Auction Company, *Louisiana Purchase Auction*, lot 672.
13. In 1894, New Orleans adopted the decimal system of house numbering, rapidly becoming popular in other large cities, whereby city blocks were numbered in 100s from a specific starting point, and properties within blocks were numbered sequentially, facilitating postal delivery. A description of this new system can be seen in *Soards' New Orleans City Directory for 1897* (New Orleans: L. Soards, 1897), 36. All other Storyville-era blue books postdate the change in street numbering, so while their street names may have changed, the numerical addresses printed in the books would remain the same today had the neighborhood not been largely demolished.
14. Heartman, "*Blue Book*," 50.
15. Rose, *Storyville*, 135.
16. Heartman, "*Blue Book*," 46.
17. Rose, *Storyville*, 135.
18. Heartman, "*Blue Book*," 40.
19. "T. W. Reeves Rites to be Held Saturday," *Hattiesburg American*, June 24, 1966, p. 10, c. 3.
20. Jennifer Brannock, email to author, June 21, 2012; Sean Farrell, email to author, September 18, 2012.
21. "Blue Books? Various Kinds of Them," *Times-Picayune*, April 26, 1951, p. 56, c. 6.
22. Justin D. Winston, interview with author, October 27, 2012.
23. Buddy Stall, undated telephone conversation, in response to author's letter of April 10, 2010.
24. THNOC had a compact disc copy made of the cassette tape in 2013 for archival purposes.
25. Kirt Stall, telephone interview with author, October 20, 2012.
26. Now inactive, ILMF was registered with the State of Louisiana in 1974 by Donald R. Perry (1928–2002), a cameraman with WDSU-TV who filmed segments of the inaugural New Orleans Jazz and Heritage Festival in 1970. Perry donated this footage to the Louisiana State Museum in 1978.
27. Moynahan also cites my 1987 article in *Louisiana History* in his essay on Storyville.
28. Moynahan, *Blue Book of New Orleans*, 17n4.
29. Ibid., 14.
30. Moynahan, *Chickadee Publishing Catalog of Books*, inside back cover; Moynahan, *Blue Book of New Orleans*, 117–18.
31. Phil Zuckerman, telephone interview with author, October 6, 2015.

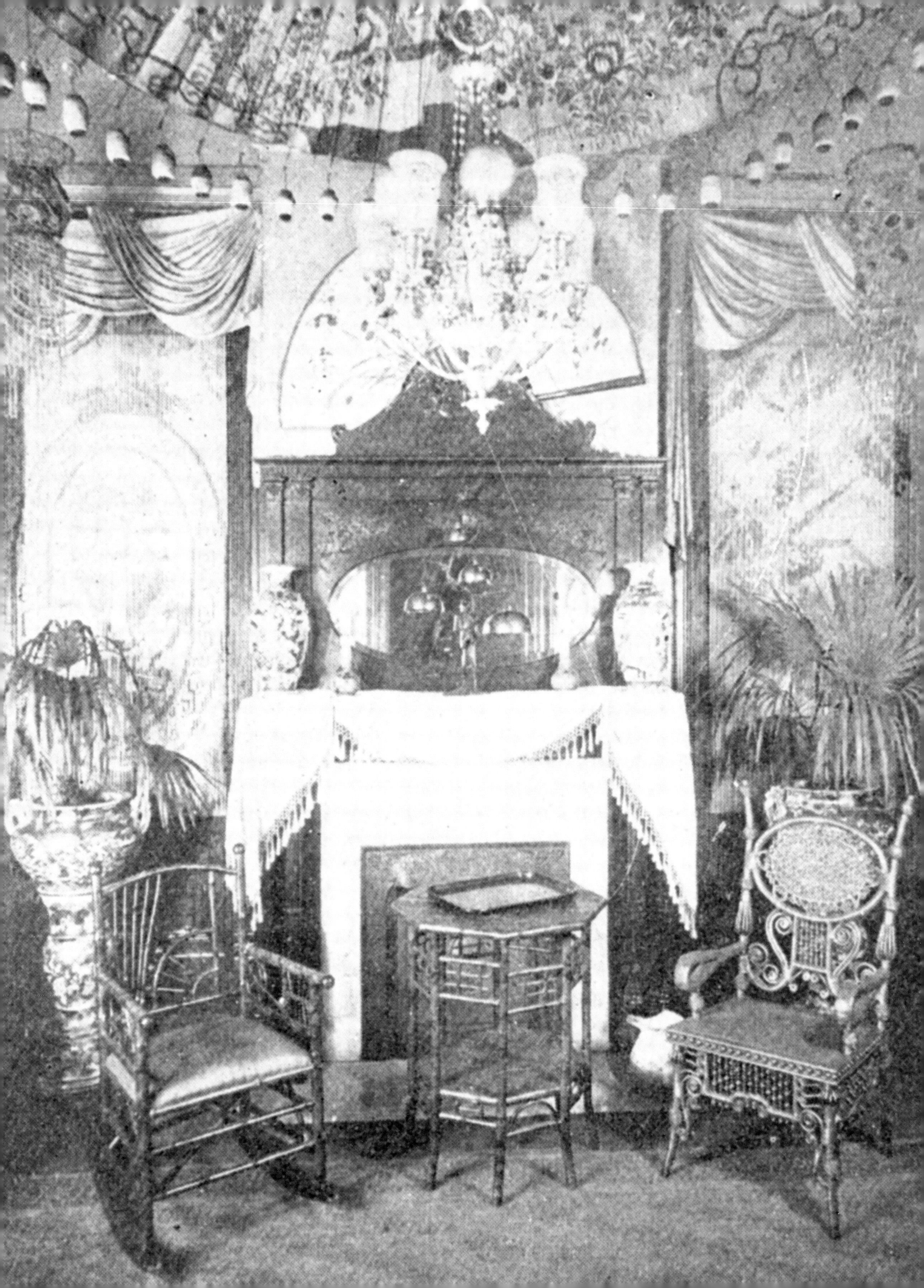

# KEY TO NOS. 1–25

|  | TITLE | YEAR OF PUBLICATION | STATED EDITION | HEARTMAN'S NUMBER | IN THIS BIBLIOGRAPHY |
|---|---|---|---|---|---|
| **EDITIONS OF *BLUE BOOK*** | | | | | |
| No. 1 | *Blue Book* | [1900] | – | – | pp. 66–69 |
| No. 2 | *Blue Book* | [1901] | – | IV | pp. 70–73 |
| No. 3 | *Blue Book* | [1903] | – | – | pp. 74–77 |
| No. 4 | *Blue Book* | [1905] | 6 | VI | pp. 78–81 |
| No. 5 | *Blue Book* | 1906 | 7 | VII | pp. 82–85 |
| No. 6 | *Blue Book* | 1907 | 8 | VIII | pp. 86–89 |
| No. 7 | *Blue Book* | [1908] | 9 | IX | pp. 90–93 |
| No. 8 | *Blue Book* | [1909] | 10 | X | pp. 94–97 |
| No. 9 | *Blue Book* | [1912] | – | XI | pp. 98–101 |
| No. 10 | *Blue Book* | [1913–15] | – | XII, XIII | pp. 102–5 |
| **ALTERNATIVE STORYVILLE-ERA GUIDES** | | | | | |
| No. 11 | *New Mahogany Hall* | [1898–99] | – | – | pp. 106–9 |
| No. 12 | *The Red Book* | [1901] | – | V | pp. 110–13 |
| No. 13 | *Sporting Guide* | [1902] | – | III | pp. 114–17 |
| No. 14 | *Hell-O* | [1903] | – | II | pp. 118–19 |
| No. 15 | *"The Lid"* | [1906] | – | I | pp. 120–21 |
| **FAKES AND FACSIMILES** | | | | | |
| No. 16 | *From the Scarlet Past of Fabulous New Orleans* | 1951 | – | – | pp. 122–23 |
| No. 17 | *Hell-O* | [mid-1960s] | – | – | pp. 124–25 |
| No. 18 | *The Blue Book* | 1963 | – | – | pp. 126–29 |
| No. 19 | *Blue Book* | [1970s] | – | – | pp. 130–31 |
| No. 20 | *Blue Book* | [1970s] | – | – | pp. 132–33 |
| No. 21 | *Blue Book* | [1970s] | – | – | pp. 134–35 |
| No. 22 | *Blue Book* | [1970s] | – | – | pp. 136–37 |
| No. 23 | *Blue Book* | [1980s] | – | – | pp. 138–39 |
| No. 24 | *The Blue Book of New Orleans* | 2006 | – | – | pp. 140–41 |
| No. 25 | *Blue Book* | 2013 | – | – | pp. 142–43 |

# WORKS CONSULTED

Abbott, Karen. *Sin in the Second City: Madams, Ministers, Playboys, and the Battle for America's Soul*. 2007. Reprint, New York: Random House, 2008.

Agnew, Jean-Christophe. "The Consuming Vision of Henry James," in *The Culture of Consumption: Critical Essays in American History, 1880–1980*, edited by Richard Wightman Fox and T. J. Jackson Lears. New York: Pantheon Books, 1983.

*American Chap-Book* 1, no. 3 (November 1904).

American Social Hygiene Association. *Why Let It Burn? The Case Against the Red Light District*. New York: American Social Hygiene Association, [1919].

Anderson Galleries. *The Library of Mr. Simon J. Shwartz, New Orleans, La., Sold by His Order. Part One: Americana Consisting of Books, Broadsides, Autographs, Maps Relating to the Louisiana Territory, the Mississippi Valley and the Development of the West Together with Currier and Ives Colored Prints of American Subjects*. New York: Anderson Galleries, 1926.

———. *The Library of Mr. Simon J. Shwartz, New Orleans, La., Sold by His Order. Part Two: Consisting of Fine Bindings, Manuscripts, Napoleonana, Colored Costume Plates, First Editions, Autographs, Original Drawings, etc*. New York: Anderson Galleries, 1926.

Arceneaux, Pamela D. "Guidebooks to Sin: The Blue Books of Storyville." *Louisiana History* 28, no. 4 (Fall 1987): 397–405.

———. "Guidebooks to Sin: The Blue Books of Storyville." In *Visions and Revisions: Perspectives on Louisiana Society and Culture*. Louisiana Purchase Bicentennial Series in Louisiana History, vol. 15, Lafayette: Center for Louisiana Studies, University of Louisiana at Lafayette, 2000.

———. "New Orleans Blue Books." In *KnowLA Encyclopedia of Louisiana*, edited by David Johnson. Louisiana Endowment for the Humanities, 2010–. Article published November 23, 2010. Revised and updated September 17, 2013. http://www.knowla.org/entry/734/&view=article.

———. "Storyville's Blue Books." *The Historic New Orleans Collection Quarterly* 13, no. 1 (Winter 1995): 8–9.

Asbury, Herbert. *The Barbary Coast: An Informal History of the San Francisco Underworld*. 1933. Reprint, New York: Thunder's Mouth, 2002.

———. *The French Quarter: An Informal History of the New Orleans Underworld*. 1936. Reprint, Garden City, NY: Garden City Publishing, 1938.

Barthes, Roland. *Mythologies*. Translated by Annette Lavers. New York: Hill and Wang, 1972.

Josie Arlington's Japanese Parlor, from No. 7

Berendt, Joachim-Ernst. *Jazz: A Photo History*. Translated by William Odom. New York: Schirmer, 1979.

Bernstein, Patricia. *The First Waco Horror: The Lynching of Jesse Washington and the Rise of the NAACP*. Centennial Series of the Association of Former Students, Texas A&M University, no. 101. College Station: Texas A&M University Press, 2005.

Blesh, Rudi, and Harriet Janis. *They All Played Ragtime: The True Story of an American Music*, 1950. Reprint, New York: Grove Press, 1959.

*Blue Book*. Applewood after Dark. Carlisle, MA: Applewood Books, 2013.

Brasseaux, Carl A., and James D. Wilson Jr., eds. *A Dictionary of Louisiana Biography Ten-Year Supplement, 1988–1998*. Lafayette: The Louisiana Historical Association in cooperation with the Center for Louisiana Studies of the University of Southwestern Louisiana, 1999.

Brock, Eric J. *Red Light: Shreveport's St. Paul's Bottoms Red Light District: An Experiment in Controlled Vice, Including "A Look Back": Red Light Shreveport a Century Ago and The District and Its People in Pictures*. Shreveport, LA: Ramble House, 2004.

———. "Shreveport's St. Paul's Bottoms Red Light District: An Experiment in Controlled Vice." *North Louisiana History* 31, no. 2–3 (Spring–Summer 2000): 3–23.

Charles B. Wood III. *One Hundred Rare Books and Manuscripts*. Catalogue 155. Cambridge, MA: Charles B. Wood III, 2012.

Clark, Emily. *The Strange History of the American Quadroon: Free Women of Color in the Revolutionary Atlantic World*. Chapel Hill: University of North Carolina Press, 2013.

Cohen, Patricia Cline. *The Murder of Helen Jewett: The Life and Death of a Prostitute in Nineteenth-Century New York*. 1998. Reprint, New York: Vintage Books, 1999.

Collins, Nancy Sharon. *The Complete Engraver: Monograms, Crests, Ciphers, Seals, and the Etiquette of Social Stationery*. New York: Princeton Architectural Press, 2012.

Collins, R. *New Orleans Jazz: A Revised History*. New York: Vantage, 1996.

Conrad, Glenn R., ed. *A Dictionary of Louisiana Biography*. 2 vols. New Orleans: The Louisiana Historical Association in cooperation with the Center for Louisiana Studies of the University of Southwestern Louisiana, 1988.

Corrales, Barbara Smith. "Prurience, Prostitution, and Progressive Improvements: The Crowley Connection, 1909–1918." *Louisiana History* 45, no.1 (2004): 37–70.

Flexner, Abraham. *Prostitution in Europe*. Publications of the Bureau of Social Hygiene. New York: Century, 1914.

Flexner, Stuart Berg. *Listening to America: An Illustrated History of Words and Phrases from Our Lively and Splendid Past*. New York: Simon and Schuster, 1982.

Foster, Craig L. "Tarnished Angels: Prostitution in Storyville, New Orleans, 1900–1910." *Louisiana History* 31, no. 4 (1990): 387–97.

Gilfoyle, Timothy J. "Prostitutes in the Archives: Problems and Possibilities in Documenting the History of Sexuality." *American Archivist* 57, no. 3 (Summer 1994): 514–27.

Goldman, Marion S. *Gold Diggers and Silver Miners: Prostitution and Social Life on the Comstock Lode*. Women and Culture Series. Ann Arbor: University of Michigan Press, 1981.

*Guide to Research at The Historic New Orleans Collection*. 2nd ed. New Orleans: The Historic New Orleans Collection, 1980.

Haraway, Donna. "Teddy Bear Patriarchy: Taxidermy in the Garden of Eden, 1908–1936," in *Cultures of United States Imperialism*, edited by Amy Kaplan and Donald E. Pease. Durham and London: Duke University Press, 1993.

Hardy, Arthur. *Mardi Gras in New Orleans: An Illustrated History*. Metairie, LA: Arthur Hardy, 2001.

Heartman, Charles F. [Semper Idem, pseud.] "An Exciting Bibliographical Adventure. The 'Blue Book': A Bibliographical Attempt to Describe the Guide Books to the Houses of Ill Fame in New Orleans as They Were Published There. Together with Some Pertinent and Illuminating Remarks Pertaining to the Establishments and Courtesans as Well as to Harlotry in General in New Orleans. By Semper Idem." New York: Mayco, 1936. Prospectus for *The "Blue Book."*

———. *The "Blue Book": A Bibliographical Attempt to Describe the Guide Books to the Houses of Ill Fame in New Orleans as They Were Published There. Together with Some Pertinent and Illuminating Remarks Pertaining to the Establishments and Courtesans as Well as to Harlotry in General in New Orleans*. Heartman's Historical Series, no. 50. Privately printed [New York: Mayco], 1936.

Heartman (Charles F.) Papers. M94. McCain Library and Archives, University of Southern Mississippi, Hattiesburg, MS.

Hewes, Lauren B. "Thomas W. Streeter (1883–1965), 1961," in *Portraits at the American Antiquarian Society*. American Antiquarian Society. http://www.americanantiquarian.org/Inventories/Portraits/113.htm. Text originally published in *Portraits in the Collection of the American Antiquarian Society*, edited by Catherine F. Sloat and Katherine A. St. Germaine. Worcester, MA: American Antiquarian Society, 2004.

Hughes Books. *Catalog 44*. New Orleans: Hughes Books, 2011.

Krist, Gary. *Empire of Sin: A Story of Sex, Jazz, Murder, and the Battle for Modern New Orleans*. New York: Crown, 2014.

Landau, Emily Epstein. "'Spectacular Wickedness': New Orleans, Prostitution, and the Politics of Sex, 1897–1917." PhD diss., Yale University, 2005.

———. *Spectacular Wickedness: Sex, Race, and Memory in Storyville, New Orleans*. Baton Rouge: Louisiana State University Press, 2013.

Leach, William. *Land of Desire: Merchants, Power, and the Rise of a New American Culture*. New York: Vintage Books, 1994.

Lears, T. J. Jackson. "From Salvation to Self-Realization: Advertising and the Therapeutic Roots of the Consumer Culture, 1880–1930," in *The Culture of Consumption: Critical Essays in American History, 1880–1980*, edited by Richard Wightman Fox and T. J. Jackson Lears. New York: Pantheon Books, 1983.

Leathem, Karen Trahan. "'A Carnival According to Their Own Desires': Gender and Mardi Gras in New Orleans, 1870–1941." PhD diss., University of North Carolina at Chapel Hill, 1994.

Levine, Lawrence. *Highbrow/Lowbrow: The Emergence of Cultural Hierarchy in America*. Cambridge, MA: Harvard University Press, 1988.

Library Company of Philadelphia, The. *Capitalism by Gaslight: The Shadow Economies of 19th-Century America*. 2012. http://www.librarycompany.org/shadoweconomy/index.htm.

Long, Alecia P. *The Great Southern Babylon: Sex, Race, and Respectability in New Orleans, 1865–1920*. Baton Rouge: Louisiana State University Press, 2004.

Longstreet, Stephen, ed. *Nell Kimball, Her Life as an American Madam by Herself*. New York: Macmillan, 1970.

Mackey, Thomas Clyde. "Red Lights Out: A Legal History of Prostitution, Disorderly Houses, and Vice Districts, 1870–1917." PhD diss., Rice University, 1984.

MacLeod, Kirsten. *American Little Magazines of the 1890s: A Revolution in Print*. Sunderland, UK: Bibelot, 2013.

Marchand, Roland. *Advertising the American Dream: Making Way for Modernity, 1920–1940*. Berkeley: University of California Press, 1985.

Mir, Jasmine. "Marketplace of Desire: Storyville and the Making of a Tourist City in New Orleans, 1890–1920." PhD diss., New York University, 2005.

Morgan, Lael. "The San Antonio Blue Book: Proof of a Secret Era." *The Compass Rose: Special Collections, The University of Texas at Arlington Library* 21, no. 2 (Fall 2007): 1–3.

Moynahan, Jay, ed. *The Blue Book of New Orleans*. Spokane, WA: Chickadee, 2006.

———. *Chickadee Publishing Catalog of Books. Number 1, 2011*. Spokane, WA: Chickadee, 2011.

———. *Prostitutes of Storyville, New Orleans 1897–1917: With Over 1600 Listed Names*. Spokane, WA: Chickadee, 2011.

Mulvey, Laura. "Visual Pleasure and Narrative Cinema," in *Film Theory and Criticism: Introductory Readings*, edited by Gerald Mast and Marshall Cohen. Oxford: Oxford University Press, 1985.

Myers, William E. *The Israelites of Louisiana: Their Religious, Civic, Charitable, and Patriotic Life*. New Orleans: W. E. Myers, [1905].

Nasaw, David. *Going Out: The Rise and Fall of Public Amusements*. Cambridge, MA: Harvard University Press, 1993.

Neal Auction Company. *Louisiana Purchase Auction, October 6 and 7, 2007*. New Orleans: Neal Auction Company, 2007.

New Orleans Chamber of Commerce and Industry of Louisiana. *The City of New Orleans: The Book of the Chamber of Commerce and Industry of Louisiana and Other Public Bodies of the "Crescent City."* New Orleans: Geo. W. Engelhardt, 1894.

O'Connor, Richard. *The Golden Summers: An Antic History of Newport*. New York: G. P. Putnam's Sons, 1974.

Palmer, Robert. *Rock and Roll: An Unruly History*. New York: Harmony, 1995.

Parke-Bernet Galleries. *The Celebrated Collection of Americana Formed by the Late Thomas Winthrop Streeter, Morristown, New Jersey, Sold by Order of the Trustees*. 7 vols. and an index. New York: Parke-Bernet Galleries, 1966–70.

Platt, R. Eric, and Lilian H. Hill. "A Storyville Education: Spatial Practices and the Learned Sex Trade in the City That Care Forgot." *Adult Education Quarterly* 64 (November 2014): 285–305. doi: 10.1177/0741713614539030.

*Polk's New Orleans City Directory*. New Orleans: R. L. Polk, 1949, 1952–58, 1960–62, 1964–66.

Porter, Lewis. *Jazz: A Century of Change*. New York: Schirmer, 1997.

Price, Peggy. "The Book Farm: Charles F. Heartman's Utopia for Intellectuals." *Fine Books and Collections*, April 2010. http://www.finebooksmagazine.com/issue/201004/heartman-1.phtml.

Rose, Al. *Miss Lulu White de Basin Street, Nouvelle Orléans*. Translated by Raymond Manicacci. Paris: Gaston Lachurié, 1991.

———. *Storyville, New Orleans: Being an Authentic Account of the Notorious Red-Light District*. 1974. Reprint, Tuscaloosa: University of Alabama Press, 1979.

Rydell, Robert W. *All the World's a Fair: Visions of Empire at American International Exhibitions, 1876–1916*. Chicago and London: The University of Chicago Press, 1984.

Sanborn Map Company. *Insurance Maps of New Orleans, Louisiana*. Volume 2. Plates 129, 130, 134, and 135. New York: Sanborn Map, 1908.

Schafer, Judith Kelleher. *Brothels, Depravity, and Abandoned Women: Illegal Sex in Antebellum New Orleans*. 2009. Reprint, Baton Rouge: Louisiana State University Press, 2011.

*Soards' Blue Book of New Orleans, for 1890–91. . . .* New Orleans: L. Soards, 1890. Not to be confused with a Storyville blue book.

*Soards' Elite Book of New Orleans. . . .* New Orleans: Soards, 1908.

*Soards' New Orleans City Directory*. New Orleans: L. Soards, 1896–1920.

Stearns, Marshall W. *The Story of Jazz*. New York: Oxford University Press, 1956.

Stott, Richard. *Jolly Fellows: Male Milieus in Nineteenth-Century America*. Gender Relations in the American Experience. Baltimore: Johns Hopkins University Press, 2009.

Streeter, Ruth Cheney. "Streeter, Thomas Winthrop." In *Handbook of Texas Online*. Texas State Historical Association. Article published June 15, 2010. http://www.tshaonline.org/handbook/online/articles/fst73.

Temperley, Harold, and Lillian M. Penson, eds. *A Century of Diplomatic Blue Books: 1814–1914*. 1938. Reprint, London: Frank Cass, 1966.

Tirro, Frank. *Jazz: A History*. New York: W. W. Norton, 1977.

Topping, Elizabeth. "Fact and Fiction Regarding Prostitution in Mid-Nineteenth Century American Cities." *Nineteenth Century* 20, no. 2 (Fall 2000): 8–12.

Trachtenberg, Alan. *The Incorporation of America: Culture and Society in the Gilded Age*. New York: Hill and Wang, 1982.

Ward, Geoffrey C., and Ken Burns. *Jazz: A History of America's Music*. New York: Alfred A. Knopf, 2000.

Weiss, Harry B. *The Bibliographical, Editorial, and Other Activities of Charles F. Heartman, With an Annotated Bibliography*. Privately printed [New Orleans: Rogers Printing], 1938.

William Reese Company. *Catalogue Two Hundred Fifty-Seven: The Streeter Sale Revisited*. New Haven, CT: William Reese Company, 2007.

———. *Catalogue Two Hundred Ninety-Seven: Recent Acquisitions in Americana*. New Haven, CT: William Reese Company, 2012.

Williams, L. Kemper and Leila Hardie Moore, Papers. 97-63-L. The Historic New Orleans Collection, New Orleans, LA.

Wunsch, James L. Review of *Nell Kimball: Her Life as an American Madam by Herself*, edited by Stephen Longstreet. *Journal of Social History* 6, no. 1 (1972): 121 26. http://www.jstor.org/stable/3786441.

Young, Perry. *Carnival and Mardi-Gras in New Orleans*. New Orleans: Harmanson's, 1939.

Zacks, Richard. *Island of Vice: Theodore Roosevelt's Doomed Quest to Clean Up Sin-Loving New York*. New York: Doubleday, 2012.

# IMAGE CREDITS

Front of jacket
:   Illustration from *Blue Book*, [1908], *The Historic New Orleans Collection*, 1969.19.9

Back of jacket
:   Pages from *Blue Book*, [1900], *The Historic New Orleans Collection*, 94-092-RL

Back of jacket
:   Pages from *Blue Book*, 1907, *The Historic New Orleans Collection*, 1969.19.8

Case
:   Illustration from *Blue Book*, [1903], *The Historic New Orleans Collection*, 2006.0237

Front endpapers
:   Photograph of Josie Arlington's Turkish Parlor from *Blue Book*, 1907, *The Historic New Orleans Collection*, 1969.19.8

Facing half title
:   Illustration from *Blue Book*, 1907, *The Historic New Orleans Collection*, 1969.19.8

2   Typography from advertisement for Willie Piazza's brothel from *Blue Book*, [1909], *The Historic New Orleans Collection*, 1969.19.10

3   Graphic element from *Blue Book*, [1905], *The Historic New Orleans Collection*, 1969.19.6

5   Illustration from *Blue Book*, [1908], *The Historic New Orleans Collection*, 1969.19.9

6   View of Basin Street, ca. 1908 (photoprint made between 1950 and 1973), *The Historic New Orleans Collection*, gift of Albert Louis Lieutaud, 1957.101

8   Typography from preface from *Blue Book*, [1905], *The Historic New Orleans Collection*, 1969.19.6

11  *Vestibule of the Fertility Symbol*, gelatin silver print by Clarence John Laughlin, 1945, *The Clarence John Laughlin Archive at The Historic New Orleans Collection*, 1981.247.1.363

12  Typography from directory from *Blue Book*, [1901], *The Historic New Orleans Collection*, 1969.19.4

15  Illustration from *Blue Book*, [1905], *The Historic New Orleans Collection*, 1969.19.6

16  Postcard showing view of Storyville (New Orleans: C. B. Mason, [1904–8]), *The Historic New Orleans Collection*, 1979.362.16

19  Photographs of prostitutes taken upon their arrests in the Storyville era. Top row: Mable Brown, Cora McIntyre, Ethel Jackson; middle row: Gussie Conner, Louisa Barnes, Maude Comm; bottom row: Carrie Gross, May Morlock, Elizabeth Monnier, *courtesy Louisiana Division/City Archives, New Orleans Public Library*

25  Photograph of a boudoir in Hilma Burt's mansion from *Blue Book*, [1909], *The Historic New Orleans Collection*, 1969.19.10

26  Typography from introduction from *Blue Book*, [1900], *The Historic New Orleans Collection*, 94-092-RL

28  Prostitution license for Mary Brooks, 1857, *The Historic New Orleans Collection*, 69-19-L.10

29  Bertillon card for Rosie Gibson, 1913, *courtesy Louisiana Division/City Archives, New Orleans Public Library*

29  Bertillon card for Jessie Knotts, 1912, *courtesy Louisiana Division/City Archives, New Orleans Public Library*

30  Map by Alison Cody

31  *Soards' Blue Book of New Orleans* (New Orleans: Soards, 1890), *The Historic New Orleans Collection*, 69-49-LP.6

31  *Soards' Elite Book* (New Orleans: Soards, [1908]), *The Historic New Orleans Collection*, 77-391-RL

32  Cover and detail of page 16 from *A Guide to the Stranger* (Philadelphia, 1849), *courtesy Library Company of Philadelphia*

34  Directory excerpt from *Blue Book*, [1900], *The Historic New Orleans Collection*, 94-092-RL

34  Photograph of Billy Struve from his obituary "Billy Struve of Night Life Fame Passes," *Item*, October 21, 1937, p. 1, col. 2

34  Photograph of Tom Anderson from souvenir program for the Elks Burlesque Circus, 1906, *The Historic New Orleans Collection*, 92-48-L.78.220

35  Rose bush Mission Toy from *Blue Book*, 1907, *The Historic New Orleans Collection*, 1969.19.8

35  Rocking horse Mission Toy from *Blue Book*, 1907, *The Historic New Orleans Collection*, 1969.19.8

35  Scribe Mission Toy from *Blue Book*, [1908], *The Historic New Orleans Collection*, 1969.19.9

36  Advertisement for the French balls from *Blue Book*, [1903], *The Historic New Orleans Collection*, 2006.0237

36  Advertisement for the French balls from *The Red Book*, [1901], *The Historic New Orleans Collection*, 1969.19.5

37  Photograph of Rita Walker from *Blue Book*, [1913–15], *The Historic New Orleans Collection*, 85-517-RL

38  Cover of *Hell-O*, [1903], *The Historic New Orleans Collection*, 1969.19.2

150

| Page | Description |
|---|---|
| 38 | Excerpt from *The Blue Book*, [1963], The Historic New Orleans Collection, gift of Linda Kaplan, 2006.0423 |
| 39 | Excerpt from *Blue Book*, [1913–15], The Historic New Orleans Collection, 85-517-RL |
| 40 | Photograph of Josie Arlington's mirrored ballroom from *Blue Book*, [1905], The Historic New Orleans Collection, 1969.19.6 |
| 40 | Photograph of Josie Arlington's Japanese Parlor from *Blue Book*, [1903], The Historic New Orleans Collection, 2006.0237 |
| 41 | Drawing of Josie Arlington's brothel from *Blue Book*, [1913–15], The Historic New Orleans Collection, 85-517-RL |
| 42 | Photograph of a boudoir in Hilma Burt's mansion from *Blue Book*, [1909], The Historic New Orleans Collection, 1969.19.10 |
| 43 | Photograph of Estelle Russell from *New Mahogany Hall*, [1898–99], The Historic New Orleans Collection, 56-15 |
| 43 | Directory excerpt from *Blue Book*, [1903], The Historic New Orleans Collection, 2006.0237 |
| 44 | Photograph of Sadie Reed from *New Mahogany Hall*, [1898–99], The Historic New Orleans Collection, 56-15 |
| 44 | Directory excerpt from *Blue Book*, 1906, The Historic New Orleans Collection, 1969.19.7 |
| 44 | Photograph of the Star Mansion from *Blue Book*, 1906, The Historic New Orleans Collection, 1969.19.7 |
| 45 | Photograph of Josie Arlington from photograph by John N. Teunisson, February 8, 1908, The Historic New Orleans Collection, 1993.55 |
| 45 | Photograph of Willie Piazza from *Sporting Guide*, [1902], The Historic New Orleans Collection, 1969.19.3 |
| 45 | Photograph of Emma Johnson's from *Blue Book*, [1909], The Historic New Orleans Collection, 1969.19.10 |
| 46 | Directory excerpt from *Blue Book*, [1913–15], The Historic New Orleans Collection, 85-517-RL |
| 46 | Photograph of a scene in Hilma Burt's mirrored ballroom, courtesy Al Rose Collection, Louisiana Research Collection, Tulane University |
| 47 | Photograph of Jelly Roll Morton, ca. 1906, The Historic New Orleans Collection, William Russell Jazz Collection, MSS 536, 92-48-L.73 |
| 47 | Advertisement for Antonia Gonzales's brothel from *Blue Book*, [1905], The Historic New Orleans Collection, 1969.19.6 |
| 48 | Whiskey advertisement from *Blue Book*, [1913–15], The Historic New Orleans Collection, 85-517-RL |
| 48 | Budweiser advertisement from *Blue Book*, [1905], The Historic New Orleans Collection, 1969.19.6 |
| 49 | Advertisement for Tom Anderson's restaurants from *Blue Book*, 1906, The Historic New Orleans Collection, 1969.19.7 |
| 49 | Advertisement for venereal disease cure from *Blue Book*, [1900], The Historic New Orleans Collection, 94-092-RL |
| 49 | Advertisement for laundry services from *Blue Book*, [1913–15], The Historic New Orleans Collection, 85-517-RL |
| 50 | Cover of *The Blue Book for Visitors, Tourists and Those Seeking a Good Time While in San Antonio, Texas*, 1911, courtesy Special Collections, The University of Texas at Arlington Libraries, Arlington, Texas |
| 50 | Storyville cartoon by Trist Wood, *Item*, November 13, 1917 |
| 51 | Cover of *Why Let It Burn?* (New York: American Social Hygiene Association, [1919]), The Historic New Orleans Collection, 2016.0201 |
| 54 | Photograph of a den in Josie Arlington's mansion from *Blue Book*, [1905], The Historic New Orleans Collection, 1969.19.6 |
| 55 | Photograph of Simon James Shwartz from *The Israelites of Louisiana* (New Orleans: W. E. Myers, [1905]), The Historic New Orleans Collection, 69-81-LP.4 |
| 56 | Photograph of Charles Frederick Heartman, courtesy McCain Library and Archives, The University of Southern Mississippi |
| 57 | Title page of Heartman's *The "Blue Book"* (privately printed [New York: Mayco], 1936), The Historic New Orleans Collection, 1969.19.13 |
| 58 | Heartman's mark from *Blue Book*, [1901], The Historic New Orleans Collection, 1969.19.4 |
| 58 | Heartman's mark from *Blue Book*, [1909], The Historic New Orleans Collection, 1969.19.10 |
| 58 | Photograph of Thomas Winthrop Streeter, courtesy The Winterthur Library: Joseph Downs Collection of Manuscripts and Printed Ephemera |
| 59 | Streeter's mark from *Blue Book*, 1907, The Historic New Orleans Collection, 1969.19.8 |
| 59 | Photograph of Lewis Kemper Williams, ca. 1950, The Historic New Orleans Collection, gift of Florence D. Landry, 2004.0078.2.3 |
| 60 | Patch from *Blue Book*, 1906, The Historic New Orleans Collection, 1969.19.7 |
| 60 | Patch from *Blue Book*, [1901], The Historic New Orleans Collection, 1969.19.4 |
| 63 | Fan light over the front door of Lulu White's Mahogany Hall, photograph by Felix Julius Dreyfous, 1930–37, The Historic New Orleans Collection, 1990.2.2 |
| 64 | Photograph of Rita Walker from *Blue Book*, [1913–15], The Historic New Orleans Collection, 85-517-RL |
| 66–69 | Images from *Blue Book*, [1900], The Historic New Orleans Collection, 94-092-RL |
| 70–73 | Images from *Blue Book*, [1901], The Historic New Orleans Collection, 1969.19.4 |
| 74–77 | Images from *Blue Book*, [1903], The Historic New Orleans Collection, 2006.0237 |
| 78–81 | Images from *Blue Book*, [1905], The Historic New Orleans Collection, 1969.19.6 |

brothels
  advertising, 38–43, *41*, *45*, *47*, 47, 80–81, 83, 91–92, 96–97, 114–16
  Arlington. *See* Arlington, Josie
  Cairo, 37, 39–40
  class, 9, 17, 18, 40
  closures, 50
  Club, 71, *100*
  Cottage, 44
  Crescent, 71
  discretion, 41–42
  exclusivity, 40, 41, 42, 43
  Firm, 119
  Mahogany Hall. *See* White, Lulu
  Mansion, 117
  music, 46–47
  Phoenix, 42, *89*
  Star Mansion, *11*, 42, 44, *44*, 80, *80*, *81*, 83, 100, *101*, 120, 134
  Studio, 71
Brown, Jessie, 35, 39, *104*, 115
Burnett and Gayle, *114*, 114–15
Burnett's, 48
Burt, Hilma, 23, 25, 34, 42, *42*, 44, 46, 47, 83, 84, 88, 97, *97*, 101, *104*, 120, 121, 136, 141
Burton, Mae, 111, *112*

California Historical Society, 58
Camay, 21
Camille, H., *129*
Carlton, Jean, *88*
Carnival season, 35, 36, *36*, 37, 66, 74, 82, 103
  *See also* Mardi Gras
Casey, Anna (Annie), 45, 101, 103
C. C. C. Club Ball, 36, *36*, 70, 75, 87, 95, 99, 111, *135*, *137*, *139*
  *See also* French balls
*Celebrated Collection of Americana Formed by the Late Thomas Winthrop Streeter, The*, 59
Central Glass Co., 49, 84, *85*
Charles B. Wood III Antiquarian Bookseller, 32
Charles Meyer and Co., 48
Chicago, 30, 33
Chickadee Publishing, 141
City Park, New Orleans, 131
Civil War, 20
Club (brothel), 71, *100*
Clysmic Table Water, *105*
Coburn and Carroll High Class Decorators, 83–84, *85*
Collins, Nancy Sharon, 35
Colorado, 33
Comstock, Anthony, 37
Comstock Law, 37, 71, 116
Concord (NH), 58
Connecticut, 60
Cook, Middie, *109*
Cooke's Taxis, 49
Cooney, James, 111
Cottage (brothel), 44
Countess, the. *See* Piazza, Willie V.
Crescent (brothel), 71
cribs, 18, 45, 87, *88*
Cummings, Bessie, 40
Curtis, Lizzie, 119
Custer, Frank P., 68
  Olympic Saloon, 48, 68, *69*

*Daily Picayune*, 28
Dartmouth College, 58
Deering, Eunice, 44
Denning, Dorothy, 41–42, 44, 45, 69, 117
department stores, 21–22, 24, 55
Deubler, Mary. *See* Arlington, Josie
Dewar's, 48
DeWitt, Cora, 127–28, *128*
DeWitt, Vivian, 40
directories of prostitutes. *See under* prostitution
*Directory to the Seraglios in New York, Philadelphia, Boston and All the Principal Cities in the Union*, 32
disease, 29, 30, 37, 49, *49*, 68
District, the. *See* Storyville
Dix, Gertrude, 34, 44, 47, 88, 104, *104*
Dollars, Dollie, *129*
Dr. Miles' No. 150 Specific-Mixture, 49
drugs, 30, 71
Dudley, Effie, 95

E. A. Rosenham Co., 48
El Albert (cigar), 48
Elias Aaron and Bro., 48
*Elle*, 18
Evans, May, 47, *88*, *133*
exoticism, 37, 39–40, *40*, 42, 43, 51
explicitness, 38–39, 43, 51, 57, 71, 92, 127–28, *127*, *128*, *129*

fakes and facsimiles of blue books, *38*, 39, 65, 122–43
Falstaff (beer), 48
Famous National Cocktail, *101*
Famous Number Seven Specifics, 49
*Fast Man's Directory and Lovers' Guide to the Ladies of Fashion and Houses of Pleasure in New-York and Other Large Cities*, 32
F. B. Williams Cypress Company, 60
fees for services, 32, 34
F. Hollander and Co., 48
*Fiesta de Los Angeles Souvenir Sporting Guide, La*, 33
Fisher, Lottie, 23, 45, *72*
*Floradora*, 46
Forbidden Fruit, 84, *85*
Ford Foundation, 61
Fort Worth (TX), 30
Foster, Craig L., 30–31
Fourchy, Paul Louis, 49, 76, *76*, 79, 92, *93*, 97
Frank Toro's New Monte Carlo Café and Restaurant, 48
*Free Blue Guide (La Guía Azul)*, 31
French balls, 35, 36, *36*, 66–67, 70, *70*, 74–75, *75*, 78, 79, 82–83, 86, 87, 90, 95, *95*, 98–99, *99*, 103, 111, *135*, *137*, *139*
French Pallace Studio, *115*, 116
Friedman, Josie, 76
Friends of City Park, 131
*From the Scarlet Past of Fabulous New Orleans* (No. 16, Reeves), 59, *122*, 122–23, *123*, 140

Gallagher & Burton, *84*
*G. A. R. Souvenir Sporting Guide*, 33
gender. *See* men; women
*Gentleman's Companion: New York City in 1870, The*, 32
Geo. A. Kessler and Co., 48
George A. Dickel and Co., 48

INDEX | 154

Germany, 31, 56
G. H. Mumm, 48
Gibson, Charles Dana, 70
Gibson, Rosie, *29*
Gold, Saidie, *129*
Golden, Bertha, 47, 76, 97, *115*, 116
Gonzales, Antonia, 47, *47*, 84, 115, *115*, 119
Goodspeed's Book Shop, 60
Grand Army of the Republic, 33
Green, Nettie, 116, *117*
*Green Book, or Gentlemen's Guide to New Orleans, The*, 33
Green River Whiskey, 48, 85
Grotto Dance Hall, *110*, 111
"Guidebooks to Sin: The Blue Books of Storyville" (Arceneaux article), 9
*Guides Bleus*, 17–18, 31
*Guide to the Stranger, A*, *32*, 32–33


Hachette, 17
    *Guides Bleus*, 17–18, 31
Haitian Revolution, 27
Hall, Victoria, 107, *107*
Hanover, Germany, 56
Happy Hollow Saloon, *110*, 111
Haraway, Donna, 18
Harris, Jack, 32
*Harris's List of Covent-Garden Ladies*, 32
Harvard Law School, 58
Hattiesburg (MS), 56, 123
Heartman, Charles F., 9, 33, 35, 36, 39, 55, *56*, 56–58, *58*, 59, 60, 61, 65, 67, 71, 75, 81, 85, 87, 92, 98, 104–5, 108, 111, 116, 119, 121, 124, 140
    The "Blue Book," 9, 39, 55, 57, 58, 60
    Book Farm, 56
    Heartman's Historical Series, 56, 57, 58
Hellmann's No. 206 Mixture, 49
*Hell-O* (No. 14, genuine), 27, 38, *38*, *118*, 118–19, *119*, 120, 121, 124
*Hell-O* (No. 17, fake), 119, 124, *124*–25, *125*
Henry, Maria, 128, *129*
Higgins Industries, 123
Historic New Orleans Collection, The, 55–61
*Historic New Orleans Collection Quarterly*, 9, 61
Hogan Jazz Archive, Tulane University, 124
"honi soit qui mal y pense," 5, 50, *82*, 82–83, *90*–91, *91*, 96, 99, *99*, 135, *137*, 139


*Il Catalogo di tutte le principlai et più honorate cortigiane di Venezia*, 32
ILMF (Institute of Louisiana Music and Folklore), 132–33
Ingalls Shipbuilding, 123
*In Remembrance of a Visit to Lulu White's*, 108
Institute of Louisiana Music and Folklore (ILMF), 132–33
International Trade Mart, 60
Irwin, Lillian, 40–41, 44
*Item*, 34
I. W. Harper, 48


Jackson, Nina, 44, 119
Jackson, Tony, 47
Jacobs Candies, 49
Joe Toro's Saloon and Ladies Cafe, 79
Johnson, Emma, 9, 45, *45*, 47, 80, *80*, 83, 87, 92, 97, 101, 104, 116
Joiner, Isabelle, *129*
Judge, the, 120
    *See also* Struve, William (Billy)

Junior League of New Orleans, 60
J. W. Davis, 116


Kansas City (MO), 33
*Kelley Blue Book*, 31
Kemper and Leila Williams Foundation, 60
Key West (FL), 48
Knight, Pearl, 106
Knotts, Jessie, *29*
*KnowLA Encyclopedia of Louisiana*, 9
Krug and Co., 48, 94


*La Fiesta de Los Angeles Souvenir Sporting Guide*, 33
Lafitte, Judith, 143
Lake Pontchartrain, 48
Lambert, Fanny, *89*
LaMothe, Ferdinand Joseph, 47, *47*
Lamothe, Frank, 48, 88
Lamothe's City Park Restaurant, 48, 88, *88*, 99, *99*
Landau, Emily Epstein, 50, 61
La Turina Cigars, 89
Laurel (MS), 123
law enforcement, 19, 29, 30, 37, 38, 103
Law Enforcement League of Louisiana, 103
laws and legality. *See under* prostitution
Leach, William, 20, 22
Lears, Jackson, 20
legal services, 49
Lemp's (beer), 70
Leverie, Jennie, *109*
Levine, Lawrence, 18
Levy, Margaret, 106, *109*
"Lid, The" (No. 15), 38, 119, *120*, 120–21, *121*
Lighthouse Louisiana, 55
Lines, Como, 40, 44
Listerine, 21
Little Arlington Cafe and Oyster House, *101*, 136, *139*
*Little Black Book*, 33
*Little Johnny Jones*, 46
Little Salty, 119, 120
    *See also* Struve, William (Billy)
Little Willie, 74
    *See also* Struve, William (Billy)
Lloyd, Grace, 40
Lobrano, Josie. *See* Arlington, Josie
London, England, 32
Londonderry Lithia Water, 97
Los Angeles (CA), 33
Loubat Glassware and Cork Company, 49–50, 99, 132, *133*
Louisiana Civil Service League, 60
Louisiana Club, 60
Louisiana Commission for the Blind, 55
Louisiana Endowment for the Humanities, 9
*Louisiana History*, 9
Louisiana Purchase, 27, 41
Louisiana Purchase Exposition, 41, 78
Louisiana State Museum, 137
Louisiana Supreme Court, 28
Louisville (KY), 33
Lowenburg, Tom, 143

Mahogany Hall (brothel). *See* White, Lulu
"Mahogany Hall Stomp" (Williams), 45
Maison Blanche, 55
male gaze, 18, 24
Manetta, Manuel (Fess), 46–47
Mansion (brothel), *117*
Mantley, Florence, 76, *76*, *109*
Mantley, Irene, *109*
Marchand, Roland, 20, 21
Mardi Gras, 33, 36, *36*, 66, 70, 74, 78, 82, 86, 90, 95, 103, 111
   *See also* Carnival season
*Mascot*, 33
Massachusetts, 58
Mayco Press, 57
Mayflower Society, 60
Mayor of Storyville. *See* Anderson, Thomas C. (Tom)
McAllister, Ward, 17, 21
McClelland, Ida, *109*
McDowell, Nellie, *72*, 75, 76
McKee, Chippie, *109*
Meeker, Flo, 23, 34, 41, 44, 74–75, 88
men
   advertising, 48–49
   African American, 18, 50
   discretion, 41–42
   fantasy, 37, 51
   male gaze, 18, 24
   sexual power, 37
   social status, 37
   white, 18, 37, 39
Metairie (LA), 124, 131
Metuchen (NJ), 56
*Mexican Imprints Relating to Texas* (Streeter), 59
Mexico, 31
Meyers, Corine, *109*
Milwaukee (WI), 33
Milwaukee Saloon, 48
Minit Printit, Inc., 137
Mission Toys, 35, *35*
Mississippi, 56, 57, 123
Moerlein's Barbarossa (beer), *89*
Moët and Chandon, 48, *79*
Molly's Irish Pub, *133*
Monaco, 60
Monte Carlo Saloon, *117*
Moore, Leila, 60
Morris, Frances, 41–42
Morris, Lulu, *109*
Morristown (NJ), 58
Morton, Jelly Roll, 47, *47*
Most Noble Order of the Garter, 82
Mountain Dew Old Scotch Whiskey, *85*
Moynahan, Jay, 140–41
Mulvey, Laura, 18
Mumm's, *76*
music and dancing, 46–47, 104

Napoleon House, 132, *133*
Nasaw, David, 18
National Bank of Commerce, 60
Neal Auction Company, 108
Ned Palfrey Co., 48
New Braunfels (TX), 57

New Hampshire, 58
New Jersey, 56, 58, 59
New London (CT), 60
*New Mahogany Hall* (No. 11), 27, 38, 43, *43*, 44, *44*, 60, 106, 106–9, *107*, *108*, *109*, 122, 123
   *See also* White, Lulu
New Orleans
   Anderson County, 67, 71
   cabarets and clubs, 46
   Carnival season, 35, 36, *36*, 37, 66, 74, 82, 103
   Chinatown, 71
   city directories, 123
   City Park, 131
   French Market, 81
   French Quarter, 29, 30, 67, 71, 103, 133
   immigration, 27, 31
   jazz, 123
   Lorette ordinance, 27–28, 29
   Louisiana Purchase, 27
   Mardi Gras, 36, *36*, 66, 70, 74, 78, 82, 86, 90, 95, 103, 111
   printers and stationers, 35–36
   prostitution, 27–29, *28*, 31–32, 33–37, 57
   self-promotion, 30
   taxation and fines, 28
   tourism, 18, 27, 37, 47, 65
   *See also* Storyville
New Orleans Country Club, 60
New Orleans Housing Authority, 60
New Orleans Jazz Museum, 137
New Orleans Loan and Pledge Co., 49
New Orleans Philharmonic Society, 60
New Orleans Symphony, 60
News, Billy. *See* Struve, William (Billy)
New York (NY), 17, 30, 32, 48, 51, 56, 57, 58
New-York Historical Society, 58
New York Society for the Suppression of Vice, 37
Nicholls, Ollie, 75, *117*
*Nocturnal Paris, An Indispensable Companion for the Stranger*, 32

Octavia Books, 143
octoroon women, 17, 18, 37, 43, 44, 47, 68, 71, *71*, 80, 83, 104, 106, 108
   madams, 87, 97, 101, 104, 106, *109*, 112, *112*, 119
   terminology, 65
   *See also* Piazza, Willie V.; White, Lulu
O'Ferrell, Trilby, 45
Offel Offset, 133
Old Scotch Whiskey, *89*
Olympic Saloon, 48, 68, *69*
Omaha (NE), 29
Orleans Club, 60
Orleans Medalarts, 133
Orloff, Jessie, 100
Owens, Ray, 23, 42, 44, 80, *80*, *81*, 88, 101, 119
Ozone Water, *89*

Pabst Blue Ribbon (beer), 48
Paddock Dry Gin, *130*, 131, 137, *138*
Palmer, Robert, 46
Paris, France, 32, 128
*Paris after Dark, Containing a Description of the Fast Women, Their Haunts, Habits, etc. . . .*, 32
Parke-Bernet Galleries, 59

Patterson (LA), 59
Perrottet, Tony, 32
Perth Amboy (NJ), 56
Peter, Charles G., 49
Philadelphia, *32*, 32–33, 51
Phoenix (brothel), 42, *89*
Piazza, Willie V., *2*, 45, *45*, 46–47, 50, *84*, 87, 97, 101, 106, 116, *116*
Piper-Heidsieck, 48, *79*
P. L. Fourchy, Attorney and Counsellor-at-Law. *See* Fourchy, P. L.
Plimsoll Club, 60
police. *See* law enforcement
Port of New Orleans Storyville Ball, 133
Preferencia Cigars, *101*
Price, Jessie, 123
Principe de Gales (cigar), *93*
prostitution
    alcoholism, 30
    class, 17, 18, 31–32, 32–33, 39, 40, 45, 51, 78–79, 114
    criminalization, *29*, 29–30
    decline, 50–51, *51*
    directories of prostitutes, *43*, 43–46, *44*, 75, 75–76, *76*, 79–80, *80*, 83, *83*, 86–87, *87*, *88*, 91, *91*, 96, 96–97, 100, *100*, 104, *104*, 112, 119, 120, 134
    disease, 20, 29, 30, 37, 49, *49*, 68
    drug addiction, 30
    laws and legality, 27–30, 37, 50–51, 76, 111, 116
    licensing, *28*, 29–30
    race, 17, 34, 37, 43, 71, *71*, 75–76, 80, 83, 86–87, 91, 92, 97, 100–101, 104, 106, 108, 112, 119, 120
    tourism, 31–32

race, 17, 18, 31, 34, 37, 43, 71, *71*, 75–76, 80, 83, 86–87, 91, 92, 97, 100–101, 104, 106, 108, 112, 119, 120
    segregation, 28, 43, 50, 76
    terminology, 65
Radiofone, 131
Raleigh Rye, *93*, *114*
Ralph's on the Park, 99
Ramos, Henry C., 121
Randella, Flora (Snooks), 39–40
Ravain, A. E. 49, 68, *68*, 72
*Red Book, The* (No. 12), 27, *36*, 38, *110*, 110–13, *111*, *112*, 113
"Red-Light Look at New Orleans History, A" (Arceneaux), 9
Reed, Sadie, 44, *44*
Reeves, Thomas W., 123, 140
Reeves, Thurman W., 59, 122–23
Reeves, Viola, 123
Renault Taxi Service, 49
Ritz-Carlton Hotel, 55
Rose, Al, 9, 33, 36, 38, 66, 67, 75, 98, 107, 108, 111, 120, 124, 137
Ross, Annie, 44, 101
Russell, Estelle, *43*, *109*
Russell, Olive, 23, *77*
Russell, William (Bill), 46–47, 123, 137
Ruy Lopez Cigars, *79*
Rydell, Robert, 18

San Antonio (TX), 30, 50, *50*
Sanborn Insurance Maps, 45
San Francisco (CA), 30, 50
Sapho, *96*
Schlitz (beer), 48
Schwartz, Ella, 103

"*Scout, The*", 119, 121
Semper Idem, 58
    *See also* Heartman, Charles F.
Sewanee (TN), 59
sex acts, 34, 39, 43, 51, 67, 83, 87, 108
Shaffer, Gipsy, 94, 95
Shwartz, Simon J., 55, *55*–56, 57, 58, 61
Simms Petroleum Corporation, 58
Simpson, Grace, 42, 44, *92*
Smith, Mary, 42
Smith's Private Detective Agency, 9, 83, 85
Soards Directory Company, *31*, 31–32, 45
social register, 17
Social Science and Research Council, 61
Society of the Cincinnati, 60
Sons of the American Revolution, 60
Southern aristocracy, 37
Sparks, Claudie, 44
Speakeasies, 87
"'Spectacular Wickedness': New Orleans, Prostitution, and the Politics of Sex, 1897–1917" (Landau), 61
Spencer, May, 44
*Sporting and Club House Directory, Chicago*, 33
*Sporting and Club House Guide to Milwaukee*, 33
*Sporting Guide, of the Tenderloin-District of New Orleans, LA.* (No. 13), 38, 45, *114*, 114–17, *115*, *116*, *117*
*Sporting Life*, 111, *113*
Stall, Gaspar (Buddy), 130–31
Stanley, Lulu, *129*
Star Mansion (brothel), *11*, 42, 44, *44*, 80, *80*, *81*, 83, 100, 101, 120, 134
St. Charles Hotel, 88
St. Louis (MO), 29, 41, 44, 78, 83, 120
Stone, Annie, 106, *109*
Story, Sidney, 29
Storyville
    advertising, 17, 18, 20, 22–23, 24, 27, 30, 31, 32, 34–35, *36*, 36, 37, 38–42, 43, 45, 47, *47*, 48–50, 78–79
        cigars, 48
        dining and drinking establishments, 48
    cabarets and clubs, 46, 47
    census data, 30–31
    class, 20, 22, 23, 24, 27, 30, 31, 43, 51
    consumerism, 17, 20, 24, 48–50
    decline, 50–51, *51*
    desire, 18, 21, 22–23, 37, 51
    escapism, 20, 23
    fantasy, 22, 51
    jazz, 46
    money, 20
    prostitution, 17, 20, 27, 31–32, 37
    race, 17, 18, 24, 31, 34, 37, 43, 75–76
    ragtime, 46, 47
    street names, 36
    tourism, 18, 37, 51, 78–79
*Storyville, New Orleans* (Rose), 9, 36, 38, 66, 124
Streeter, Thomas W., 55, 58, 58–59, *59*, 60–61, 94, 98, 123, 124
    publications by, 59
Struve, William (Billy), 34, 34–35, 47, 49, 65, 67, 70, *70*, 74, 78, 78–79, 86, 90, 100, 103, 119, 120
Studio (brothel), 71
*Sunday Sun*, 35–36

Tadema Cigar, 48, 93
Tann Tonic, 97
Tennessee, 59
Texas, 50, 50, 57, 58, 59
*Texas Imprints* (Streeter), 59
Texas State Historical Association, 58
"Those Who Are Still Alive But On The Q. T.," 44, 45, 71, 71
*Times-Picayune*, 55, 60, 123
    Doll and Toy Fund, 60
    Loving Cup, 55, 60
Tin Pan Alley, 46
tourism, 37, 51, 78–79
Trachtenberg, Alan, 21–22
*Traveler's Night Guide of Colorado*, 33
Traverse, Joe, 49, 93, 101, 139
Tube Rose Rye, 130, 131, 137, 138
Tuckerman, May (Mai), 40, 96, 119
Turk, Faruk von, 124, 133
Two Well-Known Gentlemen Ball, 36, 36, 70, 70, 75, 87, 88, 95, 111, 135, 137, 139
    See also French balls

Unexpected Saloon and Restaurant, 48, 72
United States
    advertising industry, 20, 21, 24
    commercial capitalism, 17, 20
    Comstock Law, 37
    consumerism, 17, 20–22
    equality, 21
    Louisiana Purchase, 27
    obscenity laws, 37, 57–58
    progressive movements, 29
    prostitution, 29–30, 31–33, 50
    social anxiety, 20–21
    War Department, 60
    wealth disparity, 21
United States Army, 60
United States Postal Service, 37, 57, 71, 116
University of the South, 59
Uptown Storyville, 18, 30, 50

Venice, Italy, 32
Vermont, 56
Veuve Cliquot, 48, 99, 134, 135, 136, 137, 139, 140–41
Victor Hugo (street name), 128
*Vieux Carré Courier*, 133
Viking Saloon, 117
Virginia City (NV), 29
Virginia Dare Wine, 101
*Visions and Revisions* (Baker), 9
Voodoo Museum, 133

Waco (TX), 29
Wagner, Fred, 111
Waldorf Café, 48
Walker, Rita, 37, 37, 64, 103, 104
Walsh, Michael J., 60
Walton, C. D., 47, 105
Washington, DC, 60
WDSU-TV, 132, 133
Weinthal, Bertha, 103, 103, 104
Weiss, Harry B., 57

Wells, Dolly, 143
White, Birdie, 109
White, Lulu, 22, 38, 39, 41, 43, 44, 44, 45, 47, 60, 63, 71, 77, 87, 97, 101, 106, 106–8, 107, 109, 111, 112, 112, 120, 122, 123, 127
    See also New Mahogany Hall (No. 11)
William Reese Company, 55
William Russell Jazz Collection, 123, 126, 137
Williams Research Center of The Historic New Orleans Collection, 61
Williams, Emily Seyburn, 59
Williams, Francis Bennett, 59
Williams, Leila Moore, 60
Williams, L. Kemper, 55, 59, 59–61, 123
Williams, Spencer, 45
Wilson, Georgie, 107, 107
Winston, Justin D., 124, 133
Wm. C. Moulton and Co., 111
women
    African American, 17, 18, 31, 43, 50, 65, 71, 75, 76, 80, 83, 86, 87, 92, 97, 100, 101, 104
    enslaved, 37
    exoticism, 37
    free women of color, 37
    Jewish, 17, 37, 43, 52, 67, 68, 71, 76, 83
    male gaze, 18, 24
    objectification, 18
    octoroon, 37, 43, 44, 47, 65, 68, 71, 71, 75, 80, 83, 87, 97, 101, 104, 106, 108, 112, 119
    pseudonyms, 44
    white, 43, 71, 75, 76, 80, 83, 86, 92, 97, 100, 104
World War I, 50, 60
World War II, 60

Yale University, 59, 61

Ziegfeld Follies, 46
Zuckerman, Phil, 142

**Pamela D. Arceneaux** is senior librarian and rare books curator at The Historic New Orleans Collection, where she has worked since 1981. A native of Panama City, Florida, she grew up in Thomasville, Georgia, before receiving a BA in history from West Georgia College (now the University of West Georgia) and an MLS from Louisiana State University. In recognition of her contributions as an outstanding librarian in a specialized field, the Louisiana Library Association presented the Lucy B. Foote Award to her in 1999. She resides in Metairie, Louisiana, with her husband, Paul.

※ ※ ※

**Emily Epstein Landau** received her PhD in American history from Yale University. She is the author of *Spectacular Wickedness: Sex, Race, and Memory in Storyville, New Orleans* (Louisiana State University Press, 2013). She teaches history at St. Albans School in Washington, DC, where she lives with her husband and two daughters.

## THE HISTORIC NEW ORLEANS COLLECTION

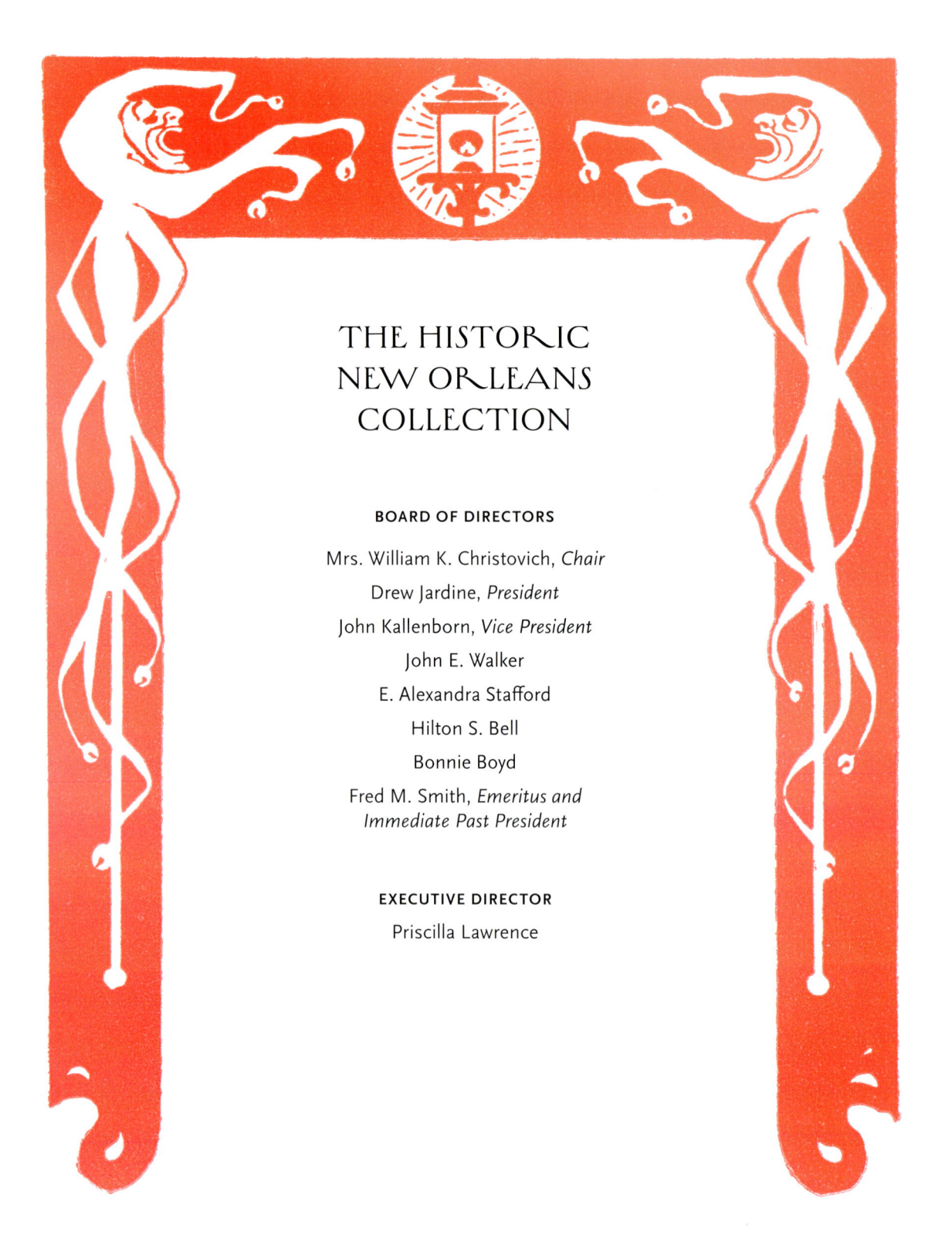

**BOARD OF DIRECTORS**

Mrs. William K. Christovich, *Chair*

Drew Jardine, *President*

John Kallenborn, *Vice President*

John E. Walker

E. Alexandra Stafford

Hilton S. Bell

Bonnie Boyd

Fred M. Smith, *Emeritus and Immediate Past President*

**EXECUTIVE DIRECTOR**

Priscilla Lawrence

This book was composed in Bradley Chicopee, Bradley Wayside, Adobe Jenson, and Scala Sans. It was printed on 100-pound Garda Silk White and bound in Arlington cotton by Friesens of Altona, Manitoba, Canada. Frames, fleurons and other type flourishes seen throughout its pages were borrowed from the blue books in the holdings of The Historic New Orleans Collection.